BOOK 2 – ECONOMICS

W9-BFW-406

SCHWESERNOTES™ 2015 CFA LEVEL I BOOK 2: ECONOMICS

©2014 Kaplan, Inc. All rights reserved.

Published in 2014 by Kaplan, Inc.

Printed in the United States of America.

ISBN: 978-1-4754-2757-8 / 1-4754-2757-3

PPN: 3200-5523

Reading Assignments and Learning Outcome Statements

The following material is a review of the Economics principles designed to address the learning outcome statements set forth by CFA Institute.

STUDY SESSION 4

Reading Assignments

Economics, CFA Program Level I 2015 Curriculum, Volume 2 (CFA Institute, 2014)

STUDY SESSION 5

Reading Assignments

Economics, CFA Program Level I 2015 Curriculum, Volume 2 (CFA Institute, 2014)

STUDY SESSION 6

Reading Assignments

Economics, CFA Program Level I 2015 Curriculum, Volume 2 (CFA Institute, 2014)

LEARNING OUTCOME STATEMENTS (LOS)

STUDY SESSION 4

The topical coverage corresponds with the following CFA Institute assigned reading:

13. Demand and Supply Analysis: Introduction

The candidate should be able to:

a. distinguish among types of markets. (page 9)
b. explain the principles of demand and supply. (page 10)
c. describe causes of shifts in and movements along demand and supply curves. (page 12)
d. describe the process of aggregating demand and supply curves. (page 13)
e. describe the concept of equilibrium (partial and general), and mechanisms by which markets achieve equilibrium. (page 14)
f. distinguish between stable and unstable equilibria, including price bubbles, and identify instances of such equilibria. (page 16)
g. calculate and interpret individual and aggregate demand, and inverse demand and supply functions, and interpret individual and aggregate demand and supply curves. (page 17)
h. calculate and interpret the amount of excess demand or excess supply associated with a non-equilibrium price. (page 17)
i. describe types of auctions and calculate the winning price(s) of an auction. (page 18)
j. calculate and interpret consumer surplus, producer surplus, and total surplus. (page 20)
k. describe how government regulation and intervention affect demand and supply. (page 24)
l. forecast the effect of the introduction and the removal of a market interference (e.g., a price floor or ceiling) on price and quantity. (page 24)
m. calculate and interpret price, income, and cross-price elasticities of demand and describe factors that affect each measure. (page 32)

The topical coverage corresponds with the following CFA Institute assigned reading:

14. Demand and Supply Analysis: Consumer Demand

The candidate should be able to:

a. describe consumer choice theory and utility theory. (page 48)
b. describe the use of indifference curves, opportunity sets, and budget constraints in decision making. (page 49)
c. calculate and interpret a budget constraint. (page 49)
d. determine a consumer's equilibrium bundle of goods based on utility analysis. (page 52)
e. compare substitution and income effects. (page 52)
f. distinguish between normal goods and inferior goods, and explain Giffen goods and Veblen goods in this context. (page 55)

The topical coverage corresponds with the following CFA Institute assigned reading:

15. Demand and Supply Analysis: The Firm

The candidate should be able to:

a. calculate, interpret, and compare accounting profit, economic profit, normal profit, and economic rent. (page 60)

b. calculate and interpret and compare total, average, and marginal revenue. (page 64)
c. describe a firm's factors of production. (page 66)
d. calculate and interpret total, average, marginal, fixed, and variable costs. (page 68)
e. determine and describe breakeven and shutdown points of production. (page 72)
f. describe approaches to determining the profit-maximizing level of output. (page 76)
g. describe how economies of scale and diseconomies of scale affect costs. (page 78)
h. distinguish between short-run and long-run profit maximization. (page 80)
i. distinguish among decreasing-cost, constant-cost, and increasing-cost industries and describe the long-run supply of each. (page 81)
j. calculate and interpret total, marginal, and average product of labor. (page 82)
k. describe the phenomenon of diminishing marginal returns and calculate and interpret the profit-maximizing utilization level of an input. (page 83)
l. determine the optimal combination of resources that minimizes cost. (page 83)

The topical coverage corresponds with the following CFA Institute assigned reading:
16. **The Firm and Market Structures**
The candidate should be able to:
a. describe characteristics of perfect competition, monopolistic competition, oligopoly, and pure monopoly. (page 94)
b. explain relationships between price, marginal revenue, marginal cost, economic profit, and the elasticity of demand under each market structure. (page 96)
c. describe a firm's supply function under each market structure. (page 114)
d. describe and determine the optimal price and output for firms under each market structure. (page 96)
e. explain factors affecting long-run equilibrium under each market structure. (page 96)
f. describe pricing strategy under each market structure. (page 114)
g. describe the use and limitations of concentration measures in identifying market structure. (page 115)
h. identify the type of market structure within which a firm operates. (page 117)

STUDY SESSION 5

The topical coverage corresponds with the following CFA Institute assigned reading:
17. **Aggregate Output, Prices, and Economic Growth**
The candidate should be able to:
a. calculate and explain gross domestic product (GDP) using expenditure and income approaches. (page 126)
b. compare the sum-of-value-added and value-of-final-output methods of calculating GDP. (page 127)
c. compare nominal and real GDP and calculate and interpret the GDP deflator. (page 127)
d. compare GDP, national income, personal income, and personal disposable income. (page 129)
e. explain the fundamental relationship among saving, investment, the fiscal balance, and the trade balance. (page 130)

    f.   explain the IS and LM curves and how they combine to generate the aggregate demand curve. (page 131)

    g.   explain the aggregate supply curve in the short run and long run. (page 135)

    h.   explain causes of movements along and shifts in aggregate demand and supply curves. (page 136)

    i.   describe how fluctuations in aggregate demand and aggregate supply cause short-run changes in the economy and the business cycle. (page 140)

    j.   distinguish between the following types of macroeconomic equilibria: long-run full employment, short-run recessionary gap, short-run inflationary gap, and short-run stagflation. (page 140)

    k.   explain how a short-run macroeconomic equilibrium may occur at a level above or below full employment. (page 140)

    l.   analyze the effect of combined changes in aggregate supply and demand on the economy. (page 144)

    m. describe sources, measurement, and sustainability of economic growth. (page 145)

    n.   describe the production function approach to analyzing the sources of economic growth. (page 146)

    o.   distinguish between input growth and growth of total factor productivity as components of economic growth. (page 147)

The topical coverage corresponds with the following CFA Institute assigned reading:

18. Understanding Business Cycles

The candidate should be able to:

    a.   describe the business cycle and its phases. (page 157)

    b.   describe how resource use, housing sector activity, and external trade sector activity vary as an economy moves through the business cycle. (page 158)

    c.   describe theories of the business cycle. (page 161)

    d.   describe types of unemployment and measures of unemployment. (page 162)

    e.   explain inflation, hyperinflation, disinflation, and deflation. (page 163)

    f.   explain the construction of indices used to measure inflation. (page 164)

    g.   compare inflation measures, including their uses and limitations. (page 167)

    h.   distinguish between cost-push and demand-pull inflation. (page 168)

    i.   describe economic indicators, including their uses and limitations. (page 170)

The topical coverage corresponds with the following CFA Institute assigned reading:

19. Monetary and Fiscal Policy

The candidate should be able to:

    a.   compare monetary and fiscal policy. (page 179)

    b.   describe functions and definitions of money. (page 179)

    c.   explain the money creation process. (page 180)

    d.   describe theories of the demand for and supply of money. (page 182)

    e.   describe the Fisher effect. (page 184)

    f.   describe roles and objectives of central banks. (page 184)

    g.   contrast the costs of expected and unexpected inflation. (page 185)

    h.   describe tools used to implement monetary policy. (page 187)

    i.   describe the monetary transmission mechanism. (page 187)

    j.   describe qualities of effective central banks. (page 188)

    k.   explain the relationships between monetary policy and economic growth, inflation, interest, and exchange rates. (page 189)

l. contrast the use of inflation, interest rate, and exchange rate targeting by central banks. (page 190)

m. determine whether a monetary policy is expansionary or contractionary. (page 191)

n. describe limitations of monetary policy. (page 192)

o. describe roles and objectives of fiscal policy. (page 193)

p. describe tools of fiscal policy, including their advantages and disadvantages. (page 194)

q. describe the arguments about whether the size of a national debt relative to GDP matters. (page 197)

r. explain the implementation of fiscal policy and difficulties of implementation. (page 198)

s. determine whether a fiscal policy is expansionary or contractionary. (page 199)

t. explain the interaction of monetary and fiscal policy. (page 200)

STUDY SESSION 6

The topical coverage corresponds with the following CFA Institute assigned reading:

20. International Trade and Capital Flows

The candidate should be able to:

a. compare gross domestic product and gross national product. (page 211)

b. describe benefits and costs of international trade. (page 211)

c. distinguish between comparative advantage and absolute advantage. (page 212)

d. explain the Ricardian and Heckscher–Ohlin models of trade and the source(s) of comparative advantage in each model. (page 215)

e. compare types of trade and capital restrictions and their economic implications. (page 216)

f. explain motivations for and advantages of trading blocs, common markets, and economic unions. (page 219)

g. describe common objectives of capital restrictions imposed by governments. (page 221)

h. describe the balance of payments accounts including their components. (page 221)

i. explain how decisions by consumers, firms, and governments affect the balance of payments. (page 223)

j. describe functions and objectives of the international organizations that facilitate trade, including the World Bank, the International Monetary Fund, and the World Trade Organization. (page 223)

The topical coverage corresponds with the following CFA Institute assigned reading:

21. Currency Exchange Rates

The candidate should be able to:

a. define an exchange rate, and distinguish between nominal and real exchange rates and spot and forward exchange rates. (page 231)

b. describe functions of and participants in the foreign exchange market. (page 233)

c. calculate and interpret the percentage change in a currency relative to another currency. (page 234)

d. calculate and interpret currency cross-rates. (page 234)

e. convert forward quotations expressed on a points basis or in percentage terms into an outright forward quotation. (page 235)

f. explain the arbitrage relationship between spot rates, forward rates, and interest rates. (page 236)

g. calculate and interpret a forward discount or premium. (page 237)

h. calculate and interpret the forward rate consistent with the spot rate and the interest rate in each currency. (page 238)

i. describe exchange rate regimes. (page 239)

j. explain the effects of exchange rates on countries' international trade and capital flows. (page 240)

The following is a review of the Economics: Microeconomic Analysis principles designed to address the learning outcome statements set forth by CFA Institute. This topic is also covered in:

DEMAND AND SUPPLY ANALYSIS: INTRODUCTION

Study Session 4

EXAM FOCUS

In this topic review, we introduce basic microeconomic theory. Candidates will need to understand the concepts of supply, demand, equilibrium, and how markets can lead to the efficient allocation of resources to all the various goods and services produced. The reasons for and results of deviations from equilibrium quantities and prices are examined. Finally, several calculations are required based on supply functions and demand functions, including price elasticity of demand, cross price elasticity of demand, income elasticity of demand, excess supply, excess demand, consumer surplus, and producer surplus.

LOS 13.a: Distinguish among types of markets.

CFA® Program Curriculum, Volume 2, page 7

The two types of markets considered here are markets for **factors of production** (factor markets) and markets for **services and finished goods** (goods markets or product markets).

Sometimes this distinction is quite clear. Crude oil and labor are factors of production, and cars, clothing, and liquor are finished goods, sold primarily to consumers. In general, firms are buyers in factor markets and sellers in product markets.

Intel produces computer chips that are used in the manufacture of computers. We refer to such goods as **intermediate goods,** because they are used in the production of final goods.

Capital markets refers to the markets where firms raise money for investment by selling debt (borrowing) or selling equities (claims to ownership), as well as the markets where these debt and equity claims are subsequently traded.

LOS 13.b: Explain the principles of demand and supply.

CFA® Program Curriculum, Volume 2, page 8

The Demand Function

We typically think of the quantity of a good or service demanded as depending on price but, in fact, it depends on income, the prices of other goods, as well as other factors. A general form of the demand function for Good X over some period of time is:

$$Q_{Dx} = f(P_x, I, P_y, ...)$$

where:

P_x = price of Good X
I = some measure of individual or average income per year
$P_y ...$ = prices of related goods

Consider an individual's demand for gasoline over a week. The price of automobiles and the price of bus travel may be independent variables, along with income and the price of gasoline.

Consider the function $Q_{D\,gas} = 10.75 - 1.25P_{gas} + 0.02I + 0.12P_{BT} - 0.01P_{auto}$ where income and car price are measured in thousands, and the price of bus travel is measured in average dollars per 100 miles traveled. Note that an increase in the price of automobiles will decrease demand for gasoline (they are complements), and an increase in the price of bus travel will increase the demand for gasoline (they are substitutes).

To get quantity demanded as a function of only the price of gas, we must insert values for all the other independent variables. Assuming that the average car price is $25,000, income is $45,000, and the price of bus travel is $30, our demand function above becomes $Q_{D\,gas} = 10.75 - 1.25(P_{gas}) + 0.02(45) + 0.12(30) - 0.01(25) = 15.00 - 1.25P_{gas}$, and at a price of $4 per gallon, the quantity of gas demanded per week is 10 gallons.

The quantity of gas demanded is a (linear) function of the price of gas. Note that different values of income or the price of automobiles or bus travel result in different demand functions. We say that, other things equal (for a given set of these values), the quantity of gas demanded equals $15.00 - 1.25P_{gas}$.

In this form, we can see that each $1 increase in the price of gasoline reduces the quantity demanded by 1.25 gallons. We will also have occasion to use a different functional form that shows the price of gasoline as a function of the quantity demanded. While this seems a bit odd, we graph demand curves with price (the independent variable) on the vertical y-axis and quantity (the dependent variable) on the horizontal x-axis by convention. In order to get this functional form, we *invert* the function to show price as a function of the quantity demanded. For our function, $Q_{D\,gas} = 15.00 - 1.25P_{gas}$, we simply use algebra to solve for $P_{gas} = 12.00 - 0.80Q_{D\,gas}$.

This is our demand curve for gasoline (based on current prices of cars and bus travel and the consumer's income). The graph of this function for positive prices is shown in

Figure 1. The fact that the quantity demanded typically increases at lower prices is often referred to as the **law of demand**.

Figure 1: Demand for Gasoline

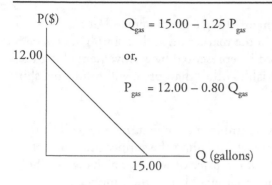

$$Q_{gas} = 15.00 - 1.25\,P_{gas}$$

or,

$$P_{gas} = 12.00 - 0.80\,Q_{gas}$$

The Supply Function

For the producer of a good, the quantity he will willingly supply depends on the selling price as well as the costs of production which, in turn, depend on technology, the cost of labor, and the cost of other inputs into the production process. Consider a manufacturer of furniture that produces tables. For a given level of technology, the quantity supplied will depend on the selling price, the price of labor (wage rate), and the price of wood (for simplicity, we will ignore the price of screws, glue, finishes, and so forth).

An example of such a function is $Q_{S\ tables} = -274 + 0.80P_{tables} - 8.00\text{Wage} - 0.20P_{wood}$ where the wage is in dollars per hour and the price of wood is in dollars per 100 board feet. To get quantity supplied as a function solely of selling price, we must assume values for the other independent variables and hold technology constant. For example, with a wage of $12 per hour and wood priced at $150, $Q_{S\ tables} = -400 + 0.80P_{tables}$.

In order to graph this producer's supply curve we simply invert this supply function and get $P_{tables} = 500 + 1.25Q_{S\ tables}$. This resulting supply curve is shown in Figure 2. The fact that a greater quantity is supplied at higher prices is referred to as the **law of supply**.

Figure 2: Supply of Tables

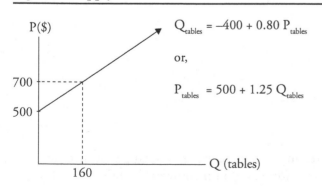

$$Q_{tables} = -400 + 0.80\,P_{tables}$$

or,

$$P_{tables} = 500 + 1.25\,Q_{tables}$$

LOS 13.c: Describe causes of shifts in and movements along demand and supply curves.

CFA® Program Curriculum, Volume 2, page 11

It is important to distinguish between a movement along a given demand or supply curve and a shift in the curve itself. A change in the market price that simply increases or decreases the quantity supplied or demanded is represented by a movement along the curve. A change in one of the independent variables other than price will result in a shift of the curve itself.

For our gasoline demand curve in our previous example, a change in income will shift the curve, as will a change in the price of bus travel. Recalling the supply function for tables in our previous example, either a change in the price of wood or a change in the wage rate would shift the curve. An increase in either would shift the supply curve to the left as the quantity willingly supplied at each price would be reduced.

Figure 3 illustrates a decrease in the quantity demanded from Q_0 to Q_1 in response to an increase in price from P_0 to P_1. Figure 4 illustrates an increase in the quantity supplied from Q_0 to Q_1 in response to an increase in price from P_0 to P_1.

Figure 3: Change in Quantity Demanded

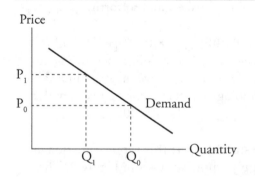

Figure 4: Change in Quantity Supplied

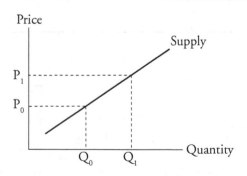

In contrast, Figure 5 illustrates shifts (changes) in demand from changes in income or the prices of related goods. An increase (decrease) in income or the price of a substitute will increase (decrease) demand, while an increase (decrease) in the price of a complement will decrease (increase) demand.

Figure 6 illustrates an increase in supply, which would result from a decrease in the price of an input, and a decrease in supply, which would result from an increase in the price of an input.

Figure 5: Shift in Demand

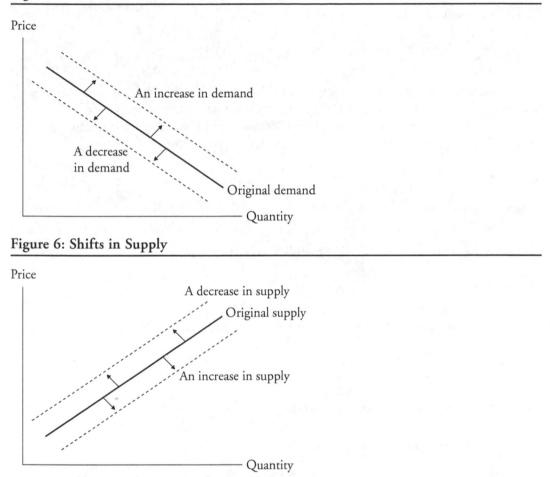

Figure 6: Shifts in Supply

LOS 13.d: Describe the process of aggregating demand and supply curves.

CFA® Program Curriculum, Volume 2, page 17

Given the supply functions of the firms that comprise market supply, we can add them together to get the market supply function. For example, if there were 50 table manufacturers with the supply function $Q_{S\ tables} = -400 + 0.80P_{tables}$, the market supply would be $Q_{S\ tables} = -(50 \times 400) + (50 \times 0.80) P_{tables}$, which is $-20,000 + 40 P_{tables}$. Now, to get the market supply curve, we need to invert this function to get:

$$P_{tables} = 0.025 Q_{S\ tables} + 500$$

Note that the slope of the supply curve is the coefficient of the independent (in this form) variable, 0.025.

The following example illustrates the aggregation technique for getting market demand from many individual demand curves.

Example: Aggregating consumer demand

If 10,000 consumers have the demand function for gasoline:

$$Q_{D\ gas} = 10.75 - 1.25P_{gas} + 0.02I + 0.12P_{BT} - 0.01P_{auto}$$

where income and car price are measured in thousands, and the price of bus travel is measured in average dollars per 100 miles traveled. Calculate the market demand curve if the price of bus travel is $20, income is $50,000, and the average automobile price is $30,000. Determine the slope of the market demand curve.

Answer:

Market demand is:

$$Q_{D\ gas} = 107,500 - 12,500P_{gas} + 200I + 1,200P_{BT} - 100P_{auto}$$

Inserting the values given, we have:

$$Q_{D\ gas} = 107,500 - 12,500P_{gas} + 200 \times 50 + 1,200 \times 20 - 100 \times 30$$

$$Q_{D\ gas} = 138,500 - 12,500P_{gas}$$

Inverting this function, we get the market demand curve:

$$P_{gas} = 11.08 - 0.00008Q_{D\ gas}$$

The slope of the demand curve is –0.00008, or if we measure quantity of gas in thousands of gallons, we get –0.08.

LOS 13.e: Describe the concept of equilibrium (partial and general), and mechanisms by which markets achieve equilibrium.

CFA® Program Curriculum, Volume 2, page 20

When we have a market supply and market demand curve for a good, we can solve for the price at which the quantity supplied equals the quantity demanded. We define this as the **equilibrium price** and the **equilibrium quantity**; graphically, these are identified by the point where the two curves intersect, as illustrated in Figure 7.

Figure 7: Movement Toward Equilibrium

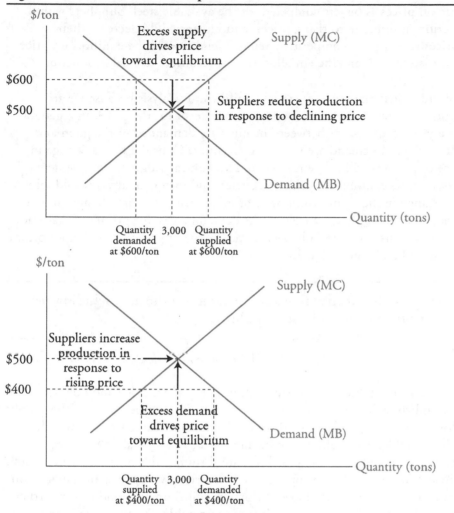

Under the assumptions that buyers compete for available goods on the basis of price only, and that suppliers compete for sales only on the basis of price, market forces will drive the price to its equilibrium level.

Referring to Figure 7, if the price is above its equilibrium level, the quantity willingly supplied exceeds the quantity consumers are willing to purchase, and we have **excess supply**. Suppliers willing to sell at lower prices will offer those prices to consumers, driving the market price down towards the equilibrium level. Conversely, if the market price is below its equilibrium level, the quantity demanded at that price exceeds the quantity supplied, and we have **excess demand**. Consumers will offer higher prices to compete for the available supply, driving the market price up towards its equilibrium level.

Consider a situation where the allocation of resources to steel production is not efficient. In Figure 7, we have a disequilibrium situation where the quantity of steel supplied is greater than the quantity demanded at a price of $600/ton. Clearly, steel inventories will build up, and competition will put downward pressure on the price of steel. As the price falls, steel producers will reduce production and free up resources to be used in the production of other goods and services until equilibrium output and price are reached.

If steel prices were $400/ton, inventories would be drawn down, which would put upward pressure on prices as buyers competed for the available steel. Suppliers would increase production in response to rising prices, and buyers would decrease their purchases as prices rose. Again, competitive markets tend toward the equilibrium price and quantity consistent with an efficient allocation of resources to steel production.

Our analysis of individual markets is a **partial equilibrium** analysis because we are taking the factors that may influence demand as fixed except for the price. In a **general equilibrium analysis**, relationships between the quantity demanded of the good and factors that may influence demand are taken into account. Consider that a change in the market price of printers will influence demand for ink cartridges (a complementary good) and, therefore, its equilibrium price. A general equilibrium analysis would take account of this change in the equilibrium price of ink cartridges (from changes in the equilibrium price of printers) in constructing the demand curve for printers. That said, for many types of analysis and especially over a small range of prices, partial equilibrium analysis is often useful and appropriate.

LOS 13.f: Distinguish between stable and unstable equilibria, including price bubbles, and identify instances of such equilibria.

CFA® Program Curriculum, Volume 2, page 25

An equilibrium is termed **stable** when there are forces that move price and quantity back towards equilibrium values when they deviate from those values. Even if the supply curve slopes downward, as long as it cuts through the demand curve from above, the equilibrium will be stable. Prices above equilibrium result in excess supply and put downward pressure on price, while prices below equilibrium result in excess demand and put upward pressure on price. If the supply curve is less steeply sloped than the demand curve, this is not the case, and prices above (below) equilibrium will tend to get further from equilibrium. We refer to such an equilibrium as **unstable**. We illustrate both of these cases in Figure 8, along with an example of a nonlinear supply function, which produces two equilibria—one stable and one unstable.

Figure 8: Stable and Unstable Equilibria

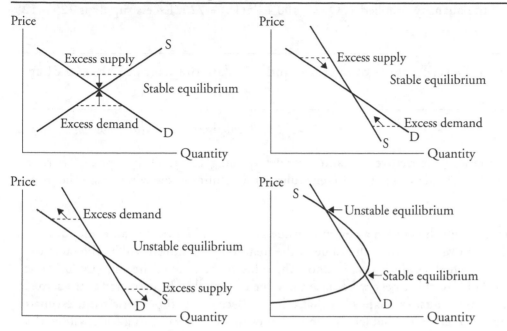

Bubbles, or unsustainable increases in asset prices, are evident in real estate prices and prices of other assets at various times. In these situations, market participants take recent price increases as an indication of higher future asset prices. The expectation of higher future prices then increases the demand for the asset (i.e., shifts the demand curve to the right) which again increases the equilibrium price of the asset. At some point, the widely held belief in ever-increasing prices is displaced by a realization that prices can also fall. This leads to a "breaking of the bubble," and the asset price falls rapidly towards a new and sustainable equilibrium price (and perhaps below it in the short run).

LOS 13.g: Calculate and interpret individual and aggregate demand, and inverse demand and supply functions, and interpret individual and aggregate demand and supply curves.

LOS 13.h: Calculate and interpret the amount of excess demand or excess supply associated with a non-equilibrium price.

CFA® Program Curriculum, Volume 2, page 10

Earlier in this topic review, we illustrated the technique of defining and inverting linear demand and supply functions. We then aggregated individuals' demand functions and firms' supply functions to form market demand and supply curves.

Given a supply function, $Q_S = -400 + 75P$, and a demand function, $Q_D = 2,000 - 125P$, we can determine that the equilibrium price is 12 by setting the functions equal to each other and solving for P.

At a price of 10, we can calculate the quantity demanded as $Q_D = 2,000 - 125(10) = 750$ and the quantity supplied as $Q_S = -400 + 75(10) = 350$. Excess demand is $750 - 350 = 400$.

At a price of 15, we can calculate the quantity demanded as $Q_D = 2,000 - 125(15) = 125$ and the quantity supplied as $Q_S = -400 + 75(15) = 725$. Excess supply is $725 - 125 = 600$.

LOS 13.i: Describe types of auctions and calculate the winning price(s) of an auction.

CFA® Program Curriculum, Volume 2, page 27

An **auction** is an alternative to markets for determining an equilibrium price. There are various types of auctions with different rules for determining the winner and the price to be paid.

We can distinguish between a **common value auction** and a **private value auction**. In a common value auction, the value of the item to be auctioned will be the same to any bidder, but the bidders do not know the value at the time of the auction. Oil lease auctions fall into this category because the value of the oil to be extracted is the same for all, but bidders must estimate what that value is. Because auction participants estimate the value with error, the bidder who most overestimates the value of a lease will be the highest (winning) bidder. This is sometimes referred to as the **winner's curse**, and the winning bidder may have losses as a result. An example of a private value auction is an auction of art or collectibles. The value that each bidder places on an item is the value it has to him, and we assume that no bidder will bid more than that.

One common type of auction is an **ascending price auction**, also referred to as an *English auction*. Bidders can bid an amount greater than the previous high bid, and the bidder that first offers the highest bid of the auction wins the item and pays the amount bid.

In a **sealed bid auction**, each bidder provides one bid, which is unknown to other bidders. The bidder submitting the highest bid wins the item and pays the price bid. The term *reservation price* refers to the highest price that a bidder is willing to pay. In a sealed bid auction, the optimal bid for the bidder with the highest reservation price would be just slightly above that of the bidder who values the item second-most highly. For this reason, bids are not necessarily equal to bidders' reservation prices.

In a **second price sealed bid auction** (*Vickrey auction*), the bidder submitting the highest bid wins the item but pays the amount bid by the second highest bidder. In this type of auction, there is no reason for a bidder to bid less than his reservation price. The eventual outcome is much like that of an ascending price auction, where the winning bidder pays one increment of price more than the price offered by the bidder who values the item second-most highly.

A **descending price auction**, or **Dutch auction**, begins with a price greater than what any bidder will pay, and this offer price is reduced until a bidder agrees to pay it. If there are many units available, each bidder may specify how many units she will purchase when accepting an offered price. If the first (highest) bidder agrees to buy three of ten units at $100, subsequent bidders will get the remaining units at lower prices as descending offered prices are accepted.

Sometimes, a descending price auction is modified (*modified Dutch auction*) so that winning bidders all pay the same price, which is the reservation price of the bidder whose bid wins the last units offered.

A single price is often determined for securities through the following method. Consider a firm that wants to buy back 1 million shares of its outstanding stock through a tender offer. The firm solicits offers from shareholders who specify a price and how many shares they are willing to tender. After such solicitation, the firm has a list of offers such as those listed in Figure 9:

Figure 9: Tender Offer Indications

Shareholder	Price	# shares
A	$38.00	200,000
B	$37.75	300,000
C	$37.60	100,000
D	$37.20	400,000
E	$37.10	300,000
F	$37.00	200,000

The firm determines that the lowest price at which it can purchase all 1 million shares is $37.60, so the offers of shareholders C, D, E, and F are accepted, and all receive the single price of $37.60. The shares offered by shareholders A and B are not purchased.

With U.S. Treasury securities, a **single price auction** is held but bidders may also submit a **noncompetitive bid.** Such a bid indicates that those bidders will accept the amount of Treasuries indicated at the price determined by the auction, rather than specifying a maximum price in their bids. The price determined by this type of auction is found as in the example just given, but the amount of securities specified in the noncompetitive bids is subtracted from the total amount to be sold. This method is illustrated in the following example.

Consider that $35 billion face value of Treasury bills will be auctioned off. Non-competitive bids are submitted for $5 billion face value of bills. Competitive bids, which must specify price (yield) and face value amount, are shown in Figure 10. Note that a bid with a higher quoted yield is actually a bid at a lower price.

Figure 10: Auction Bids for Treasury Bills

Discount Rate (%)	Face Value ($ billions)	Cumulative Face Value ($ billions)
0.1081	3	3
0.1090	12	15
0.1098	8	23
0.1104	5	28
0.1117	8	36
0.1124	7	43

Because the total face value of bills offered is $35 billion, and there are non-competitive bids for $5 billion, we must select a minimum yield (maximum price) for which $30 billion face value of bills can be sold to those making competitive bids. At a discount of 0.1104%, $28 billion can be sold to competitive bidders but that would leave 35 – 5 – 28 = $2 billion unsold. At a slightly higher yield of 0.1117%, more than $30 billion of bills can be sold to competitive bidders.

The single price for the auction is a discount of 0.1117%. All bidders that bid at lower yields (higher prices) will get all the bills they bid for ($28 billion); the non-competitive bidders will get $5 billion of bills as expected. The remaining $2 billion in bills go the bidders who bid a discount of 0.1117%. Since there are bids for $8 billion in bills at the discount of 0.1117%, and only $2 billion unsold at a yield of 0.1104%, each bidder receives 2/8 of the face amount of bills they bid for.

LOS 13.j: Calculate and interpret consumer surplus, producer surplus, and total surplus.

CFA® Program Curriculum, Volume 2, page 30

The difference between the total value to consumers of the units of a good that they buy and the total amount they must pay for those units is called **consumer surplus**. In Figure 11, this is the shaded triangle. The total value to society of 3,000 tons of steel is more than the total amount paid for the 3,000 tons of steel, by an amount represented by the shaded triangle.

Figure 11: Consumer Surplus

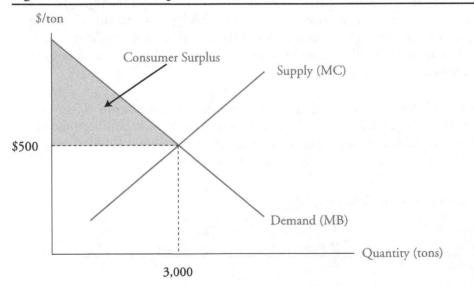

We can also refer to the consumer surplus for an individual. Figure 12 shows a consumer's demand for gasoline in gallons per week. It is downward sloping because each successive gallon of gasoline is worth less to the consumer than the previous gallon. With a market price of $3 per gallon, the consumer chooses to buy five gallons per week for a total of $15. While the first gallon of gasoline purchased each week is worth $5 to this consumer, it only costs $3, resulting in consumer surplus of $2. If we add up the maximum prices this consumer is willing to pay for each gallon, we find the total value of the five gallons is $20. Total consumer surplus for this individual from gasoline consumption is $20 – $15 = $5.

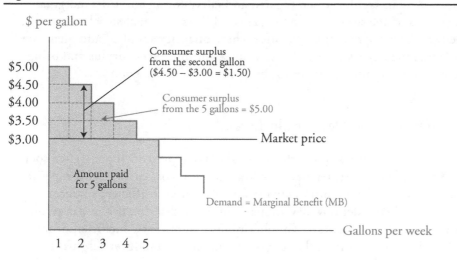

Producer Surplus

Under certain assumptions (perfect markets), the industry supply curve is also the marginal societal (opportunity) cost curve. **Producer surplus** is the excess of the market price above the opportunity cost of production; that is, total revenue minus the total variable cost of producing those units. For example, in Figure 13, steel producers are willing to supply the 2,500th ton of steel at a price of $400. Viewing the supply curve as the marginal cost curve, the cost in terms of the value of other goods and services foregone to produce the 2,500th ton of steel is $400. Producing and selling the 2,500th ton of steel for $500 increases producer surplus by $100. The difference between the total (opportunity) cost of producing steel and the total amount that buyers pay for it (producer surplus) is at a maximum when 3,000 tons are manufactured and sold.

Figure 13: Producer Surplus

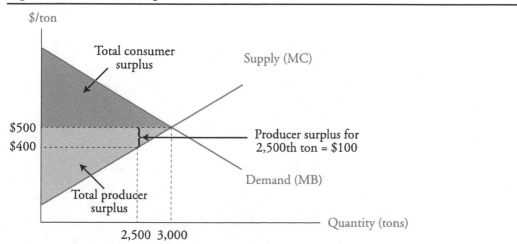

Note that the efficient quantity of steel (where marginal cost equals marginal benefit) is also the quantity of production that maximizes total consumer surplus and producer surplus. The combination of consumers seeking to maximize consumer surplus and producers seeking to maximize producer surplus (profits) leads to the efficient allocation of resources to steel production because it maximizes the total benefit to society from steel production. We can say that when the demand curve for a good is its marginal social benefit curve and the supply curve for the good is its marginal social cost curve, producing the *equilibrium quantity* at the price where quantity supplied and quantity demanded are equal maximizes the sum of consumer and producer surplus and brings about an efficient allocation of resources to the production of the good.

Obstacles to Efficiency and Deadweight Loss

Our analysis so far has presupposed that the demand curve represents the marginal social benefit curve, the supply curve represents the marginal social cost curve, and competition leads us to a supply/demand equilibrium quantity consistent with efficient resource allocation. We now will consider how deviations from these ideal conditions can result in an inefficient allocation of resources. The allocation of resources is inefficient if the quantity supplied does not maximize the sum of consumer and producer surplus. The reduction in consumer and producer surplus due to underproduction or overproduction is called a **deadweight loss**, as illustrated in Figure 14.

Figure 14: Deadweight Loss

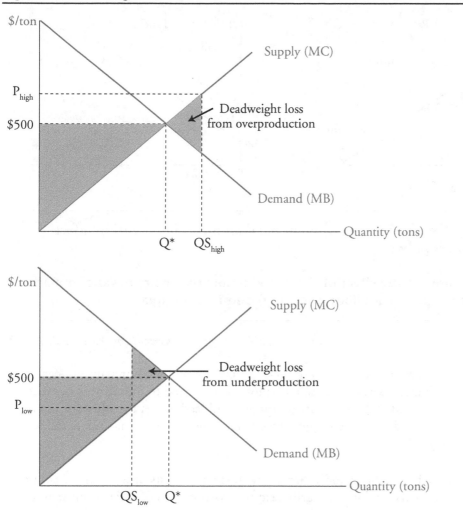

Calculating Consumer and Producer Surplus

To calculate the amount of consumer surplus or producer surplus when demand and supply are linear, we need only find the height and width of the triangles. Consider the demand function $Q = 48 - 3P$ shown in Figure 15, Panel A. Note that when P is zero, the quantity demanded is 48. Setting Q to zero and solving for P gives us $P = 16$, which is the intercept on the price axis.

Given a market price of 8, we can calculate the quantity demanded as $48 - 3(8) = 24$. Noting that the area of any triangle is ½ (base × height), we can calculate the consumer surplus as ½(8 × 24) = 96 units.

In Figure 15, Panel B, we have graphed the simple supply function $Q = -24 + 6P$. The intercept on the price axis can be found by setting Q equal to zero and solving for $P = 4$. At a price of 8, the quantity supplied is $-24 + 6(8) = 24$. Producer surplus can be seen as a triangle with height of 4 and width of 24, and we can calculate producer surplus as ½(4 × 24) = 48.

Figure 15: Calculating Consumer and Producer Surplus

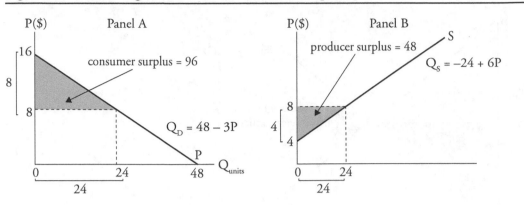

LOS 13.k: Describe how government regulation and intervention affect demand and supply.

LOS 13.l: Forecast the effect of the introduction and the removal of a market interference (e.g., a price floor or ceiling) on price and quantity.

CFA® Program Curriculum, Volume 2, page 36

Imposition by governments of minimum legal prices (price floors), maximum legal prices (price ceilings), taxes, subsidies, and quotas can all lead to imbalances between the quantity demanded and the quantity supplied and lead to deadweight losses as the quantity produced and consumed is not the efficient quantity that maximizes the total benefit to society.

In other cases, such as public goods, markets with external costs or benefits, or common resources, free markets do not necessarily lead to maximization of total surplus, and governments sometime intervene to improve resource allocation.

Obstacles to the Efficient Allocation of Productive Resources

- **Price controls**, such as price ceilings and price floors. These distort the incentives of supply and demand, leading to levels of production different from those of an unregulated market. Rent control and a minimum wage are examples of a price ceiling and a price floor.
- **Taxes and trade restrictions**, such as subsidies and quotas. *Taxes* increase the price that buyers pay and decrease the amount that sellers receive. *Subsidies* are government payments to producers that effectively increase the amount sellers receive and decrease the price buyers pay, leading to production of more than the efficient quantity of the good. *Quotas* are government-imposed production limits, resulting in production of less than the efficient quantity of the good. All three lead markets away from producing the quantity for which marginal cost equals marginal benefit.
- **External costs**, costs imposed on others by the production of goods which are not taken into account in the production decision. An example of an external cost is the cost imposed on fishermen by a firm that pollutes the ocean as part of its production process. The firm does not necessarily consider the resulting decrease in the fish

population as part of its cost of production, even though this cost is borne by the fishing industry and society. In this case, the output quantity of the polluting firm is greater than the efficient quantity. The societal costs are greater than the direct costs of production the producer bears. The result is an over-allocation of resources to production by the polluting firm.

- **External benefits** are benefits of consumption enjoyed by people other than the buyers of the good that are not taken into account in buyers' consumption decisions. An example of an external benefit is the development of a tropical garden on the grounds of an industrial complex that is located along a busy thoroughfare. The developer of the grounds only considers the marginal benefit to the firms within the complex when deciding whether to take on the grounds improvement, not the benefit received by the travelers who take pleasure in the view of the garden. External benefits result in demand curves that do not represent the societal benefit of the good or service, so the equilibrium quantity produced and consumed is less than the efficient quantity.

- **Public goods and common resources.** *Public goods* are goods and services that are consumed by people regardless of whether or not they paid for them. National defense is a public good. If others choose to pay to protect a country from outside attack, all the residents of the country enjoy such protection, whether they have paid for their share of it or not. Competitive markets will produce less than the efficient quantity of public goods because each person can benefit from public goods without paying for their production. This is often referred to as the "free rider" problem. A *common resource* is one which all may use. An example of a common resource is an unrestricted ocean fishery. Each fisherman will fish in the ocean at no cost and will have little incentive to maintain or improve the resource. Since individuals do not have the incentive to fish at the economically efficient (sustainable) level, over-fishing is the result. Left to competitive market forces, common resources are generally over-used and production of related goods or services is greater than the efficient amount.

A **price ceiling** is an upper limit on the price which a seller can charge. If the ceiling is above the equilibrium price, it will have no effect. As illustrated in Figure 16, if the ceiling is below the equilibrium price, the result will be a shortage (excess demand) at the ceiling price. The quantity demanded, Q_d, exceeds the quantity supplied, Q_s. Consumers are willing to pay P_{WS} (price with search costs) for the Q_s quantity suppliers are willing to sell at the ceiling price, P_C. Consumers are willing to expend effort with a value of $P_{WS} - P_C$ in search activity to find the scarce good. The reduction in quantity exchanged due to the price ceiling leads to a deadweight loss in efficiency as noted in Figure 16.

Figure 16: Price Ceiling

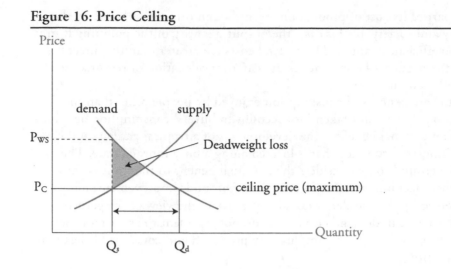

In the long run, price ceilings lead to the following:

- Consumers may have to wait in long lines to make purchases. They pay a price (an opportunity cost) in terms of the time they spend in line.
- Suppliers may engage in discrimination, such as selling to friends and relatives first.
- Suppliers "officially" sell at the ceiling price but take bribes to do so.
- Suppliers may also reduce the quality of the goods produced to a level commensurate with the ceiling price.

In the housing market, price ceilings are appropriately called **rent ceilings** or rent control. Rent ceilings are a good example of how a price ceiling can distort a market. Renters must wait for units to become available. Renters may have to bribe landlords to rent at the ceiling price. The quality of the apartments will fall. Other inefficiencies can develop. For instance, a renter might be reluctant to take a new job across town because it means giving up a rent-controlled apartment and risking not finding another (rent-controlled) apartment near the new place of work.

A **price floor** is a minimum price that a buyer can offer for a good, service, or resource. If the price floor is below the equilibrium price, it will have no effect on equilibrium price and quantity. Figure 17 illustrates a price floor that is set above the equilibrium price. The result will be a surplus (excess supply) at the floor price since the quantity supplied, Q_S, exceeds the quantity demanded, Q_D, at the floor price. There is a loss of efficiency (deadweight loss) because the quantity actually transacted with the price floor, Q_D, is less than the efficient equilibrium quantity, Q_E.

Figure 17: Impact of a Price Floor

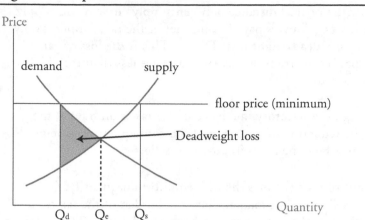

In the long run, price floors lead to inefficiencies:

- Suppliers will divert resources to the production of the good with the anticipation of selling the good at the floor price but then will not be able to sell all they produce.
- Consumers will buy less of a product if the floor is above the equilibrium price and substitute other, less expensive consumption goods for the good subject to the price floor.

In the labor market, as in all markets, equilibrium occurs when the quantity demanded (of hours worked, in this case) equals the quantity supplied. In the labor market, the equilibrium price is called the **wage rate**. The equilibrium wage rate is different for labor of different kinds and with various levels of skill. Labor that requires the lowest skill level (unskilled labor) generally has the lowest wage rate.

In some places, including the United States, there is a **minimum wage** rate (sometimes defined as a *living wage*) that prevents employers from hiring workers at a wage less than the legal minimum. The minimum wage is an example of a price floor. At a minimum wage above the equilibrium wage, there will be an excess supply of workers, since firms cannot employ all the workers who want to work at that wage. Since firms must pay at least the minimum wage for the workers, firms substitute other productive resources for labor and use more than the economically efficient amount of capital. The result is increased unemployment because even when there are workers willing to work at a wage lower than the minimum, firms cannot legally hire them. Furthermore, firms may decrease the quality or quantity of the nonmonetary benefits they previously offered to workers, such as pleasant, safe working conditions and on-the-job training.

Impact of Taxes

A tax on a good or service will increase its equilibrium price and decrease its equilibrium quantity. Figure 18 illustrates the effects of a *tax on producers* and of a *tax on buyers* (e.g., a sales tax). In Panel (a), the points indicated by P_E and Q_E describe the equilibrium prior to the tax. As a result of this tax, the supply curve shifts (decreases) from S to S_{tax}, where the quantity Q_{tax} is demanded at the price P_{tax}.

The tax is the difference between what buyers pay and what sellers ultimately earn per unit. This is illustrated by the vertical distance between supply curve S and supply curve S_{tax}. At the new quantity, Q_{tax}, buyers pay P_{tax}, but net of the tax, suppliers only receive P_S. The triangular area is a **deadweight loss** (DWL). This is the loss of gains from production and trade that results from the tax (i.e., because less than the efficient amount is produced and consumed).

Note that in Panel (b), although the statutory incidence of the tax is on buyers, the actual incidence of the tax, the reduction in output, and the consequent deadweight loss are all the same as in Panel (a), where the tax is imposed on sellers.

The **tax revenue** is the amount of the tax times the new equilibrium quantity, Q_{tax}. Economic agents (buyers and sellers) in the market share the burden of the tax revenue. The **incidence of a tax** is allocation of this tax between buyers and sellers. The rectangle denoted "revenue from buyers" represents the portion of the *tax revenue* that the buyers effectively pay. The rectangle denoted "revenue from sellers" illustrates the portion of the tax that the suppliers effectively pay.

Figure 18: Incidence of a Tax on Producers and of a Tax on Buyers

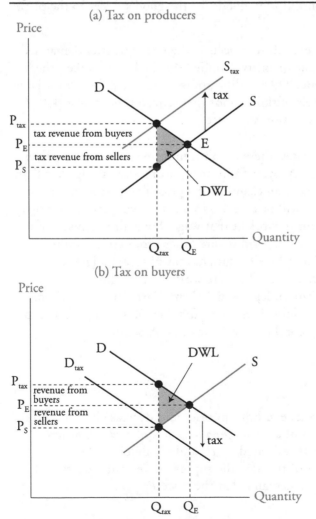

©2014 Kaplan, Inc.

Actual and Statutory Incidence of a Tax

Statutory incidence refers to who is legally responsible for paying the tax. The **actual incidence of a tax** refers to who actually bears the cost of the tax through an increase in the price paid (buyers) or decrease in the price received (sellers). In Figure 18(a), we illustrated the effect of a tax on the *sellers* of the good as opposed to the *buyers* of the good (note that the price is higher over all levels of production—the supply curve shifts up). Thus, the *statutory incidence* in Figure 18(a) is on the supplier. The result is an increase in price at each possible quantity supplied.

Statutory incidence on the *buyer* causes a downward shift of the demand curve by the amount of the tax. As indicated in Figure 18(b), prior to the imposition of a tax on buyers, the equilibrium price and quantity are at the point of intersection of the supply and demand curves (i.e., P_E, Q_E). The imposition of the tax forces suppliers to reduce output to the point Q_{tax} (a movement along the supply curve). At the new equilibrium, price and quantity are denoted by P_{tax} and Q_{tax}, respectively.

The tax that we are analyzing in Figure 18(b) could be a sales tax that is added to the price of the good at the time of sale. So, instead of paying P_E, buyers are now forced to pay P_{tax}, (i.e., tax = $P_{tax} - P_E$). The *buyer* pays the entire tax (the statutory incidence). Since, prior to the imposition of the tax, their reference point was P_E, the *buyer* only sees the price rise from P_E to P_{tax} (the buyer's tax burden). Hence, the portion of the tax borne by buyers is the area between P_E and P_{tax}, with width Q_{tax}; this is the actual tax incidence on buyers.

Note that the supply curve in Figure 18(b) does not move as a result of a tax on buyers and that given the original demand curve, D, suppliers would have supplied the equilibrium quantity Q_E at price P_E. The result is that suppliers are penalized because they would have produced at the Q_E, P_E point, but instead produce quantity Q_{tax} and receive P_S. Hence, the portion of the tax borne by sellers is the area between P_E and P_S, with width Q_{tax}; this is the actual tax incidence on sellers. Note that we are still faced with the triangular deadweight loss.

> *Professor's Note: The point you need to know is that the actual tax incidence is independent of whether the government imposes the tax (statutory incidence) on consumers or suppliers.*

How Elasticities of Supply and Demand Influence the Incidence of a Tax

When buyers and sellers share the tax burden, the relative *elasticities* of supply and demand will determine the actual incidence of a tax. Elasticity is explained in detail later in this topic review.

- If *demand is less elastic* (i.e., the demand curve is steeper) than supply, *consumers will bear a higher burden*—that is, pay a greater portion of the tax revenue than suppliers.

- If *supply is less elastic* (i.e., the supply curve is steeper) than demand, *suppliers will bear a higher burden*—that is, pay a greater portion of the tax revenue than consumers. Here, the change in the quantity supplied for a given change in price will be small—buyers have more "leverage" in this type of market. The party with the more elastic curve will be able to react more to the changes imposed by the tax. Hence, they can avoid more of the burden.

Panels (a) and (b) in Figure 19 are the same in all respects, except that the supply curve in Panel (b) is significantly steeper—it is less elastic. Comparing Panel (a) with Panel (b), we can see that the portion of tax revenue borne by the seller is much greater than that borne by the buyer as the supply curve becomes less elastic. When demand is more elastic relative to supply, buyers pay a lower portion of the tax because they have the greater ability to substitute away from the good.

Notice that as the elasticity of either demand or supply decreases, the deadweight loss is also reduced. With less effect on equilibrium quantity, the allocation of resources is less affected and efficiency is reduced less.

Figure 19: Elasticity of Supply and Tax Incidence

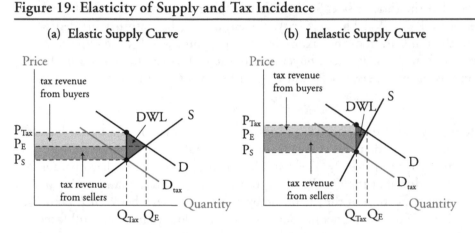

In Figure 20, we illustrate the result for differences in the elasticity of demand. In Panel (b), demand is relatively more inelastic, and we see that the size of the deadweight loss (and the decrease in equilibrium output) is smaller when demand is more inelastic. We can also see that the actual incidence of a tax falls more heavily on buyers when demand is more inelastic.

Figure 20: Elasticity of Demand and Tax Incidence

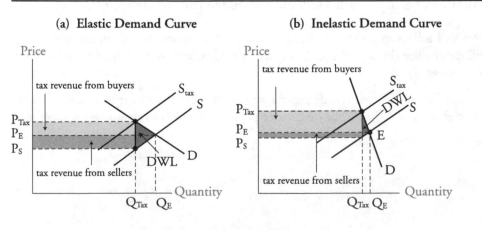

Subsidies and Quotas

Subsidies are payments made by governments to producers, often farmers. The effects of a subsidy are illustrated in Figure 21, where we use the market for soybeans as an example. Note here that with no subsidies, equilibrium quantity in the market for soybeans is 60 million tons annually at a price of $60 per ton. A subsidy of $30 per ton causes a downward shift in the supply curve from S to (S – subsidy), which results in an increase in the equilibrium quantity to 90 million tons per year and a decrease in the equilibrium price (paid by buyers) to $45 per ton. At the new equilibrium, farmers receive $75 per ton (the market price of $45, plus the $30 subsidy).

Recognizing that the (unsubsidized) supply curve represents the marginal cost and that the demand curve represents the marginal benefit, the marginal cost is greater than the marginal benefit at the new equilibrium with the subsidy. This leads to a deadweight loss from overproduction. The resources used to produce the additional 30 million tons of soybeans have a value in some other use that is greater than the value of these additional soybeans to consumers.

Figure 21: Soybean Price Subsidy

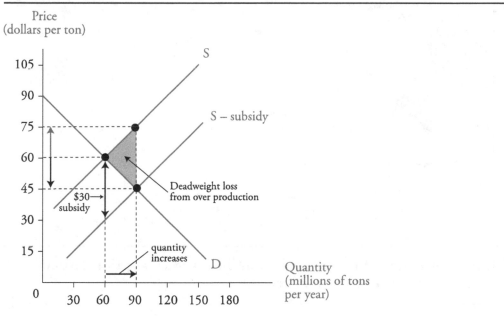

Production quotas are used to regulate markets by imposing an upper limit on the quantity of a good that may be produced over a specified time period. Quotas are often used by governments to regulate agricultural markets.

Continuing with our soybean example, let's suppose the government imposes a production quota on soybeans of 60 million tons per year. In Figure 22, we see that in the absence of a quota, soybean production is 90 million tons per year at a price of $45 per ton. With a 60 million ton quota, the equilibrium price rises to $75 per ton.

The reduction in the quantity of soybeans produced due to the quota leads to an inefficient allocation of resources and a deadweight loss to the economy. The quota not only increases the market price, but also lowers the marginal cost of producing the quota quantity. At the quota amount, marginal benefit (price) exceeds marginal cost. This explains why producers often seek the imposition of quotas.

Note that if a quota is greater than the equilibrium quantity of 90 million tons, nothing will change because farmers are already producing less than the maximum production allowed under the quota.

Further, note that the deadweight loss includes a loss of both consumer and producer surplus. The increased price, however, increases producer surplus on the 60 million tons sold by an amount greater than the producer surplus component of the deadweight loss, so that producers gain overall from the quota.

Figure 22: Soybean Production Quota

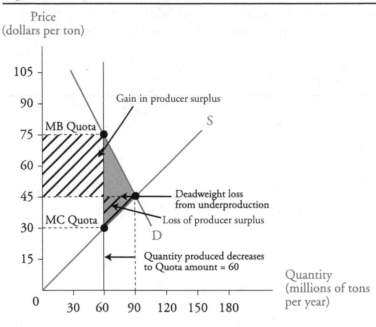

LOS 13.m: Calculate and interpret price, income, and cross-price elasticities of demand and describe factors that affect each measure.

CFA® Program Curriculum, Volume 2, page 43

Price Elasticity of Demand

Price elasticity is a measure of the responsiveness of the quantity demanded to a change in price. It is calculated as the ratio of the percentage change in quantity demanded to a percentage change in price. When quantity demanded is very responsive to a change in price, we say demand is elastic; when quantity demanded is not very responsive to a change in price, we say that demand is inelastic. In Figure 23, we illustrate the most extreme cases: perfectly elastic demand (at a higher price quantity demanded decreases to zero) and perfectly inelastic demand (a change in price has no effect on quantity demanded).

Figure 23: Inelastic and Elastic Demand

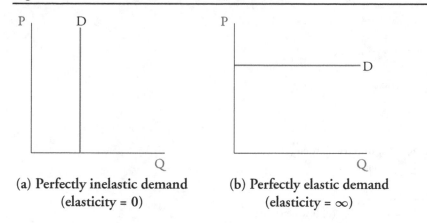

(a) Perfectly inelastic demand
(elasticity = 0)

(b) Perfectly elastic demand
(elasticity = ∞)

When there are few or no good substitutes for a good, demand tends to be relatively inelastic. Consider a drug that keeps you alive by regulating your heart. If two pills per day keep you alive, you are unlikely to decrease your purchases if the price goes up and also quite unlikely to increase your purchases if price goes down.

When one or more goods are very good substitutes for the good in question, demand will tend to be very elastic. Consider two gas stations along your regular commute that offer gasoline of equal quality. A decrease in the posted price at one station may cause you to purchase all your gasoline there, while a price increase may lead you to purchase all your gasoline at the other station. Remember, we calculate demand as well as elasticity, holding the prices of related goods (in this case, the price of gas at the other station) constant.

It is important to understand that elasticity is not slope for demand curves. Slope is dependent on the units that price and quantity are measured in. Elasticity is not dependent on units of measurement because it is based on percentage changes. Figure 24 shows how elasticity changes along a linear demand curve. In the upper part of the demand curve, elasticity is greater (in absolute value) than –1; in other words, the percentage change in quantity demanded is greater than the percentage change in price. In the lower part of the curve, the percentage change in quantity demanded is smaller than the percentage change in price.

Figure 24: Price Elasticity Along a Linear Demand Curve

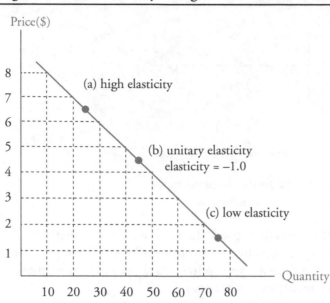

- At point (a), in a higher price range, the price elasticity of demand is greater than at point (c) in a lower price range.
- The elasticity at point (b) is –1.0; a 1% increase in price leads to a 1% decrease in quantity demanded. This is the point of greatest total revenue (P × Q), which equals 4.50 × 45 = $202.50.
- At prices less than $4.50 (inelastic range), total revenue will increase when price is increased. The percentage decrease in quantity demanded will be less than the percentage increase in price.
- At prices above $4.50 (elastic range), a price increase will decrease total revenue since the percentage decrease in quantity demanded will be greater than the percentage increase in price.

An important point to consider about the price and quantity combination for which price elasticity equals –1.0 (unitary elasticity) is that total revenue (price × quantity) is maximized at that price. An increase in price moves us to the elastic region of the curve so that the percentage decrease in quantity demanded is greater than the percentage increase in price, resulting in a decrease in total revenue. A decrease in price from the point of unitary elasticity moves us into the inelastic region of the curve so that the percentage decrease in price is more than the percentage increase in quantity demanded, resulting again in a decrease in total revenue.

Other factors affect demand elasticity in addition to the quality and availability of substitutes.

- **Portion of income spent on a good:** The larger the proportion of income that is spent on a good, the more elastic an individual's demand for that good will be. If the price of a preferred brand of toothpaste increases, a consumer may not change brands or adjust the amount used, preferring to simply pay the extra cost. When housing costs increase, however, a consumer will be much more likely to adjust consumption, because rent is a fairly large proportion of income.

- **Time:** Elasticity of demand tends to be greater the longer the time period since the price change. For example, when energy prices initially rise, some adjustments to consumption are likely made quickly. Consumers can lower the thermostat temperature. Over time, adjustments such as smaller living quarters, better insulation, more efficient windows, and installation of alternative heat sources are more easily made, and the effect of the price change on consumption of energy is greater.

Income Elasticity of Demand

Recall that one of the independent variables in our example of a demand function for gasoline was income. The sensitivity of quantity demanded to change in income is termed **income elasticity**. Holding other independent variables constant, we can measure income elasticity as the ratio of the percentage change in quantity demanded to the percentage change in income.

For most goods, the sign of income elasticity is positive—an increase in income leads to an increase in quantity demanded. Goods for which this is the case are termed **normal goods**. For other goods, it may be the case that an increase in income leads to a decrease in quantity demanded. We term goods for which this is true **inferior goods**.

A specific good may be an inferior good for some ranges of income and a normal good for other ranges of income. For a really poor person or population (think undeveloped country), an increase in income may lead to greater consumption of noodles or rice. Now, if incomes rise a bit (think college student or developing country), more meat or seafood may become part of their diet. Over this range of incomes, noodles can be an inferior good and ground meat a normal good. If incomes rise to a higher range (think graduated from college and got a job), the consumption of ground meat may fall (inferior) in favor of preferred cuts of meat (normal).

For many of us, commercial airline travel is a normal good. When our incomes rise, vacations are more likely to involve airline travel, be more frequent, and extend over longer distances so that airline travel is a normal good. For wealthy people (think hedge fund manager), an increase in income may lead to travel by private jet and a decrease in the quantity demanded of commercial airline travel.

Cross Price Elasticity of Demand

Recall that some of the independent variables in a demand function are the prices of related goods (related in the sense that their prices affect the demand for the good in question). The ratio of the percentage change in the quantity demanded of a good to the percentage change in the price of a related good is termed the **cross price elasticity of demand**.

When an increase in the price of a related good increases demand for a good, we say that the two goods are **substitutes**. If Bread A and Bread B are two brands of bread, considered good substitutes by many consumers, an increase in the price of one will lead consumers to purchase more of the other (substitute the other). When the cross price elasticity of demand is positive (price of one up, quantity demanded for the other up), we say those goods are substitutes.

When an increase in the price of a related good decreases demand for a good, we say that the two goods are **complements**. If an increase in the price of automobiles (less automobiles purchased) leads to a decrease in the demand for gasoline, they are complements. Right shoes and left shoes are perfect complements for most of us and, as a result, they are priced by the pair. If they were priced separately, there is little doubt that an increase in the price of left shoes would decrease the quantity demanded of right shoes. Overall, the cross price elasticity of demand is more positive the better substitutes two goods are and more negative the better complements the two goods are.

Calculating Elasticities

Recall the general form of our demand for gasoline function:

$$Q_{D\,gas} = 107,500 - 12,500P_{gas} + 200I + 1,200P_{BT} - 100P_{auto}$$

Note that from the coefficient on income (+200), we can tell that the good is a normal good (greater income leads to greater quantity demanded). The coefficient on the price of bus travel (+1,200) tells us that bus travel is a substitute for gasoline (higher price leads to greater quantity of gasoline demanded). The coefficient on the price of automobiles (–100) tells us that automobiles and gasoline are complements (an increase in automobile prices leads to a decrease in the quantity of gasoline demanded).

In deriving a specific demand curve for gasoline, we inserted values for income, price of bus travel, and price of automobiles to get quantity demanded as a function of only the price of the good:

$$Q_{D\,gas} = 138,500 - 12,500P_{gas}$$

The price elasticity of demand is defined as:

$$\frac{\%\Delta Q}{\%\Delta P} = \frac{\Delta Q / Q_0}{\Delta P / P_0} = \left(\frac{P_0}{Q_0}\right) \times \left(\frac{\Delta Q}{\Delta P}\right)$$

The term $\left(\dfrac{\Delta Q}{\Delta P}\right)$ is simply the slope coefficient on the price of gasoline in our demand function (–12,500).

Example: Calculating price elasticity of demand

For the previous demand curve, calculate the price elasticity at a gasoline price of $3 per gallon.

Answer:

We can calculate the quantity demanded at a price of $3 per gallon as 138,500 – 12,500(3) = 101,000. Substituting 3 for P_0, 101,000 for Q_0, and –12,500 for $\left(\dfrac{\Delta Q}{\Delta P} \right)$, we can calculate the price elasticity of demand as:

$$E_{Demand} = \frac{\%\Delta Q}{\%\Delta P} = \left(\frac{3}{101,000} \right) \times (-12,500) = -0.37$$

For this demand function, at a price and quantity of $3 per gallon and 101,000 gallons, demand is inelastic.

The technique for calculating income elasticity and cross price elasticity is identical, as we illustrate in the following example. We assume values for all the independent variables, except the one of interest, and then calculate elasticity for a given value of the variable of interest.

Example: Calculating income elasticity and cross price elasticity

An individual has the following demand function for gasoline:

$$Q_{D\,gas} = 15 - 3P_{gas} + 0.02I + 0.11P_{BT} - 0.008P_{auto}$$

where income and car price are measured in thousands, and the price of bus travel is measured in average dollars per 100 miles traveled.

Assuming the average automobile price is $22,000, income is $40,000, the price of bus travel is $25, and the price of gasoline is $3, calculate and interpret the income elasticity of gasoline demand and the cross price elasticity of gasoline demand with respect to the price of bus travel.

Answer:

Inserting the prices of gasoline, bus travel, and automobiles into our demand equation, we get:

$$Q_{D\ gas} = 15 - 3(3) + 0.02(\text{income in thousands}) + 0.11(25) - 0.008(22)$$

and

$$Q_{D\ gas} = 8.6 + 0.02(\text{income in thousands})$$

Our slope term on income is 0.02, and for an income of 40,000, $Q_{D\ gas} = 9.4$ gallons.

The formula for the income elasticity of demand is:

$$\frac{\%\Delta Q}{\%\Delta I} = \frac{\Delta Q / Q_0}{\Delta I / I_0} = \left(\frac{I_0}{Q_0}\right) \times \left(\frac{\Delta Q}{\Delta I}\right)$$

Substituting our calculated values, we have:

$$\left(\frac{40}{9.4}\right) \times (0.02) = 0.085$$

This tells us that for these assumed values (at a single point on the demand curve), a 1% increase (decrease) in income will lead to an increase (decrease) of 0.085% in the quantity of gasoline demanded.

In order to calculate the cross price elasticity of demand for bus travel and gasoline, we construct a demand function with only the price of bus travel as an independent variable:

$$Q_{D\ gas} = 15 - 3P_{gas} + 0.02I + 0.11P_{BT} - 0.008P_{auto}$$

$$Q_{D\ gas} = 15 - 3(3) + 0.02(40) + 0.11P_{BT} - 0.008(22)$$

$$Q_{D\ gas} = 6.6 + 0.11P_{BT}$$

For a price of bus travel of $25, the quantity of gasoline demanded is:

$$Q_{D\ gas} = 6.6 + 0.11P_{BT}$$

$$Q_{D\ gas} = 6.6 + 0.11(25) = 9.35 \text{ gallons}$$

The cross price elasticity of the demand for gasoline with respect to the price of bus travel is:

$$\frac{\%\Delta Q}{\%\Delta P_{BT}} = \frac{\Delta Q/Q_0}{\Delta P_{BT}/P_{0\ BT}} = \left(\frac{P_{0\ BT}}{Q_0}\right) \times \left(\frac{\Delta Q}{\Delta P_{BT}}\right) = \frac{25}{9.35} \times 0.11 = 0.294$$

As noted, gasoline and bus travel are substitutes, so the cross price elasticity of demand is positive. We can interpret this value to mean that for our assumed values, a 1% change in the price of bus travel will lead to a 0.294% change in the quantity of gasoline demanded in the same direction, other things equal.

In the previous example, we calculated the elasticity of demand at a point on the demand curve using the slope of the curve at a specific price and quantity. Given two points on the demand curve (rather than the demand function), we can calculate the elasticity over that range of the demand curve, that is, the **arc elasticity** of demand. When calculating the percentage changes in price and in quantity for arc elasticity, we use the midpoints of price and quantity over the range so that an increase and a decrease for either price or quantity will yield the same percentage change.

Example: Arc elasticity of demand

At a price of $4 per unit quantity demanded is 40,000 units and at a price of $5 per unit the quantity demanded is 35,000 units. Calculate the arc elasticity of demand over this range.

The percentage change in price over the range is $\dfrac{5-4}{(5+4)/2} = \dfrac{1}{4.5} = 22.2\%$.

The percentage change in quantity over the range is

$$\frac{35,000 - 40,000}{(35,000 + 40,000)/2} = \frac{-5,000}{37,500} = -13.3\%.$$

The elasticity over the range, $\dfrac{\%\Delta \text{ quantity}}{\%\Delta \text{ price}}$, is $\dfrac{-13.33\%}{22.2\%} = -0.6$.

KEY CONCEPTS

LOS 13.a

Markets for goods and services to consumers are referred to as goods markets or product markets.

Markets for factors of production (raw materials, goods and services used in production) are referred to as factor markets.

Goods and services used in the production of final goods and services are referred to as intermediate goods.

LOS 13.b

The quantity supplied is greater at higher prices. The quantity demanded is greater at lower prices.

A demand function provides the quantity demanded as a function of price of the good or service, the prices of related goods or services, and some measure of income.

A supply function provides the quantity supplied as a function of price of the good or service and the prices of productive inputs, and depends on the technology used to produce the good or service.

Using values for all the variables other than price and inverting a demand (supply) function produces a demand (supply) curve.

LOS 13.c

The change in quantity demanded (supplied) in response to a change in price represents a movement along a demand (supply) curve, not a change in demand (supply).

Changes in demand (supply) refer to shifts in a demand (supply) curve.

Demand is affected by changes in consumer tastes and typically increases (shifts to the right) with increases in income, increases in the price of substitute goods, or decreases in the price of complementary goods.

Supply is increased (shifted to the right) by advances in production technology and by decreases in input prices (prices of factors of production).

LOS 13.d

The aggregate or market demand (supply) function is calculated by summing the quantities demanded (supplied) at each price for individual demand (supply) functions.

LOS 13.e

In free markets, the equilibrium price is the price at which the quantity demanded equals the quantity supplied. When the market price is greater than the equilibrium price, the quantity supplied is greater than the quantity demanded (excess supply), and competition among suppliers for sales will drive the price down towards the equilibrium price. When the market price is less than the equilibrium price, the quantity demanded is greater than the quantity supplied (excess demand), and competition for the product among buyers will drive the price up towards the equilibrium price.

Analysis of the market for a single good is called partial equilibrium analysis. General equilibrium analysis also considers the effects of one good's price change on the prices of other goods that may in turn affect demand for the good.

LOS 13.f

A stable equilibrium is one for which movement of the price away from its equilibrium level results in forces that drive the price back towards equilibrium. An unstable equilibrium is one for which a movement of the price away from its equilibrium level results in forces that move the price further from its equilibrium level.

While price equilibria are typically stable, if the supply curve is downward sloping **and** less steep than the demand curve, the resulting equilibrium is unstable.

The term "bubble" refers to an unsustainable increase in price of an asset type resulting from an expecation that price increases in the current period will lead to higher future prices.

LOS 13.g

Given an individual's demand function for Good X, $Q_{DX} = f$(price of Good X, price of Good A, price of Good B, income), we can insert values for income and the prices of related goods A and B to get quantity demanded as a function of only the price of Good X. We can invert this function (solve for P_X) to get a demand curve (i.e., price as a function of quantity demanded).

Given a firm's supply function for Good X, $Q_{SX} = f$(price of Good X, price of input A, price of input B) for a specific production technology, we can insert values for input prices to get quantity supplied as a function of only the price of Good X. We can invert this function (solve for P_X) to get a supply curve (i.e., price as a function of quantity supplied).

The aggregate or market demand (supply) function is calculated by summing the quantities demanded (supplied) for individual demand (supply) functions. Inverting an aggregate demand (supply) function produces an aggregate demand (supply) curve.

LOS 13.h

Excess market supply (quantity supplied is greater than quantity demanded) or excess market demand (quantity demanded is greater than quantity supplied) for any price can be calculated by using aggregate demand and supply functions, inserting the market price of the good into each, and comparing the resulting (market) quantities supplied and demanded.

LOS 13.i

A common value auction is an auction for a good (e.g., rights to mineral extraction) which has the same value to all bidders, even though this value may not be known with certainty at the time of the auction. The highest bidder may be the one who most overvalues the item (winner's curse).

A private value auction is an auction for a good (e.g., Van Gogh painting) for which the value is different to each bidder. Bidders are not expected to bid amounts greater than their private value of the item.

In an ascending price or English auction, the highest bidder wins the item and pays the amount bid.

In a sealed bid auction, each bidder's bid is unknown to other bidders and the high bidder wins the item and pays the amount bid. The value to each bidder is referred to as the bidder's *reservation price*. The bid made by the winner may be less than his reservation price.

In a second price or Vickrey auction, the winning (highest) bidder pays the amount bid by the second-highest bidder. In this format, there is no incentive for a bidder to bid less than his reservation price.

In a descending price or Dutch auction, the auction begins with a high price which is reduced in increments until a buyer accepts the price. When multiple units are available, bidders may accept the price for some units and the price is subsequently reduced incrementally until the last of the available units are accepted.

The auction of U.S. Treasury securities is done with a modified Dutch auction in which all bidders pay the price at which the last of the units available are purchased. Non-competitive bids may be placed, which are filled in their specified amounts at the final price.

LOS 13.j

The equilibrium quantity and price lead to optimal allocation of resources because the allocation maximizes the difference between the cost of producing and the total value to consumers of the traded quantity of a good.

Consumer surplus is the excess consumers would be willing to pay above what they actually pay for the equilibrium quantity of a good or a service and is represented by the triangle bounded by the demand curve, the equilibrium price, and the left-hand axis. For a linear demand curve, consumer surplus can be calculated as the area of the triangle, or ½ × equilibrium quantity × (price at which quantity demanded is zero – equilibrium price).

Producer surplus is the excess that suppliers receive over the total cost to produce those units and is represented by the triangle bounded by market price, the supply curve, and the left-hand axis. For a linear supply curve, producer surplus can be calculated as ½ × equilibrium quantity × (equilibrium price – price at which quantity supplied is zero).

LOS 13.k

Imposition of an effective maximum price (price ceiling) by the government results in excess demand, while imposition of an effective minimum price (price floor) results in excess supply.

Imposition of an effective quota reduces supply. Payment of a subsidy to producers increases supply.

Imposition of a tax on suppliers reduces supply. Imposition of a tax on consumers reduces demand.

LOS 13.l

Imposition of a price ceiling will reduce price and decrease the traded quantity to the quantity supplied at the reduced price. Imposition of a price floor will increase price and decrease the traded quantity to the quantity demanded at the increased price. Imposition of taxes on either producers or consumers will increase price (including tax) above the previous equilibrium price, decrease price (excluding tax) below the previous equilibrium level, and decrease the traded quantity to the same amount in either case.

LOS 13.m

Elasticity is measured as the ratio of the percentage change in one variable to a percentage change in another. Three elasticities related to a demand function are of interest:

$$\text{own price elasticity} = \frac{\% \text{ change in quantity demanded}}{\% \text{ change in own price}}$$

$$\text{cross price elasticity} = \frac{\% \text{ change in quantity demanded}}{\% \text{ change in price of related good}}$$

$$\text{income elasticity} = \frac{\% \text{ change in quantity demanded}}{\% \text{ change in income}}$$

|own price elasticity| > 1: demand is elastic

|own price elasticity| < 1: demand is inelastic

cross price elasticity > 0: related good is a substitute

cross price elasticity < 0: related good is a complement

income elasticity < 0: good is an inferior good

income elasticity > 0: good is a normal good

CONCEPT CHECKERS

1. A company that manufactures airplane seats is *best* described as producing:
   A. finished goods.
   B. intermediate goods.
   C. factors of production.

2. A change in the supply of bread is *least likely* to result from a change in:
   A. wages for bakers.
   B. the price of bread.
   C. the price of wheat.

3. If quantity supplied of refrigerators exceeds quantity demanded at the current market price, the *most likely* market response would be a(n):
   A. stable market disequilibrium.
   B. increase in demand for refrigerators.
   C. decrease in the price of refrigerators.

4. In a market with an unstable equilibrium price and quantity:
   A. the demand curve must slope upward.
   B. prices do not move toward their equilibrium values.
   C. both price and output are highly variable around the equilibrium.

5. A demand function for cellular telephones is given by:

   $$QD_{cellphone} = 390 - 4\,P_{cellphone} + 0.015\ \text{income} + 2.2\,P_{landline} - 0.55\,P_{wireless}$$

   At current average prices, a cellphone costs $100, a landline costs $60, and wireless service costs $40. Average income is $20,000. The price of cellular telephones as a function of quantity demanded (QD) is *most accurately* described as:
   A. 400.
   B. $100 QD cellphone.
   C. 200 − 0.25 QD cellphone.

6. The demand function for coffee pots is given by 250 − 5P, and the supply function is given by 20P − 50. At a price of 15, the market:
   A. has excess supply of 75.
   B. has excess demand of 75.
   C. is in equilibrium with quantity supplied and demanded equal to 75.

7. Nascent Technologies solicits sealed bids for a placement of new shares and receives the following bids:

Shareholder	Price (euros per share)
Equity Partners	26.00
Wiseman Investments	25.75
Mutual Insurers	25.30
Newera Fund Management	24.85

The entire share issue is placed with Equity Partners, that pays 25.75 per share. What type of auction did Nascent Technologies conduct?
A. Dutch.
B. English.
C. Vickrey.

8. The demand function for electric motors is $120 - 6P$, and the supply function is $40P - 432$. At a price of 12, the value of consumer surplus is *closest* to:
A. 48.
B. 192.
C. 384.

9. If a market is currently in equilibrium, which of the following is *least likely* to cause an imbalance between supply and demand and a deadweight loss to the economy?
A. Subsidies to producers.
B. A legal price floor on the product.
C. A change in the equilibrium market price.

10. The long-term effects of a price ceiling on a market are *least likely* to include:
A. discrimination by sellers.
B. an increase in waiting times to purchase.
C. improvement in quality to offset the reduction in quantity supplied.

11. The imposition of a price floor above the current equilibrium price is *most likely* to result in a:
A. change in supply.
B. welfare loss to the economy.
C. decrease in quantity supplied.

12. A demand function for air conditioners is given by:

$$QD_{air\ conditioner} = 10,000 - 2\,P_{air\ conditioner} + 0.0004\ income + 30\,P_{electric\ fan} - 4\,P_{electricity}$$

At current average prices, an air conditioner costs 5,000 yen, a fan costs 200 yen, and electricity costs 1,000 yen. Average income is 4,000,000 yen. The income elasticity of demand for air conditioners is *closest* to:
A. 0.0004.
B. 0.444.
C. 40,000.

ANSWERS – CONCEPT CHECKERS

1. **B** Airplane seats are intermediate goods. The company purchases factors of production (such as fabric and labor) and sells an intermediate good (airplane seats). The airplanes into which the seats are installed are finished goods.

2. **B** Supply changes in response to a change in the cost of inputs (labor or materials). A change in the price of the product is a movement along the supply curve (change in quantity supplied), not a shift of the supply curve.

3. **C** The price of refrigerators is likely to decline as inventories build and producers compete for business. *Quantity demanded* of refrigerators is likely to increase as price decreases, but the *demand curve* for refrigerators will not change as a result. A change in price is a movement along the demand curve to a different quantity, not a change in demand.

4. **B** When an equilibrium price and quantity are unstable, both price and quantity move away from their equilibrium values rather than back toward them.

5. **C** Substituting current values for the independent variables other than price, the demand function becomes:

$$QD_{cellphone} = 390 - 4\,P_{cellphone} + 0.015(20,000) + 2.2(60) - 0.55(40)$$
$$= 390 - 4\,P_{cellphone} + 300 + 132 - 22$$
$$= 800 - 4\,P_{cellphone}$$

Solving algebraically, we have:

$$QD_{cellphone} = 800 - 4\,P_{cellphone}$$

$$QD_{cellphone} - 800 = -4\,P_{cellphone}$$

$$-0.25\,QD_{cellphone} + 200 = P_{cellphone}$$

$$P_{cellphone} = 200 - 0.25\,QD_{cellphone}$$

6. **A** At a price of 15, quantity demanded = $250 - 5(15) = 175$, and quantity supplied = $20(15) - 50 = 250$. Excess supply = $250 - 175 = 75$.

7. **C** A Vickrey auction is a sealed bid auction in which the winner pays the price bid by the second highest bidder. Dutch (descending price) and English (ascending price) auctions are not sealed bid auctions.

8. **B** The demand *curve* crosses the price-axis at Q = 0. Solving for *P* at Q = 0, we get $0 = 120 - 6P$. $P = 20$. The quantity demanded at P = 12 is $120 - 6(12) = 48$. The sides of the consumer surplus triangle measure $20 - 12 = 8$ on the price-axis and $48 - 0 = 48$ on the quantity-axis. The area of the triangle is thus $\frac{1}{2}(8 \times 48) = 192$. The supply function can also be used to calculate the equilibrium quantity of 48.

9. **C** Subsidies and price controls are both examples of government intervention in markets that can create an imbalance in supply and demand and cause a deadweight loss to the economy. The equilibrium market price is the price at which supply and demand are in balance, and there is no deadweight loss.

10. **C**   A price ceiling is a price above which producers cannot legally sell and is generally set below the market equilibrium, resulting in a decline in price. Producers often respond by reducing the quality of goods commensurate with the lower imposed price.

11. **B**   A price floor is a minimum legal price. Quantity supplied will likely increase, but supply does not change. With a minimum legal price above the equilibrium price, quantity demanded, and thus the quantity traded, is reduced. This results in a welfare loss to society compared to equilibrium without the minimum price.

12. **B**   Substituting current values for the independent variables other than income, the demand function becomes:

$$QD_{air\ conditioner} = 10,000 - 2(5,000) + 0.0004\ income + 30(200) - 4(1000)$$
$$= 0.0004\ income + 2,000$$

The slope of income is 0.0004, and for an income of 4,000,000 yen, QD = 3,600.

Income elasticity = $I_0 / Q_0 \times \Delta Q / \Delta I$ = 4,000,000 / 3,600 × 0.0004 = 0.444.

The following is a review of the Economics: Microeconomic Analysis principles designed to address the learning outcome statements set forth by CFA Institute. This topic is also covered in:

DEMAND AND SUPPLY ANALYSIS: CONSUMER DEMAND

EXAM FOCUS

In this topic review we introduce utility theory, which is a formal way of modeling consumer choice. The idea of the tangency of a curve representing preferences, with a line representing available combinations of goods indicating a consumer's most preferred or optimal combination of those goods, is an important one. We will see this analysis also used in Portfolio Management. The concept of inferior goods is useful when we try to determine which goods or industries will have increased revenues when average incomes fall, as in a recession. On the other hand, the material on income versus substitution effects of a price change, Giffen goods and Veblen goods is probably most valuable for answering exam questions.

LOS 14.a: Describe consumer choice theory and utility theory.

CFA® Program Curriculum, Volume 2, page 64

Utility theory explains consumer behavior based on preferences for various alternative combinations of goods, in terms of the relative level of satisfaction they provide. The satisfaction that consumers get from consuming a specific combination or *bundle* of goods is measured with the concept of utility. Utility theory is an important aspect of **consumer choice theory**, which relates consumers' wants and preferences to the goods and services they actually buy.

A **utility function** is of the form utility = $U(Q_A, Q_B,...,Q_N)$, where the variables are quantities consumed of goods A through N. We assume that no quantities are negative (some may be zero), and that holding all other quantities constant while increasing one always results in greater utility. This is referred to as the **condition of non-satiation** and can be simply stated as a condition that, other things equal, more is always preferred to less. If less is preferred to more, we don't have a good; instead we have a bad. An example of a bad is garbage. We are willing to pay to have less garbage.

Utility is an ordinal measure, rather than a cardinal measure. Consider two bundles of goods: Bundle 1 has 2 pizzas (*P*) and 20 beers (*B*), and Bundle 2 has 3P and 15B. If the utility of Bundle 1 equals 100, and the utility of Bundle 2 equals 200, we can say that Bundle 2 is preferred to Bundle 1 because 200 is greater than 100. We cannot infer from this, however, that Bundle 2 gives twice the satisfaction of Bundle 1 or that Bundle 2 yields the same utility as two Bundle 1s. If we assign a utility of 4,000 to Bundle 1 and 4,001 to Bundle 2, we have exactly the same information—simply that Bundle 2 is preferred to Bundle 1. We can state which bundle is preferred, but we cannot state by how much.

LOS 14.b: Describe the use of indifference curves, opportunity sets, and budget constraints in decision making.

LOS 14.c: Calculate and interpret a budget constraint.

CFA® Program Curriculum, Volume 2, page 67

A **budget constraint** can be constructed based on the consumer's income and the prices of the available goods. In Panel (a) of Figure 1, we show the budget constraint for a consumer with an income of $90 when the price of Good X is $6 and the price of Good Y is $15. The *budget line* shows all combinations of Good X and Good Y that will just exhaust the consumer's income. Combinations in the shaded area (the **opportunity set**) are also affordable.

In Panel (b), we show how the budget line would shift for an increase in income from $90 to $120. The shift is parallel because the prices of Good X and Good Y (and, therefore, the slope) are unchanged.

Panel (c) illustrates the effect of a decline in the price of Good X from $6 to $5 per unit. The slope of a budget line is equal to the (negative of the) ratio of the prices, P_X/P_Y. With the decrease in the price of Good X, the slope of the budget line has declined (in magnitude) from $-6/15$ to $-5/15$. Price ratios are referred to as **relative prices**—the price of one good in terms of another. At a price of $6, each unit of Good X costs $6/15$ of the unit of Good Y, so $6/15$ is the price of Good X in terms of Good Y. We can also easily calculate the slopes using the X- and Y-intercepts, as $-8/20$ and $-8/24$.

Figure 1: Budget Lines for Two Goods

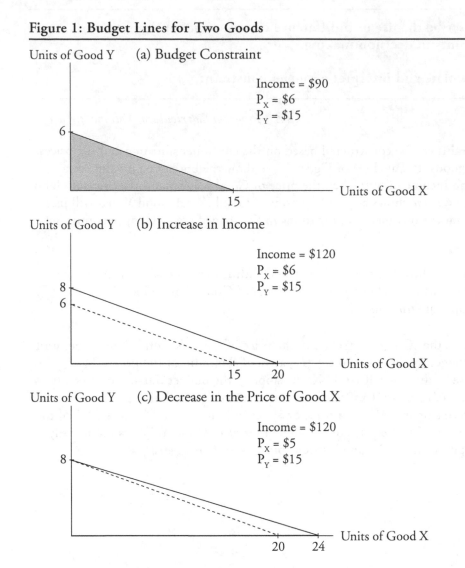

Indifference curves plot the combinations of two goods that provide equal utility to a consumer. Indifference curves must follow certain rules that can be summarized as follows:

1. *Indifference curves for two goods slope downward*: A bundle of goods with less of Good X must have more of Good Y for the two to have equal utility and lie on the same indifference curve. This is illustrated in Panel (a) of Figure 2.

2. *Indifference curves are convex towards the origin*: Convexity results when the magnitude of the slope decreases as we move toward more of Good X and less of Good Y. In Panel (a), we have shown that the tradeoff between goods X and Y changes as we move down an indifference curve. Between Point A and Point B, this consumer is willing to give up one unit of Good X to get one more unit of Good Y. Between Point C and Point D, this consumer requires two units of Good X to compensate for one less unit of Good Y.

The slope of an indifference curve at any point is referred to as the **marginal rate of substitution** (MRS), the rate at which the consumer will willingly exchange units of Good X for units of Good Y. Thus, the characteristic convexity of indifference curves reflects a diminishing marginal rate of substitution. The intuition is that when a consumer has more units of Good X and less of Good Y, he is willing to give up more units of X to get one more unit of Y.

3. *Indifference curves cannot cross*: In Panel (b) of Figure 2, we show two indifference curves that cross. If this were the case, we would have the following relationships: B is equally preferred to both A and C, while C is preferred to A because it has more of both goods. Preferences must be transitive to be consistent [i.e., if $U(B) = U(A)$, and $U(B) = U(C)$, then $U(A) = U(C)$].

Figure 2: Properties of Indifference Curves

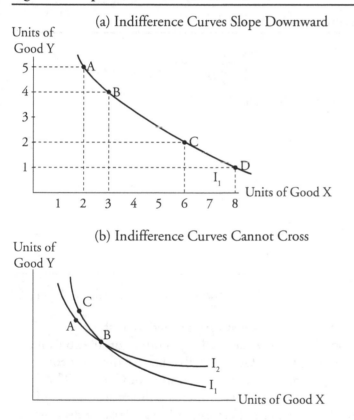

In order to use indifference curves to model consumer decision making, we need to first define the possible (affordable) consumption bundles and then use the indifference curves to identify the most preferred bundle (combination of goods) among all affordable bundles.

LOS 14.d: Determine a consumer's equilibrium bundle of goods based on utility analysis.

CFA® Program Curriculum, Volume 2, page 79

In Figure 3, we have drawn a consumer's budget constraint along with some of her indifference curves. The optimal (most preferred) consumption bundle for this consumer is at the point where indifference curve I_1 is tangent to the budget line. While there are affordable bundles along I_0, all bundles along I_0 are less preferred than those along I_1. Bundles along I_2 are preferred to those along I_1, but none are affordable. In short, we represent a consumer's **equilibrium bundle of goods**, the most preferred affordable combination of Good X and Good Y, as the point where the highest attainable indifference curve is just tangent to the budget line.

Figure 3: A Consumer's Equilibrium Bundle of Goods

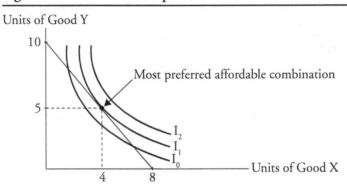

LOS 14.e: Compare substitution and income effects.

CFA® Program Curriculum, Volume 2, page 84

When the price of Good X decreases, there is a **substitution effect** that shifts consumption towards more of Good X. Because the total expenditure on the consumer's original bundle of goods falls when the price of Good X falls, there is also an **income effect**. The income effect can be toward more or less consumption of Good X. This is the key point here: the substitution effect always acts to increase the consumption of a good that has fallen in price, while the income effect can either increase or decrease consumption of a good that has fallen in price.

Based on this analysis, we can describe three possible outcomes of a decrease in the price of Good X:

1. The substitution effect is positive, and the income effect is also positive—consumption of Good X will *increase*.

2. The substitution effect is positive, and the income effect is negative but smaller than the substitution effect—consumption of Good X will *increase*.

3. The substitution effect is positive, and the income effect is negative and larger than the substitution effect—consumption of Good X will *decrease*.

Graphical representations of these three cases are illustrated in Figure 4. The initial budget line is B_0, and the new budget line after a decrease in the price of Good X is B_2. The substitution effect on the consumer's preferred consumption bundle is shown by constructing a (theoretical) budget line B_1 that is parallel to the new budget line B_2 and is also tangent to the original indifference curve I_0. We are essentially finding the consumption bundle that the consumer would prefer at the new relative prices if his utility were unchanged (i.e., the new bundle must be on I_0). The substitution effect of the decrease in the price of Good X is always positive and is shown as the increase in the quantity of X from Q_0 to Q_S.

The income effect is shown as the change in consumption from T_1 to the new tangency point T_2 (most preferred bundle) of indifference curve I_1 and the new budget line B_2, and the change in quantity from Q_S to Q_1.

In Panel (a), both the income and substitution effects increase consumption of Good X. In Panel (b), the income effect is negative but smaller in magnitude than the substitution effect, so the total effect of the price reduction on the consumption of Good X is still positive, an increase from Q_0 to Q_1. In Panel (c), the negative income effect is larger than the substitution effect, and the total effect of the reduction in the price of Good X is a *decrease* in the quantity of X from Q_0 to Q_1. This represents a case where the law of demand is violated, and a decrease in the price of Good X actually reduces the quantity of Good X demanded.

Figure 4: Income and Substitution Effects

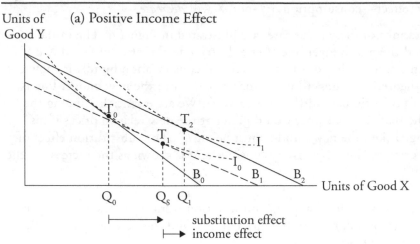

(a) Positive Income Effect

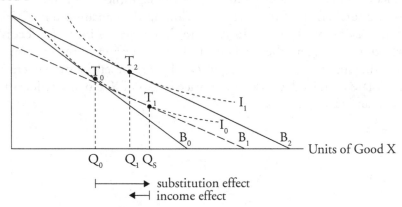

(b) Negative Income Effect, Smaller Than Substitution Effect

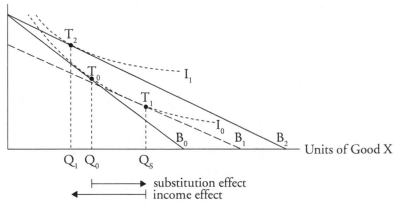

(c) Negative Income Effect, Larger Than Substitution Effect

©2014 Kaplan, Inc.

LOS 14.f: Distinguish between normal goods and inferior goods, and explain Giffen goods and Veblen goods in this context.

CFA® Program Curriculum, Volume 2, page 87

A **normal good** is one for which the income effect is positive, as in Panel (a) of Figure 4. An **inferior good** is one for which the income effect is negative, as in panels (b) and (c) of Figure 4. A **Giffen good** is an inferior good for which the negative income effect outweighs the positive substitution effect when price falls, as in Panel (c). A Giffen good is theoretical and would have an upward-sloping demand curve. At lower prices, a smaller quantity would be demanded as a result of the dominance of the income effect over the substitution effect.

A **Veblen good** is one for which a higher price makes the good more desirable. The idea is that the consumer gets utility from being seen to consume a good that has high status (think Gucci bag), and that a higher price for the good conveys more status and increases its utility. Such a good could conceivably have a positively sloped demand curve for some individuals over some range of prices. If such a good exists, there must be a limit to this process, or the price would rise without limit.

There are two important distinctions between Giffen goods and Veblen goods. First, Giffen goods are inferior goods (negative income effect), while Veblen goods certainly are not. Second, the existence of Giffen goods is theoretically supported by our rules of consumer choice, while the existence of Veblen goods is not.

KEY CONCEPTS

LOS 14.a
A consumer who selects his most preferred bundle (combination) of goods for consumption from all affordable bundles is said to be maximizing his utility. A given bundle of goods is preferred to all other bundles of goods that provide less utility.

LOS 14.b
An indifference curve shows all combinations of two goods among which a specific consumer is indifferent (i.e., all combinations of the two goods along an indifference curve are equally preferred).

An opportunity set is all the combinations of goods that are affordable to a specific consumer.

LOS 14.c
A budget constraint for two goods is all combinations of goods that will, given the prices of the two goods, just exhaust a consumer's income.

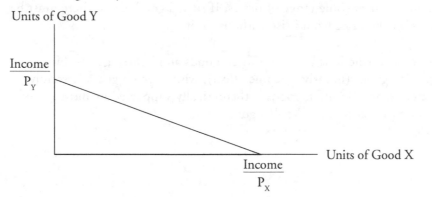

LOS 14.d
Given a budget constraint and a specific consumer's indifference curves, the consumer's most preferred combination of two goods along the budget constraint is represented by the point where one of the consumer's indifference curves is just tangent to the budget constraint.

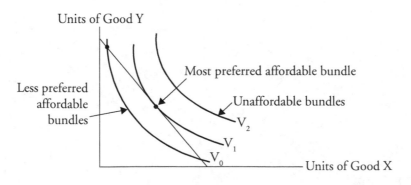

LOS 14.e
When the price of a good decreases, the substitution effect leads a consumer to consume more of that good and less of goods for which prices have remained the same.

A decrease in the price of a good that a consumer purchases leaves her with unspent income (for the same combination of goods). The effect of this additional income on consumption of the good for which the price has decreased is termed the income effect.

LOS 14.f
For a normal good, the income effect of a price decrease is positive—income elasticity of demand is positive.

For an inferior good, the income effect of a price decrease is negative—income elasticity of demand is negative. An increase in income reduces demand for an inferior good.

A Giffen good is an inferior good for which the negative income effect of a price decrease outweighs the positive substitution effect, so that a decrease (increase) in the good's price has a net result of decreasing (increasing) the quantity consumed.

A Veblen good is also one for which an increase (decrease) in price results in an increase (decrease) in the quantity consumed. However, a Veblen good is not an inferior good. The increase in consumption when the price of the good increases is due to a perception that a higher price makes consuming the good more desirable in some way, perhaps conveying higher status.

CONCEPT CHECKERS

1. Which of the following statements is *least accurate* with respect to utility theory? Utility:
   A. is an ordinal measure of a consumer's level of satisfaction.
   B. theory demonstrates that quantity demanded decreases as price increases.
   C. theory assumes that consumers can consistently rank all possible combinations of goods.

2. A consumer has a budget of 120 euros. The price of melons increases from 4 euros to 5 euros, and the price of fish increases from 6 euros to 10 euros. These changes represent an increase in the:
   A. relative price of fish.
   B. relative price of melons.
   C. opportunity set of melons and fish.

3. A consumer's equilibrium bundle of goods is *best* described as being located:
   A. at the point where an indifference curve and budget line cross.
   B. at the point of tangency of an indifference curve with a budget line.
   C. on the highest indifference curve that lies entirely below the budget line.

4. When the price of a good decreases, and an individual's consumption of that good also decreases, it is *most likely* that the:
   A. income effect and substitution effect are both negative.
   B. substitution effect is negative and the income effect is positive.
   C. income effect is negative and the substitution effect is positive.

5. If widgets are a Giffen good, which of the following describes the effect of a price decrease in widgets? Quantity demanded will *most likely*:
   A. increase in accordance with the law of demand.
   B. decrease because a lower price makes a Giffen good less desirable.
   C. decrease because the income effect will more than offset the substitution effect.

ANSWERS – CONCEPT CHECKERS

1. **B**   Utility theory is consistent with the existence of a Giffen good, one for which a price increase results in an increase in consumption.

2. **A**   The relative price of fish has increased from 6/4 = 1.5 melons to 10/5 = 2.0 melons. At the same time, the relative price of melons has decreased from 4/6 = 0.67 fish to 5/10 = 0.50 fish. Increases in the money prices of both goods decrease the opportunity set because some combinations of goods that were attainable at lower prices are no longer attainable with the same income.

3. **B**   A consumer's equilibrium bundle of goods is the one that is on the highest possible indifference curve given the budget constraint. That curve will be tangent to the budget line, and the equilibrium bundle of goods will be located at the point of tangency.

4. **C**   The substitution effect of a price decrease is always positive, but the income effect can be either positive or negative. Consumption of a good will decrease when the price of that good decreases only if the income effect is both negative and greater than the substitution effect.

5. **C**   Giffen goods are an inferior good for which the income effect is greater than the substitution effect, so that when the price decreases, quantity demanded will also decrease. Goods that are perceived as less desirable when price decreases are called Veblen goods.

DEMAND AND SUPPLY ANALYSIS: THE FIRM

EXAM FOCUS

Starting with the concept of economic profit, here we cover total, average, and marginal revenue followed by total, average, and marginal cost of production. The condition for profit maximization for a firm is a key concept and you also need to know the difference between the long run and short run for a firm. Candidates should pay special attention to the shapes of marginal cost curves, average total cost curves, and average variable cost curves. The effects of economies and diseconomies of scale on firms' long-run supply curves, the effects of industry growth on key input prices, and the slope of long-run industry supply curves are all important to know. Finally, candidates need to understand the concept of diminishing marginal productivity of a productive input and how this is used in deriving the mix of firm inputs that will minimize costs for a given output, and the condition for the quantity of each input to be at the profit-maximizing level.

LOS 15.a: Calculate, interpret, and compare accounting profit, economic profit, normal profit, and economic rent.

CFA® Program Curriculum, Volume 2, page 97

Accounting Profit

Accounting profit may be referred to as net income, net profit, net earnings, or the bottom line (of the firm's income statement). It is equal to total revenue less all accounting costs. Accounting costs are *explicit costs* that represent actual payments for the resources the firm uses in producing its output. Accounting costs include the interest cost on debt financing but not any payments to the firm's equity owners as a return on their invested capital.

accounting profit = total revenue − total accounting (explicit) costs

Example: Calculating accounting profit

Given the following financial information for the most recent accounting period, calculate the accounting profit for Patrick's Surfboard Company:

Account	Amount
Total revenue	$340,000
Expenses	
Fiberglass	$100,000
Electricity	30,000
Employee wages paid	55,000
Interest paid on debt	5,000

Answer:

$$\text{total accounting (explicit) costs} = \$100,000 + \$30,000 + \$55,000 + \$5,000$$
$$= \$190,000$$

$$\text{accounting profit} = \text{total revenue} - \text{accounting (explicit costs)}$$
$$= \$340,000 - \$190,000 = \$150,000$$

Economic Profit

Economic profit is also referred to as *abnormal profit*. It is equal to accounting profit less *implicit costs*. Implicit costs are the opportunity costs of resources supplied to the firm by its owners. For private firms, these costs may include the opportunity cost of owner-supplied capital and the opportunity cost of the time and entrepreneurial ability of the firm's owners. For publicly traded firms, implicit costs are typically only the opportunity cost of equity owners' investment in the firm. Total economic costs include both implicit and explicit costs.

economic profit = accounting profit – implicit opportunity costs

or

economic profit = total revenue – total economic costs

Example: Calculating economic profit

Continuing the example of Patrick's Surfboard Company, assume that Patrick took a pay reduction of $50,000 per year to start the company. He also invested into the business and could have earned $60,000 per year if he had invested the funds elsewhere. What is the economic profit for Patrick's Surfboard Company?

Answer:

$$\text{economic profit} = \text{accounting profit} - \text{implicit opportunity costs}$$
$$= \$150,000 - (\$50,000 + \$60,000) = \$40,000$$

Note that entrepreneurs typically earn payment or compensation in the form of profit. Note also that economic profit is lower than the accounting profit. This is because an economic profit considers both explicit and implicit costs.

Example: Economic profit for a firm

RideRight, Inc., a publicly traded company, reported $450,000 of revenue, $400,000 in expenses, and $500,000 in equity capital for the most recent accounting period. The required rate of return on RideRight's equity is 10%. Calculate RideRight's economic profit.

Answer:

For publicly traded companies, it is assumed that the cost of equity capital is the largest implicit/opportunity cost:

$$\text{economic profit} = \text{accounting profit} - \text{cost of equity capital}$$
$$= (\$450,000 - \$400,000) - (0.10 \times \$500,000) = \$0$$

RideRight's accounting profit just covered the cost of equity capital.

Normal Profit

Normal profit is the accounting profit that makes economic profit zero. It is the accounting profit that the firm must earn to just cover implicit opportunity costs. Given this definition, it follows that:

$$\text{economic profit} = (\text{accounting profit} - \text{normal profit}) = 0$$

When accounting profits exceed implicit opportunity costs, economic profit is positive and we have:

$$\text{economic profit} = (\text{accounting profit} - \text{normal profit}) > 0$$

When accounting profits are less than implicit opportunity costs, economic profit is negative and we have:

$$\text{economic profit} = (\text{accounting profit} - \text{normal profit}) < 0$$

The important thing to remember is that an economic profit of zero is what we expect in equilibrium. That's why economic profits are called abnormal profits. Firms with zero economic profit are covering all the costs of production, both explicit and implicit. Firms with zero economic profit are returning a competitive rate of return to the suppliers of debt and equity capital, paying competitive wages to their workers, and compensating top management for the opportunity cost of their entrepreneurial talent. In economics, when firms are earning zero economic profit, they have no incentive to leave the industry, and because they are just earning their required rates of return, there is no incentive for firms to enter the industry either.

With reference to RideRight, economic profit is zero, and accounting profits are $50,000, so normal profit must be $50,000.

With reference to Patrick's Surfboard Company, accounting profit is $150,000, and economic profit is $40,000, so normal profit = $150,000 − $40,000 = $110,000.

Economic Rent

Economic rent is used to describe a payment to a factor of production above its value in its next highest-valued use (its opportunity cost). Economic rent has been defined variously in the literature, but "the payment to a resource in excess of the minimum payment to retain resources in their current use" is fairly representative. Alternatively, we can think of economic rent as the portion of a payment to a resource that does not increase the quantity supplied. If we think of a supply curve as the marginal opportunity cost of an input, a perfectly inelastic supply curve would indicate that any payment to the factor is greater than its opportunity cost and would be economic rent. In the case of a perfectly elastic supply curve for a factor, there is no economic rent. We illustrate both of these cases in Figure 1.

The term *rent* is used to describe payments for the use of land for just this reason. The supply of land (think Manhattan Island) is fixed, so that supply is inelastic, and a higher price does not increase the quantity supplied. The supply of certain other factors of production may be inelastic because of government restriction (e.g., patents and copyrights) or because the natural supply is limited (oil and gold). When resources owned or otherwise employed by the firm generate economic rents, the firm earns economic profits as a result because total revenues exceed the sum of explicit and implicit costs. Firms that earn economic profits attract competition, but if the firm's resources are very difficult to replicate and produce accounting profits in excess of opportunity costs, the firm will continue to earn rents. Consider a company that owns a gold mine when the price of gold in the world market rises sharply. As its gold is in fixed (or almost fixed) supply, the price increase will generate rents to this factor, and the firm's economic profit will rise as a result. The abnormal profits of the firm will attract investment, the share price of its equity will rise as investors compete for shares, and existing firm owners will have an increase in their wealth as a result.

Figure 1: Economic Rent to Factors of Production

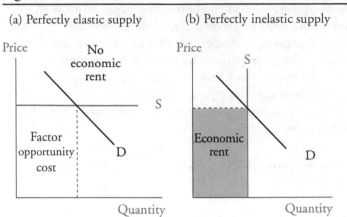

Comparing Measures of Profit

In the short run, the normal profit for a firm may be considered fixed. In the long run, it will vary with the required rate of return on equity investments. However, because accounting profit is often highly variable in both the long run and the short run, economic profit is highly variable in both the short run and long run as well.

Normal profit is a minimum requirement for a firm to continue operating in the long run. A firm unable to earn a normal profit (a firm with negative economic profit) will find it more difficult to raise equity capital, and the value of its equity in the market is likely to decline. Overall, earning a positive economic profit will increase the value of a firm's equity, and negative economic profit will decrease the value of a firm's equity.

LOS 15.b: Calculate and interpret and compare total, average, and marginal revenue.

CFA® Program Curriculum, Volume 2, page 101

Total revenue (TR) for any firm that charges a single price to all customers is calculated as price multiplied by quantity sold, or TR = P × Q.

Average revenue (AR) is equal to total revenue divided by the quantity sold, or AR = TR / Q.

Marginal revenue (MR) is the increase in total revenue from selling one more unit of a good or service. For a firm in a perfectly competitive market, all units are sold at the same price regardless of quantity, so that average revenue and marginal revenue are both equal to the market price, or AR = MR = price. We illustrate this case in Figure 2.

Figure 2: Demand and Marginal Revenue Under Perfect Competition

Price

D = Market price = MR = AR

Quantity

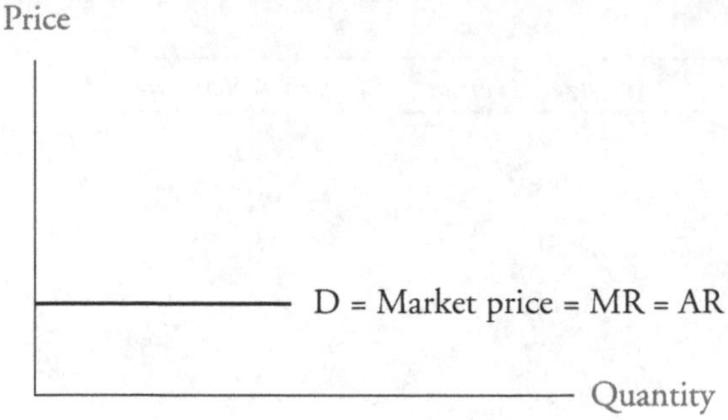

Firms operating under *imperfect competition* face downward-sloping demand curves. Unlike firms operating under *perfect competition,* firms in imperfect competition must decide what price to charge for their product. For this reason, firms that face downward-sloping demand curves are referred to as *price searchers*. To sell a greater quantity, price-searcher firms must decrease the price. Assuming (for now) that firms charge the same price to all buyers, selling one more unit requires that the price on all units sold must be decreased. It is for this reason that for firms under imperfect competition, marginal revenue is less than price for quantities greater than one. With the assumption of a single price, average revenue and price must be equal.

Under imperfect competition, average revenue and marginal revenue will decline as quantity sold increases. AR is not equal to MR for any quantities greater than one. In addition, the decrease in marginal revenue (or the rate of change in total revenue) is more than the decrease in price or AR. Total revenue is maximized when MR equals zero.

As you work through the following example of the calculation of marginal revenue for a price-searcher firm, recall that we have defined marginal revenue as the change in total revenue as a result of selling one more unit.

Example: Total revenue, average revenue, and marginal revenue for a price searcher

Given the demand curve for a firm's product below, calculate the total revenue, average revenue, and marginal revenue for the first through the eighth unit and draw the marginal revenue curve over this range.

Quantity	1	2	3	4	5	6	7	8
Price	70	65	60	55	50	45	40	35

Answer:

Quantity	Price	Total Revenue	Average Revenue	Marginal Revenue
1	70	70	70	70
2	65	130	65	60
3	60	180	60	50
4	55	220	55	40
5	50	250	50	30
6	45	270	45	20
7	40	280	40	10
8	35	280	35	0

In the following graph, we illustrate the marginal revenue curve for a firm facing the downward-sloping demand shown in the table. Note that for a firm that charges a single price to all customers, average revenue is equal to price.

Marginal Revenue for a Firm With Downward-Sloping Demand

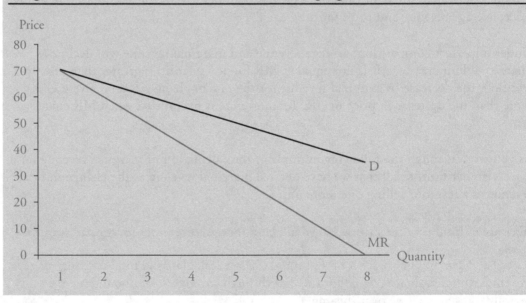

LOS 15.c: Describe a firm's factors of production.

CFA® Program Curriculum, Volume 2, page 108

Factors of production are the resources a firm uses to generate output. Factors of production include:

- *Land*—where the business facilities are located.
- *Labor*—includes all workers from unskilled laborers to top management.
- *Capital*—sometimes called *physical capital* or *plant and equipment* to distinguish it from financial capital. Refers to manufacturing facilities, equipment, and machinery.
- *Materials*—refers to inputs into the productive process, including raw materials, such as iron ore or water, or manufactured inputs, such as wire or microprocessors.

For economic analysis, we often consider only two inputs, capital and labor. The quantity of output that a firm can produce can be thought of as a function of the amounts of capital and labor employed and represented as $Q = f(K,L)$. Such a function is called a **production function**. If we consider a given amount of capital (a firm's plant and equipment), we can examine the increase in production (increase in **total product**) that will result as we increase the amount of labor employed. The output with only one worker is considered the **marginal product** of the first unit of labor. The addition of a second worker will increase total product by the marginal product of the second worker. The marginal product of (additional output from) the second worker is likely greater than the marginal product of the first. This is true if we assume that two workers can produce more than twice as much output as one because of the benefits of teamwork or specialization of tasks. At this low range of labor input (remember, we are holding capital constant), we can say that the marginal product of labor is increasing.

As we continue to add additional workers to a fixed amount of capital, at some point, adding one more worker will increase total product by less than the addition of the previous worker, although total product continues to increase. When we reach the quantity of labor for which the additional output for each additional worker begins to decline, we have reached the point of **diminishing marginal productivity** of labor, or that labor has reached the point of **diminishing marginal returns**. Beyond this quantity of labor, the additional output from each additional worker continues to decline.

There is theoretically some quantity for labor for which the marginal product of labor is actually negative, that is, the addition of one more worker actually decreases total output.

In Figure 3, we illustrate all three cases. For quantities of labor between zero and A, the marginal product of labor is increasing (slope is increasing). Beyond the inflection point in the production at quantity of labor A up to quantity B, the marginal product of labor is still positive but decreasing. The slope of the production function is positive but decreasing, and we are in a range of diminishing marginal productivity of labor. Beyond the quantity of labor B, adding additional workers decreases total output. The marginal product of labor in this range is negative, and the production function slopes downward.

Figure 3: Production Function—Capital Fixed, Labor Variable

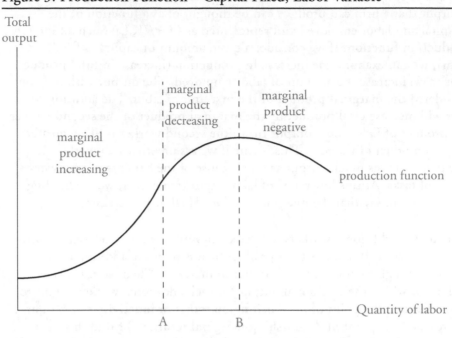

LOS 15.d: Calculate and interpret total, average, marginal, fixed, and variable costs.

CFA® Program Curriculum, Volume 2, page 109

To increase output in the short run, firms must use more labor, which increases cost. The relationship between output and cost may be explained in terms of three cost concepts: (1) total cost, (2) marginal cost, and (3) average cost.

Total fixed cost (TFC) is the cost of inputs that do not vary with the quantity of output and cannot be avoided over the period of analysis. Examples of fixed costs are property, plant, and equipment; normal profit; fixed interest costs on debt financing; and wages of management and finance employees who are not directly involved in the production of the firm's product. Note that some of these costs will remain constant over some range of output but will increase if output is increased beyond some quantity (e.g., administrative salaries and utilities). These costs can be referred to as **quasi-fixed costs**. Because fixed costs must be paid (at least over the near term) even when demand for the firm's product declines, they can result in significant losses during economic downturns or when industry competition is especially aggressive.

Total variable cost (TVC) is the cost of all inputs that vary with output over the period of analysis. The largest variable costs for most firms are wages, raw materials, or both. Variable costs increase with greater output and can be reduced if a decrease in demand leads to a decrease in production.

Total cost (TC) is the sum of all costs (fixed or variable, explicit and implicit) of producing a specific level of output.

total cost = total fixed cost + total variable cost

Once we determine total costs for various levels of output, we can calculate **marginal costs** (MCs) as the addition to total cost of producing one more unit. Given output levels that are several units of output apart, dividing the difference in total cost by the number of units will provide a measure of marginal cost per unit.

$$\text{marginal cost} = \frac{\text{change in total cost}}{\text{change in output}}, \text{ or } MC = \frac{\Delta TC}{\Delta Q}$$

average total costs (ATC) = total costs / total product

average fixed costs (AFC) = total fixed costs / total product

average variable costs (AVC) = total variable costs / total product

Figure 4 illustrates the components of total cost for Sam's Shirts at various output levels. Sam's total fixed cost is $20 per day to rent one sewing machine. Labor is Sam's only variable cost, and the wage rate is $20 per day.

Figure 4: Total Cost Curves

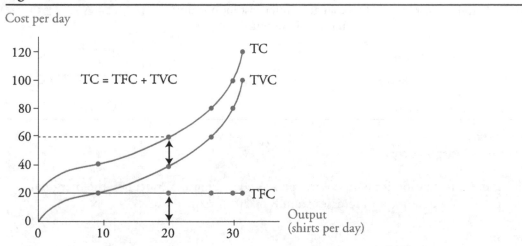

We can apply much of what we have learned so far to interpret the graph in Figure 4. Total fixed costs do not change with output, and the vertical distance between TVC and TC is equal to TFC. As the variable cost per worker is $20, examining the points plotted on either the TC or the TVC curve, we can see the increase in output associated with each additional worker.

Just as our example of a production function was drawn to illustrate first increasing and then decreasing marginal productivity of labor, both the TC and TVC curves exhibit first decreasing, and then increasing, marginal cost per shirt. With the wage fixed at $20, greater output per worker reduces the cost per shirt. We assume that marginal cost typically first decreases (as marginal product of a factor input increases) and then increases (after we reach the point of diminishing marginal productivity).

The relationships among TFC, TVC, MC, AFC, AVC, and ATC are shown for increasing amounts of labor and output in Figure 5.

Figure 5: Total, Marginal, and Average Costs for Sam's Shirts

Output (shirts)	Labor (workers/day)	TFC ($/day)	TVC	TC	MC ($/additional shirt)	AFC ($/shirt)	AVC	ATC
0	0	20	0	20				
					-----2.50-----			
8	1	20	20	40		2.50	2.50	5.00
					-----1.67-----			
20	2	20	40	60		1.00	2.00	3.00
					-----3.33-----			
26	3	20	60	80		0.77	2.31	3.08
					-----5.00-----			
30	4	20	80	100		0.67	2.67	3.33
					----10.00-----			
32	5	20	100	120		0.63	3.13	3.75

TFC = Total fixed cost	cost of fixed inputs; independent of output	
TVC = Total variable cost	cost of variable inputs; changes with output	
TC = Total cost		$TC = TFC + TVC$
MC = Marginal cost	change in total cost for one unit increase in output	$MC = \Delta TC / \Delta Q$
AFC = Average fixed cost		$AFC = TFC / Q$
AVC = Average variable cost		$AVC = TVC / Q$
ATC = Average total cost		$ATC = AFC + AVC$

Example: Marginal cost

Using the information for Sam's Shirts presented in Figure 5, calculate the marginal cost per shirt when output increases from 8 to 20 shirts per day.

Answer:

In Figure 5, we see that the change in TC when output increases from 8 to 20 shirts is $60 − $40 = $20. Because the change in output is 20 − 8 = 12 shirts, the marginal cost can be calculated as:

$MC = \$20 / 12$ shirts $= \$1.67$ per shirt

Average costs at the various output levels for Sam's have been calculated and tabulated in Figure 5. The marginal cost (MC) and average cost curves (ATC, AVC, and AFC) for Sam's Shirts are shown in Figure 6.

Figure 6: Average and Marginal Costs

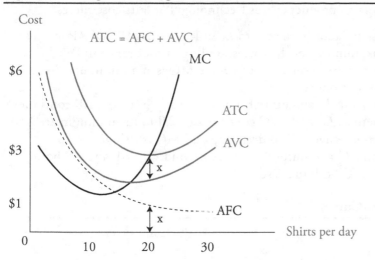

Important relationships among the marginal and average cost curves illustrated in Figure 6 are:

- *AFC slopes downward.* This is because fixed costs are constant but are distributed over a larger and larger number of products as output quantity increases.
- *The vertical distance between the ATC and AVC curves is equal to AFC.* This is indicated by the arrows marked *x* at an output of 20 shirts per day.
- *MC declines initially, then increases.* At low output quantities, efficiencies are realized from the specialization of labor. However, as more and more labor is added, marginal cost increases. This is due to *diminishing returns*, which means that at some point, each added worker contributes less to total output than the previously added worker.
- *MC intersects AVC and ATC at their minimum points.* The intersection comes from below, which implies that when MC is less than ATC or AVC, respectively, ATC or AVC are decreasing. This also implies that when MC exceeds ATC or AVC, respectively, ATC or AVC are increasing. The MC curve is considered to have a J-shape due to the declining MC over lower production quantities and because the minimum points of the ATC and the AVC curves are not the same.
- *ATC and AVC are U-shaped.* AVC decreases initially, but as output increases, the effect of diminishing returns sets in and AVC eventually slopes upward, giving the curve its U shape. However, because fixed costs are spread out over a larger and larger quantity of output, AFC decreases as output increases, and eventually flattens out. ATC gets its U shape because as output increases we are adding a curve that goes from downward sloping to flat (AFC) to a U-shaped curve (AVC), which results in a U-shaped ATC curve. Remember, ATC = AVC + AFC.
- *Minimum point on the ATC curve represents the lowest cost per unit,* but it is not necessarily the profit-maximizing point. It means the firm is maximizing profit per unit at that point.
- *The MC curve above AVC is the firm's short-run supply curve* in a perfectly competitive market.

The relationship between product curves and cost curves is illustrated in Figure 7, where average and marginal product curves for a firm are presented in Panel (a), and marginal and average cost curves are presented in Panel (b). Figure 7 illustrates the following important links between a firm's product curves (technology) and its cost curves.

- Over the initial increase in labor from zero to L_1 in Panel (a), MP and AP increase and MP reaches its maximum. Over the corresponding output range in Panel (b), MC and AVC decrease to output quantity Q_1 where MC is at a minimum. Note that L_1 is the labor required to produce Q_1.
- As labor increases from L_1 to L_2 and output increases from Q_1 to Q_2, AP continues to increase to a maximum at L_2, and AVC continues to fall to its minimum at Q_2. Over this same production range, MP is declining and MC is rising.
- As labor increases beyond L_2 and output increases beyond Q_2, MP and AP both decrease, and MC and AVC both increase.

Figure 7: Product and Cost Curves

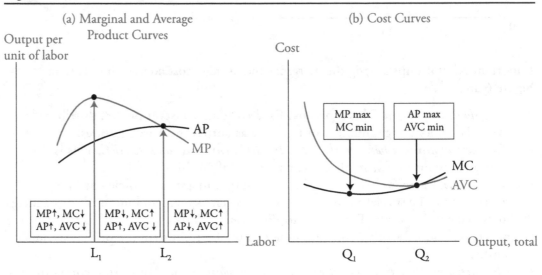

LOS 15.e: Determine and describe breakeven and shutdown points of production.

CFA® Program Curriculum, Volume 2, page 116

In economics, we define the **short run** for a firm as the time period over which some factors of production are fixed. Typically, we assume that capital is fixed in the short run so that a firm cannot change its scale of operations (plant and equipment) over the short run. All factors of production (costs) are variable in the **long run**. The firm can let its leases expire and sell its equipment, thereby avoiding the costs that are fixed in the short run.

Shutdown and Breakeven Under Perfect Competition

As a simple example of shutdown and breakeven analysis, consider a retail store with a 1-year lease (fixed cost) and one employee (quasi-fixed cost), so that variable costs are simply its cost of merchandise. If the total sales (total revenue) just covers both fixed and variable costs, price equals average revenue and average total cost, so we are at the breakeven output quantity and economic profit equals zero. During the period of the lease (short run), as long as items are being sold for more than their cost (AR > AVC), the store should continue in operation. If items are sold for less than their cost, losses would be reduced by shutting down the business in the short run. In the long run, if the difference between the total revenue on items sold and their total cost is not great enough to pay for the lease and one employee, the firm should shut down. This means that in the long run, a firm should shut down if the price is less than average total cost.

In the case of a firm under perfect competition, price = marginal revenue = average revenue, as we have noted. For a firm under perfect competition (a price taker), we can use a graph of cost functions to examine the profitability of the firm at different output prices. In Figure 8, based on the cost curves for Sam's Shirts, at price P_1, price and average revenue equal average total cost. At the output level of Point A, the firm is making an economic profit of zero. At a price above P_1, economic profit is positive, and at prices less than P_1, economic profit is negative (the firm has economic losses).

Because some costs are fixed in the short run, it will be better for the firm to continue production in the short run as long as average revenue is greater than average variable costs. At prices between P_1 and P_2 in Figure 8, the firm has losses, but the loss is less than the losses that would occur if all production were stopped. As long as total revenue is greater than total variable cost, at least some of the firm's fixed costs are covered by continuing to produce and sell its product. If the firm were to shut down, losses would be equal to the fixed costs that still must be paid. As long as price is greater than average variable costs, the firm will minimize its losses in the short run by continuing in business.

If average revenue is less average variable cost, the firm's losses are greater than its fixed costs, and it will minimize its losses by shutting down production in the short run. In this case (a price less than P_2 in Figure 8), the loss from continuing to operate is greater than the loss (total fixed costs) if the firm is shut down.

In the long run, all costs are variable, so a firm can avoid its (short-run) fixed costs by shutting down. For this reason, if price is expected to remain below minimum ATC (Point A in Figure 8) in the long run, the firm will shut down rather than continue to generate losses.

Figure 8: Shutdown and Breakeven

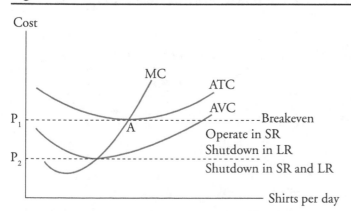

To sum up, if average revenue is less than average variable cost in the short run, the firm should shut down. This is its **short-run shutdown point**. If average revenue is greater than average variable cost in the short run, the firm should continue to operate, even if it has losses. In the long run, the firm should shut down if average revenue is less than average total cost. This is the **long-run shutdown point**. If average revenue is just equal to average total cost, total revenue is just equal to total (economic) cost, and this is the firm's **breakeven point**.

- If AR ≥ ATC, the firm should stay in the market in both the short and long run.
- If AR ≥ AVC, but AR < ATC, the firm should stay in the market in the short run but will exit the market in the long run.
- If AR < AVC, the firm should shut down in the short run and exit the market in the long run.

Shutdown and Breakeven Under Imperfect Competition

For price-searcher firms (those that face downward-sloping demand curves), we could compare average revenue to ATC and AVC just as we did for price-taker firms to identify shutdown and breakeven points. However, marginal revenue is no longer simply equal to price.

We can also explain when a firm is breaking even, should shut down in the short run, and should shut down in the long run in terms of total costs and total revenue. These conditions are:

- TR = TC: break even.
- TC > TR > TVC: firm should continue to operate in the short run but shutdown in the long run.
- TR < TVC: firm should shut down in the short run and the long run.

Because price does not equal marginal revenue for a firm in imperfect competition, analysis based on total costs and revenues is better suited for examining breakeven and shutdown points.

The previously described relations hold for both price-taker and price-searcher firms. We illustrate these relations in Figure 9 for a price-taker firm (TR increases at a constant rate with quantity). Total cost equals total revenue at the breakeven quantities Q_{BE1} and Q_{BE2}. The quantity for which economic profit is maximized is shown as Q_{max}.

 Professor's Note: Remember that total costs include a normal profit.

Figure 9: Breakeven Point Using the Total Revenue/Total Cost Approach

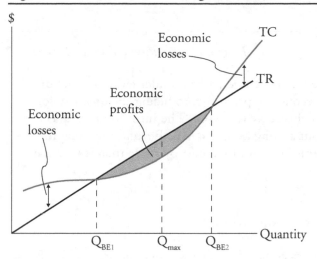

If the entire TC curve exceeds TR (i.e., no breakeven point), the firm will want to minimize the economic loss in the short run by operating at the quantity corresponding to the smallest (negative) value of TR – TC.

Example: Short-run shutdown decision

For the last fiscal year, Legion Gaming reported total revenue of $700,000, total variable costs of $800,000, and total fixed costs of $400,000. Should the firm continue to operate in the short run?

Answer:

The firm should shut down. Total revenue of $700,000 is less than total costs of $1,200,000 and also less than total variable costs of $800,000. By shutting down, the firm will lose an amount equal to fixed costs of $400,000. This is less than the loss of operating, which is TR – TC = $500,000.

Example: Long-run shutdown decision

Suppose instead that Legion reported total revenue of $850,000. Should the firm continue to operate in the short run? Should it continue to operate in the long run?

Answer:

In the short run, TR > TVC, and the firm should continue operating. The firm should consider exiting the market in the long run, as TR is not sufficient to cover all of the fixed costs and variable costs.

LOS 15.f: Describe approaches to determining the profit-maximizing level of output.

CFA® Program Curriculum, Volume 2, page 120

Under the assumptions we have made for cost curves, a firm under either perfect or imperfect competition will maximize economic profit by producing the quantity for which marginal revenue equals marginal cost (MR = MC). The intuition is that a firm should continue to increase output as long as MC < MR. Beyond that quantity, producing and selling an additional unit increases total cost by more than it increases total revenue, and profit is decreased.

Profit Maximization Under Perfect Competition

In Figure 10, we show total cost for a price-taker firm facing a market price of 90. From this, we can calculate marginal cost and total revenue and identify the profit-maximizing quantity of output by comparing marginal cost to marginal revenue or by comparing total costs to total revenue.

Figure 10: Profit Maximization

Quantity	Price	Total Revenue (TR)	Total Costs (TC)	Profits (TR – TC)	Marginal Revenue (MR)	Marginal Costs (MC)
0	90	0	50	n/a	n/a	n/a
1	90	90	135	–45	90	85
2	90	180	215	–35	90	80
3	90	270	285	–15	90	70
4	90	360	350	10	90	65
5	90	450	430	20	90	80
6	90	540	520	20	90	90
7	90	630	620	10	90	100
8	90	720	732	–12	90	112
9	90	810	857	–47	90	125

In Figure 10, marginal revenue is greater than marginal cost for the first 5 units produced, and profit is at a maximum of 20 when 5 units are produced. For the sixth unit produced, MC = MR, and profit remains at 20. For the seventh unit, MC is 100 and MR is 90, so profit is reduced to 10. For quantities greater than 7, total cost is greater than total revenue, and the firm will experience losses. A firm can determine (estimate) its profit-maximizing output by either comparing total cost to total revenue or by comparing marginal cost to marginal revenue. Profit can be maximized by:

- *Producing up to the point where MR = MC and not producing additional units for which MR < MC.* Under this method, the firm estimates the change in revenue for each additional unit and the change in cost for each additional unit. The firm expands production while MR is greater than MC and stops when MR = MC.

- *Producing the quantity for which TR – TC is at a maximum.* Under this approach, the firm must estimate total cost for various output quantities (or ranges) and compare it to total revenue for those quantities.

Note that maximizing profit is sometimes equivalent to minimizing losses. For a firm that is operating at MR = MC but is selling at a price below AVC, shutting down is really the profit-maximizing decision in the short and long run.

In Figure 11, we show the profit-maximizing output for three different prices under perfect competition at the quantities for which MR = MC. At P_1, the profit-maximizing output is Q^*_1, price = average revenue (AR) is greater than ATC, and the firm has positive economic profits equal to area A. At P_2, the profit-maximizing output is Q^*_2, price = AR = ATC, and economic profit is zero. In Panel (b), at P_3, the profit-maximizing output is Q^*_3, price = AR < ATC, and the firm has economic losses equal to area B.

Figure 11: Profit Maximizing Output Under Perfect Competition

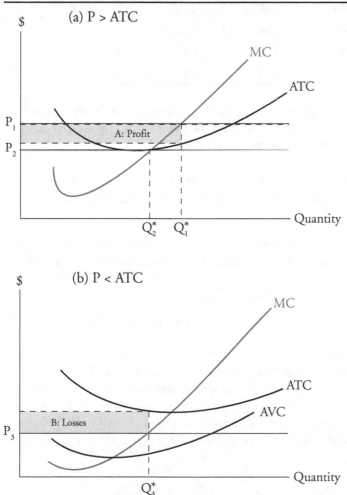

Profit Maximization Under Imperfect Competition

Recall that for firms facing downward-sloping demand curves, marginal revenue is less than price, as price must be reduced to sell additional units. Figure 12 contains the demand schedule and total costs of production for a price-searcher firm. Again, we have calculated marginal cost, marginal revenue, total revenue, and profit for each output quantity.

Figure 12: Profit Maximization—Total Revenue Less Total Cost Method

Quantity	Price	Total Revenue (TR)	Total Costs (TC)	Profits (TR – TC)	Marginal Revenue (MR)	Marginal Costs (MC)
0	130	0	100	–100	n/a	n/a
1	125	125	165	–40	125	65
2	115	230	225	5	105	60
3	100	300	280	20	70	55
4	90	360	340	20	60	60
5	80	400	405	–5	40	65
6	70	420	475	–55	20	70

Marginal revenue is greater than marginal cost for the first three units of output and MR = MC for the fourth unit of output. Profit decreases with the fifth unit of output, and, in fact, the firm experiences losses if it produces five or more units.

Just as we saw under perfect competition, a firm in imperfect competition maximizes profits by producing the quantity of output for which MR = MC, the same quantity for which TR – TC is at its maximum.

LOS 15.g: Describe how economies of scale and diseconomies of scale affect costs.

CFA® Program Curriculum, Volume 2, page 125

While plant size is fixed in the short run, in the long run, firms can choose their most profitable scale of operations. Because the long-run average total cost (LRATC) curve is drawn for many different plant sizes or scales of operation, each point along the curve represents the minimum ATC for a given plant size or scale of operations. In Figure 13, we show a firm's LRATC curve along with short-run average total cost (SRATC) curves for many different plant sizes, with $SRATC_{n+1}$ representing a larger scale of operations than $SRATC_n$.

We draw the LRATC curve as U-shaped. Average total costs first decrease with larger scale and eventually increase. The lowest point on the LRATC corresponds to the scale or plant size at which the average total cost of production is at a minimum. This scale is sometimes called the **minimum efficient scale**. Under perfect competition, firms must operate at minimum efficient scale in long-run equilibrium, and LRATC will equal the market price. Recall that under perfect competition, firms earn zero economic profit in long-run equilibrium. Firms that have chosen a different scale of operations with higher average total costs will have economic losses and must either leave the industry or change to minimum efficient scale.

The downward-sloping segment of the long-run average total cost curve presented in Figure 13 indicates that **economies of scale** (or *increasing returns to scale*) are present. Economies of scale result from factors such as labor specialization, mass production, and investment in more efficient equipment and technology. In addition, the firm may be able to negotiate lower input prices with suppliers as firm size increases and more resources are purchased. A firm operating with economies of scale can increase its competitiveness by expanding production and reducing costs.

Figure 13: Economies and Diseconomies of Scale

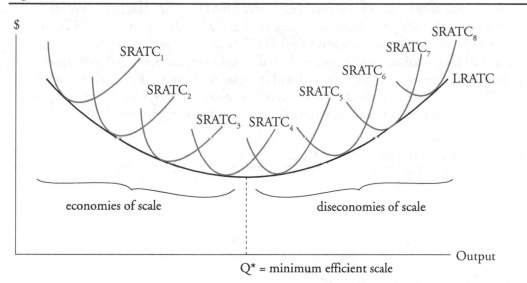

The upward-sloping segment of the LRATC curve indicates that **diseconomies of scale** are present. Diseconomies of scale may result as the increasing bureaucracy of larger firms leads to inefficiency, problems of motivating a larger workforce, and greater barriers to innovation and entrepreneurial activity. A firm operating under diseconomies of scale will want to decrease output and move back toward the minimum efficient scale. The U.S. auto industry is an example of an industry that has exhibited diseconomies of scale.

There may be a relatively flat portion at the bottom of the LRATC curve that exhibits *constant returns to scale*. Over a range of constant returns to scale, costs are constant for the various plant sizes.

LOS 15.h: Distinguish between short-run and long-run profit maximization.

CFA® Program Curriculum, Volume 2, page 129

We have described the determination of the profit-maximizing output in the short run for both price-taker and price-searcher firms. For a given plant size, producing up to the quantity where marginal revenue equals marginal cost will maximize profits as long as price at that output quantity is greater than average variable cost.

In the long run, when plant size is variable, firms under perfect competition will all choose to operate at the minimum average cost, considering all possible plant sizes (scales of operation). In Figure 14, we have reproduced the long-run average total cost curve derived previously, with short-run average cost for two firm sizes. Consider first firm-size 1 with short-run average total cost curve $SRATC_1$ when the market price is P_1. A firm at this scale can increase its size to firm-size 2, decreasing its SRATC to the level of P_2 at the minimum point of $SRATC_2$. If the market price remains at P_1, the firm will now earn economic profits. But all firms have the option of increasing scale to the minimum efficient scale and will increase to this scale in search of profits. In equilibrium, they will be back to zero economic profit, however, as the increase in market supply (as firms increase size to Q_2) causes the market price to decline to P_2.

Figure 14: Long-Run Average Total Cost

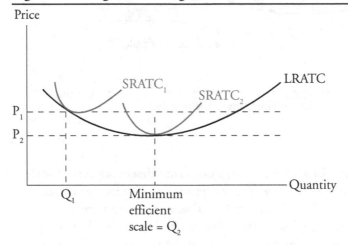

For a price below P_2 under perfect competition, firms will have economic losses, and some will exit the industry. This exit of firms from the industry reduces market supply and increases market price. Firms will exit the industry until market price increases to P_2 and firms are again earning economic profits of zero. In sum, entry of firms into the industry or increases in firm size in response to positive economic profit opportunities put downward pressure on market price. The exit of firms from the industry when economic profit is negative decreases industry supply, and the equilibrium market price increases. From this analysis, we can conclude that the long-run industry supply curve is perfectly elastic at the ATC for the minimum efficient scale, P_2 in our example. In practice, this result will hold only if the cost of the firms' inputs is constant as the industry expands output. Next, we consider industries for which input costs (or input quality) change as an industry expands output.

LOS 15.i: Distinguish among decreasing-cost, constant-cost, and increasing-cost industries and describe the long-run supply of each.

CFA® Program Curriculum, Volume 2, page 131

What we did not consider in describing the effects of firms that increase output or scale in response to positive economic profits is that resource prices may increase as industry output increases. While the output decision of a single firm does not affect market price, increases in output by many or all firms can drive up the price of resources. Consider an increase in demand that results in an increase in the market price. In the short run, all firms earn positive economic profits when the market price rises. As firms enter the industry in pursuit of profits, the demand for the productive inputs specific to the industry increases, and their market prices increase as well. This results in an **increasing-cost industry**. This can also result from a reduction in the quality of inputs as production expands. The long-run supply curve for the industry is upward-sloping as a result. Higher output is associated with more firms but also higher ATC as input prices rise or input quality deteriorates. Oil is an example of an increasing cost industry because as demand for oil increases over time, the costs of finding and producing a barrel of oil increase as more and more is produced.

For some industries, resource prices fall as the industry expands. In this case, the industry is said to be a **decreasing-cost industry**, and the long-run industry supply curve is downward sloping. A recent example is the flat-panel television industry. As the industry grew and demand for the electronic components for flat-panel televisions grew, the manufacturing cost of these inputs fell significantly. Economies of scale in the production of components reduced prices and the ATC for flat-panel television manufacturers, and prices fell each year as the industry grew to replace conventional televisions.

For ranges of industry output in which input prices do not increase or decrease, the industry supply curve is perfectly elastic at minimum average cost. We refer to this as a **constant-cost industry**.

Figure 15 illustrates the long-run industry supply (S_{LR}) curve for increasing-, decreasing- and constant-cost industries. In each panel, from an initial equilibrium at Point 1, an increase in market demand to D_1 increases both price and output in the short run (Point 2). Over time, the increase in market price produces economic profits for firms. The resulting entry of firms to the industry and expansion of scale by existing firms increases supply to S_1 (Point 3). Whether the new long-run equilibrium price is above or below the initial equilibrium price as the industry expands depends on the effect of industry expansion on input prices. For decreasing-cost industries, the equilibrium price falls with industry growth; for increasing-cost industries, price rises; and for constant-cost industries, price returns to its initial level at the minimum LRATC of a representative firm.

Figure 15: Long-Run Industry Supply Curves

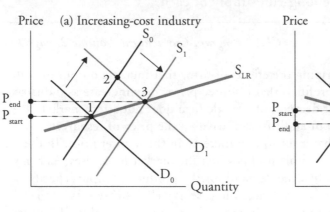

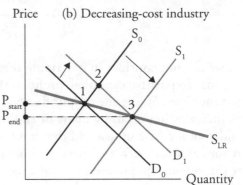

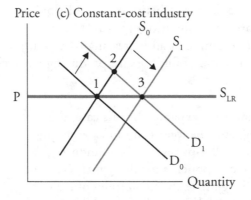

Example: Long-run industry supply

Minifone, Ltd. produces personal electronics, currently a decreasing-cost industry. Demand for the products has increased recently. What is most likely to happen in the long run to selling prices and per-unit production costs?

Answer:

Because Minifone operates in a decreasing-cost industry, the most likely equilibrium response to an increase in demand is for prices and per-unit production costs to decrease.

LOS 15.j: Calculate and interpret total, marginal, and average product of labor.

CFA® Program Curriculum, Volume 2, page 134

We discussed the marginal product of labor and diminishing returns to a factor of production in connection with our analysis of a firm's production function. For a production process with a fixed amount of capital, we can define the following terms:

- The **total product of labor** is the output for a specific amount of labor.

- The **average product of labor** per worker (or other unit of labor input) is the total product of labor divided by the number of workers (or units of labor employed).
- The **marginal product of labor** is the addition to the total product of labor from employing one more unit of labor.

We illustrate these calculations for Sam's Shirts in Figure 16 based on the production schedule given in terms of output employing different quantities of labor. Note that the marginal product of labor at first increases as more workers are employed, and then it decreases as additional workers are added. This is consistent with an average product of labor that first increases, and then it decreases as more workers are added. Recall that the quantity of labor employed at which the marginal product of labor begins to decrease is the point of diminishing marginal productivity of (or diminishing marginal returns to) labor. Note in the table that total product in measured in shirts, and average and marginal product are measured in shirts per worker.

Figure 16: Short-Run Output as a Function of Labor Employed

Workers	Total Product	Marginal Product	Average Product
1	8	8	8.0
2	20	12	10.0
3	26	6	8.7
4	30	4	7.5
5	32	2	6.4
6	33	1	5.5

For analysis, the usefulness of the total product measure is limited, as it does not measure the efficiency of any one firm. It provides information on the output of the firm relative to industry output. Average product is a measure of overall efficiency, not the efficiency of any one worker. Marginal product is a better measure of the productivity of an individual worker and is preferred over average product or total product. However, average product may be an appropriate measure when it is difficult to determine the productivity of any one worker (e.g., a team that performs tasks collectively).

LOS 15.k: Describe the phenomenon of diminishing marginal returns and calculate and interpret the profit-maximizing utilization level of an input.

LOS 15.l: Determine the optimal combination of resources that minimizes cost.

CFA® Program Curriculum, Volume 2, page 136

Previously, we introduced the concept of **diminishing marginal returns** to a factor of production, which is equivalent to *diminishing marginal productivity* of a factor. We have developed this concept for labor with the quantity of capital held constant. We can also apply the concept to capital, examining the addition to total output from additional capital while holding the quantity of labor constant. As we saw with labor, increasing the quantity of capital for a given quantity of labor will at first result in increasing marginal returns to capital. At some point, however, employing additional units of capital will result in smaller increases in output. This is the point of diminishing marginal returns to capital.

Professor's Note: To convince yourself that there is a point of diminishing marginal returns for both labor and capital, consider the result if this were not the case. If the marginal product of labor continued to increase, all the output ever required could be produced (given enough workers) with a given amount of capital (one factory). If the marginal product of capital continued to increase, one group of laborers could (with enough capital) produce all the output ever required. Neither seems likely.

Profit-Maximizing Utilization of an Input

The marginal product of a resource is measured in output units and is sometimes called the *marginal physical product* of the resource. In order for profit to be at a maximum, a firm must use the mix of inputs that minimizes the cost of producing any given quantity of output. For a firm with N productive inputs, cost minimization requires that:

$$\frac{MP_1}{P_1} = \frac{MP_2}{P_2} = ... = \frac{MP_N}{P_N}$$

This equation tells us that the additional output per dollar spent to employ one additional unit of each input must be the same. This result is best understood by examining the case where this does not hold. Consider a production process that uses only two inputs, capital and labor (K and L), with the following input prices and values for MP_L and MP_K:

$$P_L = \$75$$
$$P_K = \$600$$
$$MP_L = 5 \text{ units}$$
$$MP_K = 30 \text{ units}$$

Additional output from employing one more unit of labor costs 75/5 = $15 per output unit, and output per additional dollar spent on labor is 1/15 unit.

Additional output from employing one more unit of capital costs 600/30 = $20 per unit of output, and output per additional dollar spent on capital is 1/20 unit.

In this situation, production costs can be reduced by employing less capital and more labor, so this cannot be the optimal (cost-minimizing) combination of inputs. Reducing capital by one unit would reduce output by 30 units and reduce costs by $600. Spending $450 on 6 additional units of labor would increase output by 6 × 5 = 30 units, restoring output to its previous level. By employing more labor and less capital, we have decreased the cost of production by $150.

If we can produce greater output at the same cost by using more labor and less capital, the cost of producing that output was not at a minimum. Given that we have diminishing marginal productivity in each input, using more labor and less capital will decrease the MP_L and increase the MP_K, reducing the difference between MP_L / P_L and MP_K / P_K. From this example, we can see that we can reduce production costs by substituting labor for capital until we reach the input quantities for which $MP_L / P_L = MP_K / P_K$, which is the necessary condition for cost minimization.

Although the condition for cost minimization is necessary for costs to be at a minimum, it does not tell us how much of either input to use to maximize profit. That is, we could be minimizing the cost of producing an output quantity either greater or less than the profit-maximizing quantity.

To determine the quantity of each input that should be used to maximize profit, we need to introduce the concept of **marginal revenue product** (MRP). The MRP is the monetary value of the marginal product of an input. It is calculated by multiplying a production factor's marginal product by the marginal revenue of the additional output. MRP is the increase in the firm's total revenue from selling the additional output from employing one more unit of the factor.

The profit-maximizing quantity of an input i is that quantity for which $MRP_i = P_i$. A firm can increase profits by employing another unit of the input as long as $MRP_i > P_i$ because employing another unit of the input increases revenue by more that it increases costs. Conversely, if $MRP_i < P_i$, the firm could increase profits by reducing the quantity of the input employed. The decrease in total revenue is less than the cost savings from using one less unit of the input.

Recall that under perfect competition, marginal revenue is equal to price, and the MRP of a factor is its marginal product multiplied by price. For a firm that faces a downward-sloping demand curve, marginal revenue is less than price. In either case, we can multiply each factor's marginal product in the cost minimization condition, by the marginal revenue value of additional output, to get an equivalent relation necessary for cost minimization:

$$\frac{MP_1 \times MR_{output}}{P_1} = \frac{MP_2 \times MR_{output}}{P_2} = ... = \frac{MP_N \times MR_{output}}{P_N}$$

or

$$\frac{MRP_1}{P_1} = \frac{MRP_2}{P_2} = ... = \frac{MRP_N}{P_N}$$

Based on the condition for the profit-maximizing utilization of each factor, $MRP_f = P_f$, we can state that for cost minimization and profit maximization, a firm must employ inputs in quantities such that:

$$\frac{MRP_1}{P_1} = \frac{MRP_2}{P_2} = ... = \frac{MRP_N}{P_N} = 1$$

Example: Profit maximizing level of a productive input

Consider the following data for Centerline Industries. The firm's inputs can be categorized as high technology equipment, unskilled labor, and highly trained workers. The MR, MP, and cost per day of the various inputs are summarized in the following table. Assume that the inputs can substitute for each other in the production process.

Resource	Resource MP (units)	Output MR ($)	Resource $ Price/ Unit
High technology equipment	30	30	800
Unskilled labor	5	30	160
Highly trained workers	15	30	450

1. Is the firm operating at the cost-minimizing levels for its inputs?

2. Assuming diminishing marginal factor returns, what adjustments to its input mix, if any, should the firm make to increase profits?

Answer:

1. Comparing marginal product per dollar of each resource we have:

$$MP_{high\ tech} / P_{high\ tech} = 30 / 800 = 0.03750$$

$$MP_{unskilled} / P_{unskilled} = 5 / 160 = 0.03125$$

$$MP_{high\ skill} / P_{high\ skill} = 15 / 450 = 0.03333$$

Because these are not equal, the condition for cost minimization is not met.

2. Comparing the MRP for each resource to its price, we have:

$$MRP_{high\ tech} = 30 \times 30 = 900 \qquad P_{high\ tech} = 800$$

$$MRP_{unskilled} = 5 \times 30 = 150 \qquad P_{unskilled} = 160$$

$$MRP_{high\ skill} = 15 \times 30 = 450 \qquad P_{high\ skill} = 450$$

The condition for the profit-maximizing quantity of each resource, MRP = P is met only for highly skilled labor. For high technology equipment, the MRP (900) is greater than the unit cost (800), so the firm should employ more high technology equipment. For unskilled workers, the MRP (150) is less than the unit cost (160), so the firm should employ fewer unskilled workers.

KEY CONCEPTS

LOS 15.a

accounting profit = total revenue – total accounting (explicit) costs

economic profit = accounting profit – implicit opportunity costs = total revenue – total economic costs

= total revenue – explicit costs – implicit costs

Positive economic profit has a positive effect on the market value of equity. Negative economic profit has a negative effect on the market value of equity.

Normal profit is the accounting profit for which economic profit equals zero, which occurs when accounting profit is equal to implicit opportunity costs:

normal profit = accounting profit – economic profit

Economic rent to a factor of production is the difference between its earnings and its opportunity cost. When the supply curve is perfectly elastic, there is no economic rent. Perfectly inelastic supply results in the greatest economic rent.

LOS 15.b

When all units are sold at a single price, total revenue is price multiplied by quantity sold and average revenue is equal to price. Marginal revenue is the increase in total revenue from selling one more unit of a good or service.

Under perfect competition, each firm faces a horizontal demand curve so that price, average revenue, and marginal revenue are all equal. Under imperfect competition, firm demand curves are negatively sloped so that a greater quantity can be sold only by decreasing price. In this case, marginal revenue is less than average revenue and price.

LOS 15.c

Factors of production are the resources (inputs) a firm uses to produce its output and include land, labor, materials, and capital (the physical capital or plant and equipment the firm uses in production). For economic analysis, factors of production are often simply grouped into labor and capital.

LOS 15.d

Fixed costs are those costs that do not vary directly with the quantity produced (e.g., plant and equipment). Variable costs are those that vary directly with the quantity produced (e.g., labor, raw materials). Total cost of a given output is equal to total fixed costs plus total variable costs.

Marginal cost is the increase in total variable costs for one additional unit of output. For a given level of fixed costs, marginal cost first decreases and then (at some quantity of output) begins to increase.

Average fixed cost (AFC) is fixed cost per unit of output and declines with greater quantities of output.

Average variable cost (AVC) is variable cost per unit of output and first decreases and then increases with greater quantities.

Average total cost (ATC) is total cost per unit of output and is equal to average fixed costs plus average variable costs.

Both AVC and ATC are at their minimum values where they are equal to marginal cost.

The vertical distance between the ATC and AVC curves is equal to AFC.

LOS 15.e
Under perfect competition:
- The breakeven quantity of production is the quantity for which price (P) = average total cost (ATC) and total revenue (TR) = total cost (TC).
- The firm should shut down in the long run if P < ATC so that TR < TC.
- The firm should shut down in the short run (and the long run) if P < average variable cost (AVC) so that TR < total variable cost (TVC).

Under imperfect competition (firm faces downward sloping demand):
- Breakeven quantity is the quantity for which TR = TC.
- The firm should shut down in the long run if TR < TC.
- The firm should shut down in the short run (and the long run) if TR < TVC.

LOS 15.f
The profit-maximizing quantity of output is the output for which the difference between total revenue and total cost (TR –TC) is at a maximum. This is equivalent to the output for which marginal cost equals marginal revenue. A firm should increase production as long as marginal cost is less than marginal revenue, because the addition to total costs from additional production is less than the addition to total revenue from selling the additional output.

LOS 15.g
The long-run average total cost (LRATC) curve shows the minimum average total cost for each level of output assuming that the plant size (scale of the firm) can be adjusted. A downward-sloping segment of an LRATC curve indicates economies of scale (increasing returns to scale). Over such a segment, increasing the scale of the firm reduces ATC.

An upward-sloping segment of an LRATC curve indicates diseconomies of scale, where average unit costs will rise as the scale of the business (and long-run output) increases.

A flat portion of an LRATC curve represents constant returns to scale and LRATC is constant over that range of output.

A firm's minimum efficient scale is represented by the minimum point on the LRATC curve and is the firm size that will minimize average unit costs. In perfect competition, firms will eventually all operate at minimum efficient scale.

LOS 15.h

The short run is a time period during which quantities of some firm resources are fixed. A firm may continue to operate in the short run with economic losses as long as price is greater than AVC because the losses are less than total fixed costs. The firm is maximizing profit by minimizing losses.

In the long run, all factors of production are variable so a firm will maximize profits at the quantity for which marginal revenue equals marginal cost as long as price is greater than ATC. If price is less than ATC, the firm has economic losses and will minimize losses in the long run by going out of business and reducing ongoing losses to zero.

LOS 15.i

For a decreasing-cost industry, as industry output increases, input (factor) prices decrease as the industry demand for inputs increases. This results in a negatively sloped long-run industry supply curve.

For a constant-cost industry, the price of resources does not change as industry output expands, resulting in a horizontal long-run industry supply curve.

For an increasing-cost industry, as industry output increases, input (factor) prices increase as the industry demand for inputs increases. This results in a positively sloped long-run industry supply curve.

LOS 15.j

Total product of labor (TPL) is the total output of a firm that uses a specific amount of capital (i.e., plant and equipment are fixed). The marginal product of labor (MPL) is the additional output produced when one more unit of labor is employed. The average product of labor (APL) is the TPL divided by the total number of units of labor employed.

LOS 15.k

The marginal product of labor increases initially as additional units of labor are employed. For example, four workers may produce more than twice the output of two workers. This is referred to as a situation in which the MPL is increasing.

Holding physical capital constant, as labor is increased beyond some quantity, the incremental output from each additional worker declines. This is referred to as the point of diminishing marginal returns or decreasing marginal productivity.

The marginal revenue product (MRP) of labor is the additional revenue that a firm would get from selling the additional output (marginal product) of one more unit of labor. A firm can increase profits by hiring additional units of labor, as long as the MRP of labor is greater than the cost of one more unit of labor. A firm should employ more labor until the MRP of labor just equals the wage. Beyond this quantity of labor, the value of the additional output of one more worker is less than the worker's wage.

LOS 15.1

The optimal combination of labor and capital inputs is reached when the ratio of the marginal product of capital to its cost is equal to the ratio of the marginal product of labor to its cost, which is output per dollar of input cost. That is, $MP_{capital} / P_{capital} = MP_{labor} / P_{labor}$.

When this condition is met, costs for the associated level of output are at a minimum. If the $MP_{capital} / P_{capital} < MP_{labor} / P_{labor}$ so that the output per dollar of capital is less than the output per dollar of labor, a firm can reduce costs by employing more labor and less capital to produce the same output.

CONCEPT CHECKERS

1. Economic profits are zero if:
    A. implicit costs equal explicit costs.
    B. economic depreciation equals zero.
    C. total revenue equals the sum of all opportunity costs.

2. Marginal revenue is *best* interpreted as the:
    A. addition to total revenue from the next unit produced and sold.
    B. increment to average revenue from the next unit produced and sold.
    C. smallest increment of revenue that can be gained by producing and selling a unit.

3. As a firm employs additional units of either labor or capital in its production process, holding the quantity of the other input constant, the firm is *most likely* to experience diminishing returns to:
    A. labor only.
    B. capital only.
    C. either labor or capital.

4. Which of the following statements *most accurately* describes the shapes of the average variable cost (AVC) and average total cost (ATC) curves over a wide range of output?
    A. The AVC curve and the ATC curve are both U-shaped.
    B. The AVC curve declines throughout; the ATC curve is U-shaped.
    C. The AVC curve is U-shaped; the ATC curve increases initially then declines.

5. The vertical distance between the average total cost (ATC) curve and average variable cost (AVC) curve:
    A. increases as output increases.
    B. decreases as output increases.
    C. remains constant as output increases.

6. Which of the following statements *most accurately* describes the shape of the average fixed cost curve?
    A. It becomes relatively flat at large output levels.
    B. It is always below the average variable cost curve.
    C. It intersects the marginal cost curve at its minimum.

7. A firm's average revenue is greater than its average variable cost and less than its average total cost. If the firm does not expect price to change, the firm should:
    A. shut down in the short run and in the long run.
    B. shut down in the short run but operate in the long run.
    C. operate in the short run but shut down in the long run.

8. If a firm's long-run average total cost increases by 6% if output is increased by 6%, the firm is experiencing:
    A. economies of scale.
    B. diseconomies of scale.
    C. constant returns to scale.

9. A firm is considering whether to determine its profit maximizing quantity of output by maximizing the difference between total revenue and total cost or by producing up to the point where marginal revenue equals marginal cost. Which method is *most likely* to generate the greatest profit?
    A. Profit will be the same using either method.
    B. Profit will be greater with the total revenue/total cost approach.
    C. Profit will be greater with the marginal revenue/marginal cost approach.

10. Which of the following characteristics *best* describes a decreasing-cost industry? As the quantity supplied increases, the price per unit:
    A. decreases, and the long-run industry supply curve slopes upward.
    B. decreases, and the long-run industry supply curve slopes downward.
    C. increases, and the long-run industry supply curve slopes downward.

11. Which of the following statements *most accurately* describes the relationship between marginal product (MP) and average product (AP) of labor in the short run? As the quantity of output increases:
    A. AP is always less than MP.
    B. initially, AP < MP, then AP = MP, then AP > MP.
    C. initially, AP > MP, then AP = MP, then AP < MP.

12. Marginal revenue product is *best* defined as the:
    A. addition to total revenue from selling one more unit of output.
    B. additional output produced by using one more unit of a productive input.
    C. addition to revenue from selling the output produced by using one more unit of an input.

13. In a given firm, the marginal product per hour worked for a skilled worker is twice as much as it is for an unskilled worker. Skilled workers earn $20 per hour, and unskilled workers earn $8 per hour. Based on this information, the firm should increase the:
    A. salary of skilled workers to attract more of them.
    B. use of skilled workers or decrease the use of unskilled workers.
    C. use of unskilled workers or decrease the use of skilled workers.

14. A firm is using the profit-maximizing combination of labor and capital if the ratio of each input's marginal revenue product to its cost per unit is:
    A. maximized.
    B. equal to one.
    C. minimized.

ANSWERS – CONCEPT CHECKERS

1. **C** Economic profit is equal to total revenue minus both explicit and implicit opportunity costs. When total revenues are just equal to opportunity costs (explicit and implicit, including normal profit), economic profit is zero.

2. **A** Marginal revenue is the addition to total revenue from producing and selling the next unit of a good.

3. **C** Both labor and capital inputs are subject to the law of diminishing returns.

4. **A** The AVC curve is U-shaped. It declines at first due to efficiency gains, but eventually increases due to diminishing returns. AFC decreases as output increases. The ATC curve is U-shaped because ATC is the sum of AFC and AVC.

5. **B** The vertical distance between the average total cost curve and average variable cost curve is average fixed cost, which decreases as output increases because fixed costs are averaged over greater output.

6. **A** Average fixed cost initially declines rapidly, but as output increases, it declines slowly because fixed cost is being averaged over a greater amount of output.

7. **C** If a firm is generating sufficient revenue to cover its variable costs and part of its fixed costs, it should continue to operate in the short run. If average revenue is likely to remain below average total costs in the long run, the firm should shut down.

8. **B** Increasing long-run average total cost as a result of increasing output demonstrates diseconomies of scale.

9. **A** Maximum profit is the same using either approach.

10. **B** In a decreasing-cost industry, input prices decrease as industry output increases, and the long-run industry supply curve is downward-sloping as a result.

11. **B** MP intersects the AP maximum from above. MP is initially greater than AP, and then MP and AP intersect. Beyond this intersection, MP is less than AP. (Hint: draw the curves.)

12. **C** The marginal revenue product is the addition to total revenue gained by selling the marginal product (additional output) from employing one more unit of a productive resource.

13. **C** To minimize costs, the firm should hire inputs so that $MP_{skilled} / P_{skilled} = MP_{unskilled} / P_{unskilled}$. Because the $MP_{skilled}$ is twice the $MP_{unskilled}$, and the $P_{skilled}$ is more than twice the $P_{unskilled}$, costs would be reduced by employing more unskilled labor and less skilled labor.

14. **B** At the optimal combination of labor and capital (the combination that minimizes costs), the ratio of each input's marginal revenue product to its cost per unit is equal to one.

The following is a review of the Economics: Microeconomic Analysis principles designed to address the learning outcome statements set forth by CFA Institute. This topic is also covered in:

THE FIRM AND MARKET STRUCTURES

Study Session 4

EXAM FOCUS

This topic review covers four market structures: perfect competition, monopolistic competition, oligopoly, and monopoly. You need to be able to compare and contrast these structures in terms of numbers of firms, firm demand elasticity and pricing power, long-run economic profits, barriers to entry, and the amount of product differentiation and advertising. Finally, know the two quantitative concentration measures, their implications for market structure and pricing power, and their limitations in this regard. We will apply all of these concepts when we analyze industry competition and pricing power of companies in the Study Session on equity investments.

LOS 16.a: Describe characteristics of perfect competition, monopolistic competition, oligopoly, and pure monopoly.

CFA® Program Curriculum, Volume 2, page 152

In this topic review, we examine four types of markets, which we will differentiate by the following:

- Number of firms and their relative sizes.
- Elasticity of the demand curves they face.
- Ways that they compete with other firms for sales.
- Ease or difficulty with which firms can enter or exit the market.

At one end of the spectrum is **perfect competition**, in which many firms produce identical products, and competition forces them all to sell at the market price. At the other extreme, we have **monopoly**, where only one firm is producing the product. In between are **monopolistic competition** (many sellers and differentiated products) and **oligopoly** (few firms that compete in a variety of ways). Each market structure has its own characteristics and implications for firm strategy, and we will examine each in turn.

Perfect competition refers to a market in which many firms produce identical products, barriers to entry into the market are very low, and firms compete for sales only on the basis of price. Firms face perfectly elastic (horizontal) demand curves at the price determined in the market because no firm is large enough to affect the market price. The market for wheat in a region is a good approximation of such a market. Overall market supply and demand determine the price of wheat.

Monopolistic competition differs from perfect competition in that products are not identical. Each firm differentiates its product(s) from those of other firms through some combination of differences in product quality, product features, and marketing. The demand curve faced by each firm is downward sloping; while demand is elastic, it is not perfectly elastic. Prices are not identical because of perceived differences among competing products, and barriers to entry are low. The market for toothpaste is a good example of monopolistic competition. Firms differentiate their products through features and marketing with claims of more attractiveness, whiter teeth, fresher breath, and even of actually cleaning your teeth and preventing decay. If the price of your personal favorite increases, you are not likely to immediately switch to another brand as under perfect competition. Some customers would switch in response to a 10% increase in price and some would not. This is why firm demand is downward sloping.

The most important characteristic of an *oligopoly* market is that there are only a few firms competing. In such a market, each firm must consider the actions and responses of other firms in setting price and business strategy. We say that such firms are interdependent. While products are typically good substitutes for each other, they may be either quite similar or differentiated through features, branding, marketing, and quality. Barriers to entry are high, often because economies of scale in production or marketing lead to very large firms. Demand can be more or less elastic than for firms in monopolistic competition. The automobile market is dominated by a few very large firms and can be characterized as an oligopoly. The product and pricing decisions of Toyota certainly affect those of Ford and vice versa. Automobile makers compete based on price, but also through marketing, product features, and quality, which is often signaled strongly through brand name. The oil industry also has a few dominant firms but their products are very good substitutes for each other.

A *monopoly* market is characterized by a single seller of a product with no close substitutes. This fact alone means that the firm faces a downward-sloping demand curve (the market demand curve) and has the power to choose the price at which it sells its product. High barriers to entry protect a monopoly producer from competition. One source of monopoly power is the protection offered by copyrights and patents. Another possible source of monopoly power is control over a resource specifically needed to produce the product. Most frequently, monopoly power is supported by government. A **natural monopoly** refers to a situation where the average cost of production is falling over the relevant range of consumer demand. In this case, having two (or more) producers would result in a significantly higher cost of production and be detrimental to consumers. Examples of natural monopolies include the electric power and distribution business and other public utilities. When privately owned companies are granted such monopoly power, the price they charge is often regulated by government as well.

Sometimes market power is the result of *network effects* or *synergies* that make it very difficult to compete with a company once it has reached a critical level of market penetration. EBay gained such a large share of the online auction market that its information on buyers and sellers and the number of buyers who visit eBay essentially precluded others from establishing competing businesses. While it may have competition to some degree, its market share is such that it has negatively sloped demand and a good deal of pricing power. Sometimes we refer to such companies as having a moat around them that protects them from competition. It is best to remember, however, that changes in technology and consumer tastes can, and usually do, reduce market power over time. Polaroid had a monopoly on instant photos for years, but the introduction of digital photography forced the firm into bankruptcy in 2001.

The table in Figure 1 shows the key features of each market structure.

Figure 1: Characteristics of Market Structures

	Perfect Competition	*Monopolistic Competition*	*Oligopoly*	*Monopoly*
Number of sellers	Many firms	Many firms	Few firms	Single firm
Barriers to entry	Very low	Low	High	Very high
Nature of substitute products	Very good substitutes	Good substitutes but differentiated	Very good substitutes or differentiated	No good substitutes
Nature of competition	Price only	Price, marketing, features	Price, marketing, features	Advertising
Pricing power	None	Some	Some to significant	Significant

LOS 16.b: Explain relationships between price, marginal revenue, marginal cost, economic profit, and the elasticity of demand under each market structure.

LOS 16.d: Describe and determine the optimal price and output for firms under each market structure.

LOS 16.e: Explain factors affecting long-run equilibrium under each market structure.

CFA® Program Curriculum, Volume 2, page 156

Professor's Note: We cover these LOS together and slightly out of curriculum order so that we can present the complete analysis of each market structure to better help candidates understand the economics of each type of market structure.

PERFECT COMPETITION

Producer firms in perfect competition have no influence over market price. Market supply and demand determine price. As illustrated in Figure 2, the *individual firm's* demand schedule is *perfectly elastic* (horizontal).

Figure 2: Price-Taker Demand

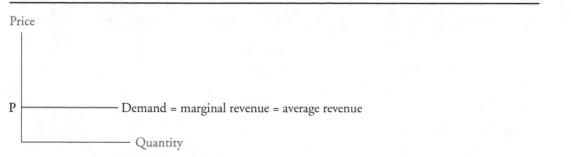

In a perfectly competitive market, a firm will continue to expand production until marginal revenue (MR) equals marginal cost (MC). Marginal revenue is the increase in total revenue from selling one more unit of a good or service. For a price taker, marginal revenue is simply the price because all additional units are assumed to be sold at the same (market) price. In *pure competition*, a firm's marginal revenue is equal to the market price, and a firm's MR curve, presented in Figure 3, is identical to its demand curve. A profit maximizing firm will produce the quantity, Q^*, when MC = MR.

Figure 3: Profit Maximizing Output For A Price Taker

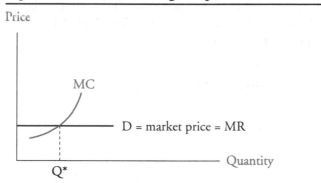

All firms maximize (economic) profit by producing and selling the quantity for which marginal revenue equals marginal cost. For a firm in a perfectly competitive market, this is the same as producing and selling the quantity for which marginal cost equals (market) price. Economic profit equals total revenues less the opportunity cost of production, which includes the cost of a normal return to all factors of production, including invested capital.

Panel (a) of Figure 4 illustrates that in the *short run*, economic profit is maximized at the quantity for which marginal revenue = marginal cost. As shown in Panel (b), profit maximization also occurs when total revenue exceeds total cost by the maximum amount.

An *economic loss* occurs on any units for which marginal revenue is less than marginal cost. At any output above the quantity where MR = MC, the firm will be generating losses on its marginal production and will maximize profits by reducing output to where MR = MC.

Figure 4: Short-Run Profit Maximization

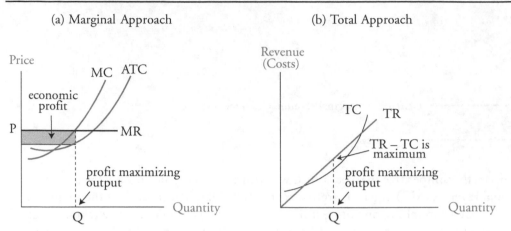

Figure 5: Equilibrium in a Perfectly Competitive Market

In a perfectly competitive market, firms will not earn economic profits for any significant period of time. The assumption is that new firms (with average and marginal cost curves identical to those of existing firms) will enter the industry to earn economic profits, increasing market supply and eventually reducing market price so that it just equals firms' average total cost (ATC). In equilibrium, each firm is producing the quantity for which P = MR = MC = ATC, so that no firm earns economic profits and each firm is producing the quantity for which ATC is a minimum (the quantity for which ATC = MC). This equilibrium situation is illustrated in Figure 5.

Figure 5: Equilibrium in a Perfectly Competitive Market

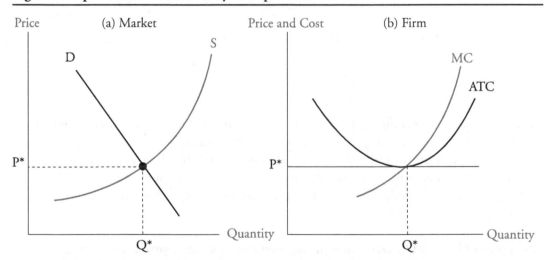

Figure 6 illustrates that firms will experience economic losses when price is below average total cost (P < ATC). In this case, the firm must decide whether to continue operating. A firm will minimize its losses in the short run by continuing to operate when price is less than ATC but greater than AVC. As long as the firm is covering its variable costs and some of its fixed costs, its loss will be less than its fixed (in the short run) costs. If the firm is only just covering its variable costs (P = AVC), the firm is operating at its **shutdown point**. If the firm is not covering its variable costs (P < AVC) by continuing to operate, its losses will be greater than its fixed costs. In this case, the firm will shut down (zero output) and lay off its workers. This will limit its losses to its fixed costs (e.g., its building lease and debt payments). If the firm does not believe price will ever exceed ATC in the future, going out of business is the only way to eliminate fixed costs.

Figure 6: Short-Run Loss

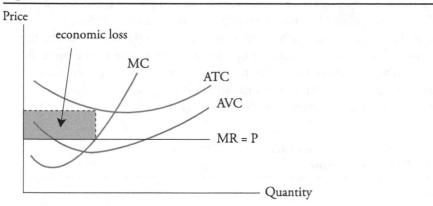

The *long-run equilibrium output* level for perfectly competitive firms is where MR = MC = ATC, which is where ATC is at a minimum. At this output, economic profit is zero and only a normal return is realized.

Recall that price takers should produce where P = MC. Referring to Panel (a) in Figure 7, a firm will shut down at a price below P_1. Between P_1 and P_2, a firm will continue to operate in the short run. At P_2, the firm is earning a normal profit—economic profit equals zero. At prices above P_2, a firm is making economic profits and will expand its production along the MC line. Thus, the **short-run supply curve for a firm** is its MC line above the average variable cost curve, AVC. The supply curve shown in Panel (b) is the **short-run market supply curve**, which is the horizontal sum (add up the quantities from all firms at each price) of the MC curves for all firms in a given industry. Because firms will supply more units at higher prices, the short-run market supply curve slopes upward to the right.

Figure 7: Short-Run Supply Curves

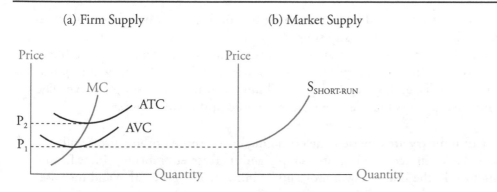

Changes in Demand, Entry and Exit, and Changes in Plant Size

In the short run, an increase in market demand (a shift of the market demand curve to the right) will increase both equilibrium price and quantity, while a decrease in market demand will reduce both equilibrium price and quantity. The change in equilibrium price will change the (horizontal) demand curve faced by each individual firm and the profit-maximizing output of a firm. These effects for an increase in demand are illustrated in Figure 8. An increase in market demand from D_1 to D_2 increases the short-run equilibrium price from P_1 to P_2 and equilibrium output from Q_1 to Q_2. In Panel (b) of Figure 8, we see the short-run effect of the increased market price on the output of an individual firm. The higher price leads to a greater profit-maximizing output, $Q_{2\ Firm}$. At the higher output level, a firm will earn an economic profit in the short run. In the long run, some firms will increase their scale of operations in response to the increase in demand, and new firms will likely enter the industry. In response to a decrease in demand, the short-run equilibrium price and quantity will fall, and in the long run, firms will decrease their scale of operations or exit the market.

Figure 8: Short-Run Adjustment to an Increase in Demand Under Perfect Competition

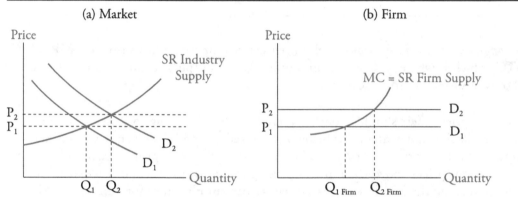

A firm's long-run adjustment to a shift in industry demand and the resulting change in price may be either to alter the size of its plant or leave the market entirely. The marketplace abounds with examples of firms that have increased their plant sizes (or added additional production facilities) to increase output in response to increasing market demand. Other firms, such as Ford and GM, have decreased plant size to reduce economic losses. This strategy is commonly referred to as *downsizing*.

If an industry is characterized by firms earning economic profits, new firms will enter the market. This will cause industry supply to increase (the industry supply curve shifts downward and to the right), increasing equilibrium output and decreasing equilibrium price. Even though industry output increases, however, individual firms will produce less because as price falls, each individual firm will move down its own supply curve. The end result is that a firm's total revenue and economic profit will decrease.

If firms in an industry are experiencing economic losses, some of these firms will exit the market. This will decrease industry supply and increase equilibrium price. Each remaining firm in the industry will move up its individual supply curve and increase production at the higher market price. This will cause total revenues to increase, reducing any economic losses the remaining firms had been experiencing.

A *permanent change in demand* leads to the entry of firms to, or exit of firms from, an industry. Let's consider the permanent increase in demand illustrated in Figure 9. The initial long-run industry equilibrium condition shown in Panel (a) is at the intersection of demand curve D_0 and supply curve S_0, at price P_0 and quantity Q_0. As indicated in Panel (b) of Figure 9, at the market price of P_0 each firm will produce q_0. At this price and output, each firm earns a normal profit, and economic profit is zero. That is, MC = MR = P, and ATC is at its minimum. Now, suppose industry demand permanently increases such that the industry demand curve in Panel (a) shifts to D_1. The new market price will be P_1 and industry output will increase to Q_1. At the new price P_1, existing firms will produce q_1 and realize an economic profit because $P_1 > $ ATC. Positive economic profits will cause new firms to enter the market. As these new firms increase total industry supply, the industry supply curve will gradually shift to S_1, and the market price will decline back to P_0. At the market price of P_0, the industry will now produce Q_2, with an increased number of firms in the industry, each producing at the original quantity, q_0. The individual firms will no longer enjoy an economic profit because ATC = P_0 at q_0.

Figure 9: Effects of a Permanent Increase in Demand

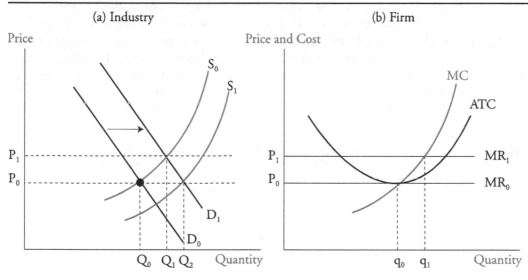

MONOPOLISTIC COMPETITION

Monopolistic competition has the following market characteristics:

- *A large number of independent sellers*: (1) Each firm has a relatively small market share, so no individual firm has any significant power over price. (2) Firms need only pay attention to average market price, not the price of individual competitors. (3) There are too many firms in the industry for collusion (price fixing) to be possible.
- *Differentiated products*: Each producer has a product that is slightly different from its competitors (at least in the minds of consumers). The competing products are close substitutes for one another.
- *Firms compete on price, quality, and marketing* as a result of product differentiation. *Quality* is a significant product-differentiating characteristic. *Price* and output can be set by firms because they face downward-sloping demand curves, but there is usually a strong correlation between quality and the price that firms can charge. *Marketing* is a must to inform the market about a product's differentiating characteristics.
- *Low barriers to entry* so that firms are free to enter and exit the market. If firms in the industry are earning economic profits, new firms can be expected to enter the industry.

Firms in monopolistic competition face *downward-sloping demand* curves (they are price searchers). Their demand curves are highly *elastic* because competing products are perceived by consumers as close substitutes. Think about the market for toothpaste. All toothpaste is quite similar, but differentiation occurs due to taste preferences, influential advertising, and the reputation of the seller.

The price/output decision for monopolistic competition is illustrated in Figure 10. Panel (a) of Figure 10 illustrates the short-run price/output characteristics of monopolistic competition for a single firm. As indicated, firms in monopolistic competition maximize economic profits by producing where marginal revenue (MR) equals marginal cost (MC), and by charging the price for that quantity from the demand curve, D. Here the firm earns positive economic profits because price, P^*, exceeds average total cost, ATC^*. Due to low barriers to entry, competitors will enter the market in pursuit of these economic profits.

Panel (b) of Figure 10 illustrates long-run equilibrium for a *representative* firm after new firms have entered the market. As indicated, the entry of new firms shifts the demand curve faced by each individual firm down to the point where price equals average total cost ($P^* = ATC^*$), such that economic profit is zero. At this point, there is no longer an incentive for new firms to enter the market, and long-run equilibrium is established. The firm in monopolistic competition continues to produce at the quantity where MR = MC but no longer earns positive economic profits.

Figure 10: Short-Run and Long-Run Output Under Monopolistic Competition

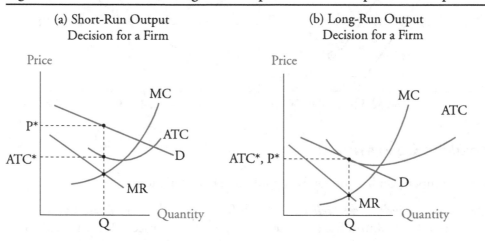

Figure 11 illustrates the differences between long-run equilibrium in markets with monopolistic competition and markets with perfect competition. Note that with monopolistic competition, price is greater than marginal cost (i.e., producers can realize a **markup**), average total cost is not at a minimum for the quantity produced (suggesting **excess capacity**, or an inefficient scale of production), and the price is slightly higher than under perfect competition. The point to consider here, however, is that perfect competition is characterized by no product differentiation. The question of the efficiency of monopolistic competition becomes, "Is there an economically efficient amount of product differentiation?"

Figure 11: Firm Output Under Monopolistic and Perfect Competition

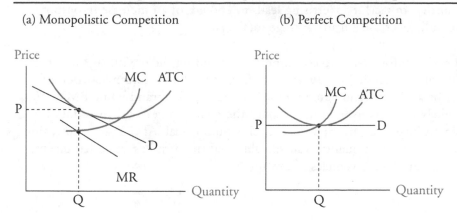

In a world with only one brand of toothpaste, clearly average production costs would be lower. That fact alone probably does not mean that a world with only one brand/type of toothpaste would be a better world. While product differentiation has costs, it also has benefits to consumers.

Consumers definitely benefit from brand name promotion and advertising because they receive information about the nature of a product. This often enables consumers to make better purchasing decisions. Convincing consumers that a particular brand of deodorant will actually increase their confidence in a business meeting or make them more attractive to the opposite sex is not easy or inexpensive. Whether the perception of increased confidence or attractiveness from using a particular product is worth the additional cost of advertising is a question probably better left to consumers of the products. Some would argue that the increased cost of advertising and sales is not justified by the benefits of these activities.

Product innovation is a necessary activity as firms in monopolistic competition pursue economic profits. Firms that bring new and innovative products to the market are confronted with less-elastic demand curves, enabling them to increase price and earn economic profits. However, close substitutes and imitations will eventually erode the initial economic profit from an innovative product. Thus, firms in monopolistic competition must continually look for innovative product features that will make their products relatively more desirable to some consumers than those of the competition.

Innovation does not come without costs. The costs of product innovation must be weighed against the extra revenue that it produces. A firm is considered to be spending the optimal amount on innovation when the marginal cost of (additional) innovation just equals the marginal revenue (marginal benefit) of additional innovation.

Advertising expenses are high for firms in monopolistic competition. This is to inform consumers about the unique features of their products and to create or increase a perception of differences between products that are actually quite similar. We just note here that advertising costs for firms in monopolistic competition are greater than those for firms in perfect competition and those that are monopolies.

As you might expect, advertising costs increase the average total cost curve for a firm in monopolistic competition. The increase to average total cost attributable to advertising decreases as output increases, because more fixed advertising dollars are being averaged over a larger quantity. In fact, if advertising leads to enough of an increase in output (sales), it can actually decrease a firm's average total cost.

Brand names provide information to consumers by providing them with signals about the quality of the branded product. Many firms spend a significant portion of their advertising budget on brand name promotion. Seeing the brand name BMW on an automobile likely tells a consumer more about the quality of a newly introduced automobile than an inspection of the vehicle itself would reveal. At the same time, the reputation BMW has for high quality is so valuable that the firm has an added incentive not to damage it by producing vehicles of low quality.

OLIGOPOLY

Compared to monopolistic competition, an oligopoly market has higher barriers to entry and fewer firms. The other key difference is that the firms are interdependent, so a price change by one firm can be expected to be met by a price change by its competitors. This means that the actions of another firm will directly affect a given firm's demand curve for the product. Given this complicating fact, models of oligopoly pricing and profits must make a number of important assumptions. In the following, we describe four of these models and their implications for price and quantity:

1. Kinked demand curve model.

2. Cournot duopoly model.

3. Nash equilibrium model (prisoner's dilemma).

4. Stackelberg dominant firm model.

One traditional model of oligopoly, the **kinked demand curve model**, is based on the assumption that an increase in a firm's product price will not be followed by its competitors, but a decrease in price will. According to the kinked demand curve model, each firm believes that it faces a demand curve that is more elastic (flatter) above a given price (the kink in the demand curve) than it is below the given price. The kinked demand curve model is illustrated in Figure 12. The kink price is at price P_K, where a firm produces Q_K. A firm believes that if it raises its price above P_K, its competitors will remain at P_K, and it will lose market share because it has the highest price. Above P_K, the demand curve is considered to be relatively elastic, where a small price increase will result in a large decrease in demand. On the other hand, if a firm decreases its price below P_K, other firms will match the price cut, and all firms will experience a relatively small increase in sales relative to any price reduction. Therefore, Q_K is the profit-maximizing level of output.

Figure 12: Kinked Demand Curve Model

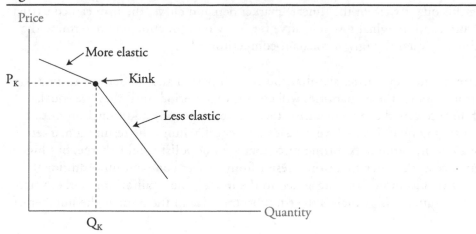

It is worth noting that with a kink in the market demand curve, we also get a gap in the associated marginal revenue curve, as shown in Figure 13. For any firm with a marginal cost curve passing through this gap, the price at which the kink is located is the firm's profit maximizing price.

Figure 13: Gap in Marginal Revenue Curve

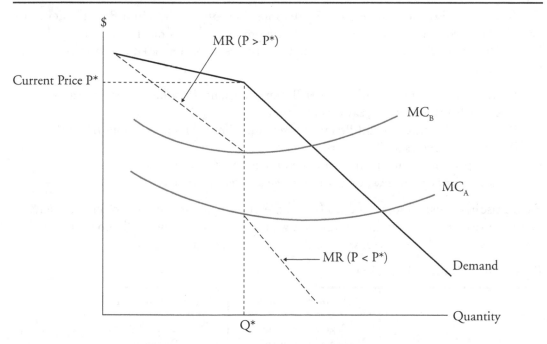

A shortcoming of the kinked demand curve model of oligopoly is that in spite of its intuitive appeal, it is incomplete because what determines the market price (where the kink is located) is outside the scope of the model.

Another model of oligopoly pricing and output is the **Cournot model**, named after the economist who developed it in the early 19th century. The model considers an oligopoly with only two firms competing (i.e., a *duopoly*), and both have identical and constant marginal costs of production. Each firm knows the quantity supplied by the other firm in the previous period and assumes that is what it will supply in the next period. By subtracting this quantity from the (linear) market demand curve, the firm can construct a demand curve and marginal revenue curve for its own production and determine the profit maximizing quantity (given constant competitor sales).

Firms determine their quantities simultaneously each period and, under the assumptions of the Cournot model, these quantities will change each period until they are equal. When each firm selects the same quantity, there is no longer any additional profit to be gained by changing quantity, and we have a stable equilibrium. The resulting market price is less than the profit maximizing price that a monopolist would charge, but higher than marginal cost, the price that would result from perfect competition. Additional analysis shows that as more firms are added to the model, the equilibrium market price falls towards marginal cost, which is the equilibrium price in the limit as the number of firms gets large.

Cournot's model was an early version of what are called *strategic games*, decision models in which the best choice for a firm depends on the actions (reactions) of other firms. A more general model of this strategic game was developed by Nobel Prize winner John Nash, who developed the concept of a **Nash equilibrium**. A Nash equilibrium is reached when the choices of all firms are such that there is no other choice that makes any firm better off (increases profits or decreases losses).

One such game is called the **prisoner's dilemma**. Two prisoners, A and B, are believed to have committed a serious crime. However, the prosecutor does not feel that the police have sufficient evidence for a conviction. The prisoners are separated and offered the following deal:

- If Prisoner A confesses and Prisoner B remains silent, Prisoner A goes free and Prisoner B receives a 10-year prison sentence.
- If Prisoner B confesses and Prisoner A remains silent, Prisoner B goes free and Prisoner A receives a 10-year prison sentence.
- If both prisoners remain silent, each will receive a 6-month sentence.
- If both prisoners confess, each will receive a 2-year sentence.

Each prisoner must choose either to betray the other by confessing or to remain silent. Neither prisoner, however, knows for sure what the other prisoner will choose to do. The result for each of these four possible outcomes is presented in Figure 14.

Figure 14: Prisoner's Dilemma

	Prisoner B is silent	*Prisoner B confesses*
Prisoner A is silent	A gets 6 months B gets 6 months	A gets 10 years B goes free
Prisoner A confesses	A goes free B gets 10 years	A gets 2 years B gets 2 years

The Nash equilibrium is for both prisoners to confess, and for each to get a sentence of two years, although clearly the best overall outcome would be for both to remain silent and get sentences of six months. However, that is not a Nash equilibrium since either prisoner can improve his situation from silent/silent by confessing, because silent/

confess and confess/silent are preferred by each in turn. Neither of these outcomes is a Nash equilibrium because the silent prisoner in both cases can improve his situation by confessing rather than remaining silent. Confess/confess is the Nash equilibrium since neither prisoner can unilaterally reduce his sentence by changing to silence. Another way to view this outcome is that no matter what the other prisoner chooses to do, the best sentence for a prisoner comes from confessing.

We can design a similar two-firm oligopoly game where the equilibrium outcome is for both firms to cheat on a **collusion** agreement by charging a low price, even though the best overall outcome is for both to honor the agreement and charge a high price. As illustrated in Figure 15, the Nash equilibrium is for both firms to cheat on the agreement.

Figure 15: Prisoner's Dilemma Type Game for Two Firms

	Firm B Honors	*Firm B Cheats*
Firm A Honors	A earns economic profit B earns economic profit	A has an economic loss B earns increased economic profit
Firm A Cheats	A earns increased economic profit B has an economic loss	A earns zero economic profit B earns zero economic profit

An example of such a two-firm oligopoly game is illustrated in Figure 16. Each firm may charge either a high price or a low price, and the profits to each firm are as shown. Assume the firms have agreed to both charge a high price. The Nash equilibrium is for Firm A and Firm B to charge a low price. This is the only combination from which neither firm can unilaterally change its action to improve its profits. Total profits are greater if both honor the agreement, but either Firm A or Firm B can improve profits from 150 to 200 by cheating on the agreement. However, the non-cheating firm can then increase profits from 50 to 100 by cheating:

Figure 16: Nash Equilibrium

	Firm B Honors	*Firm B Cheats*
Firm A Honors	A earns 150 B earns 150	A earns 50 B earns 200
Firm A Cheats	A earns 200 B earns 50	A earns 100 B earns 100

Again, this is not the best joint outcome because joint profits are maximized if both honor the agreement. This is what lies behind collusive agreements by or among firms. If firms can enter into and enforce an agreement to restrict output and charge higher prices, and share the resulting profits, they are better off. There are, however, laws (anti-trust laws) against such collusive agreements to restrain competition to protect the interests of consumers. The OPEC oil cartel is an example of such a collusive agreement, but evidence is common that cartel members regularly cheat on their agreements to share the optimal output of oil.

In general, collusive agreements to increase price in an oligopoly market will be more successful (have less cheating) when:

- There are fewer firms.
- Products are more similar (less differentiated).
- Cost structures are more similar.
- Purchases are relatively small and frequent.
- Retaliation by other firms for cheating is more certain and more severe.
- There is less actual or potential competition from firms outside the cartel.

A final model of oligopoly behavior to consider is the **dominant firm model**. In this model, there is a single firm that has a significantly large market share because of its greater scale and lower cost structure—the dominant firm (DF). In such a model, the market price is essentially determined by the dominant firm, and the other competitive firms (CF) take this market price as given.

The dominant firm believes that the quantity supplied by the other firms decreases at lower prices, so that the dominant firm's demand curve is related to the market demand curve as shown in Figure 17. Based on this demand curve (D_{DF}) and its associated marginal revenue (MR_{DF}) curve, the firm will maximize profits at a price of P^*. The competitive firms maximize profits by producing the quantity for which their marginal cost (MC_{CF}) equals P^*, quantity Q_{CF}.

A price decrease by one of the competitive firms, which increases Q_{CF} in the short run, will lead to a decrease in price by the dominant firm, and competitive firms will decrease output and/or exit the industry in the long run. The long-run result of such a price decrease by competitors below P^* would then be to decrease the overall market share of competitor firms and increase the market share of the dominant firm.

Figure 17: Dominant Firm Oligopoly

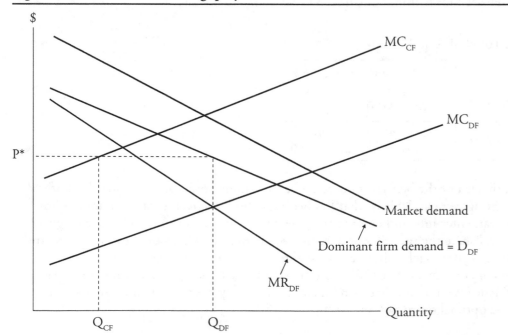

©2014 Kaplan, Inc.

Clearly, there are many possible outcomes in oligopoly markets that depend on the characteristics of the firms and the market itself. The important point is that the firms' decisions are interdependent so that the expected reaction of other firms is an important consideration. Overall, the resulting price will be somewhere between the price based on perfect collusion that would maximize total profits to all firms in the market (actually the monopoly price, which is addressed next) and the price that would result from perfect competition and generate zero economic profits in the long run. These two limiting outcomes are illustrated in Figure 18 as $P_{collusion}$ with $Q_{collusion}$ for perfect collusion and $P_{competition}$ and $Q_{competition}$ for perfect competition.

Figure 18: Collusion vs. Perfect Competition

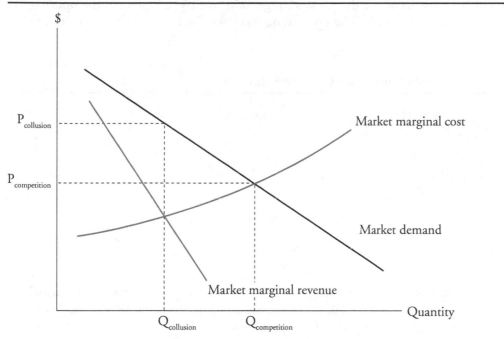

MONOPOLY

A monopoly faces a downward-sloping demand curve for its product, so profit maximization involves a trade-off between price and quantity sold if the firm sells at the same price to all buyers. Assuming a single selling price, a monopoly firm must lower its price in order to sell a greater quantity. Unlike a firm in perfect competition, a firm facing a downward-sloping demand curve must determine what price to charge, hoping to find the price and output combination that will bring the maximum profit to the firm.

Two pricing strategies that are possible for a monopoly firm are *single-price* and *price discrimination*. If the monopoly's customers cannot resell the product to each other, the monopoly can maximize profits by charging different prices to different groups of customers. When price discrimination isn't possible, the monopoly will charge a single price. Price discrimination is described in more detail after we address single-price profit maximization.

To maximize profit, monopolists will expand output until marginal revenue (MR) equals marginal cost (MC). Due to high entry barriers, monopolist profits do not attract new market entrants. Therefore, long-run positive economic profits can exist. Do monopolists charge the highest possible price? The answer is no, because monopolists want to maximize profits, not price.

Figure 19 shows the revenue-cost structure facing the monopolist. Note that production will expand until MR = MC at optimal output Q^*. To find the price at which it will sell Q^* units, you must go to the demand curve. The demand curve itself does not determine the optimal behavior of the monopolist. Just like the perfect competition model, the profit maximizing output for a monopolist is where MR = MC. To ensure a profit, the demand curve must lie above the firm's average total cost (ATC) curve at the optimal quantity so that price > ATC. The optimal quantity will be in the elastic range of the demand curve.

Figure 19: Monopoly Short-Run Costs and Revenues

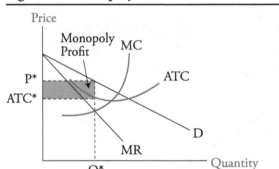

Once again, the *profit maximizing* output for a monopolistic firm is the one for which MR = MC. As shown in Figure 19, the profit maximizing output is Q^*, with a price of P^*, and an economic profit equal to $(P^* - ATC^*) \times Q^*$.

Monopolists are *price searchers* and have *imperfect information* regarding market demand. They must experiment with different prices to find the one that maximizes profit.

Price discrimination is the practice of charging different consumers different prices for the same product or service. Examples are different prices for airline tickets based on whether a Saturday-night stay is involved (separates business travelers and leisure travelers) and different prices for movie tickets based on age.

The motivation for a monopolist is to capture more consumer surplus as economic profit than is possible by charging a single price.

For price discrimination to work, the seller must:

- Face a downward-sloping demand curve.
- Have at least two identifiable groups of customers with *different price elasticities of demand* for the product.
- Be able to prevent the customers paying the lower price from reselling the product to the customers paying the higher price.

As long as these conditions are met, firm profits can be increased through price discrimination.

Figure 20 illustrates how price discrimination can increase the total quantity supplied and increase economic profits compared to a single-price pricing strategy. For simplicity, we have assumed no fixed costs and constant variable costs so that MC = ATC. In Panel (a), the single profit-maximizing price is $100 at a quantity of 80 (where MC = MR), which generates a profit of $2,400. In Panel (b), the firm is able to separate consumers, charges one group $110 and sells them 50 units, and sells an additional 60 units to another group (with more elastic demand) at a price of $90. Total profit is increased to $3,200, and total output is increased from 80 units to 110 units.

Compared to the quantity produced under perfect competition, the quantity produced by a monopolist reduces the sum of consumer and producer surplus by an amount represented by the triangle labeled *deadweight loss* (DWL) in Panel (a) of Figure 20. Consumer surplus is reduced not only by the decrease in quantity but also by the increase in price relative to perfect competition. Monopoly is considered inefficient because the reduction in output compared to perfect competition reduces the sum of consumer and producer surplus. Because marginal benefit is greater than marginal cost, less than the efficient quantity of resources are allocated to the production of the good. Price discrimination reduces this inefficiency by increasing output toward the quantity where marginal benefit equals marginal cost. Note that the deadweight loss is smaller in Panel (b). The firm gains from those customers with inelastic demand while still providing goods to customers with more elastic demand. This may even cause production to take place when it would not otherwise.

An extreme (and largely theoretical) case of price discrimination is perfect price discrimination. If it were possible for the monopolist to charge each consumer the maximum they are willing to pay for each unit, there would be no deadweight loss because a monopolist would produce the same quantity as under perfect competition. With perfect price discrimination, there would be no consumer surplus. It would all be captured by the monopolist.

Figure 20: Effect of Price Discrimination on Output and Operating Profit

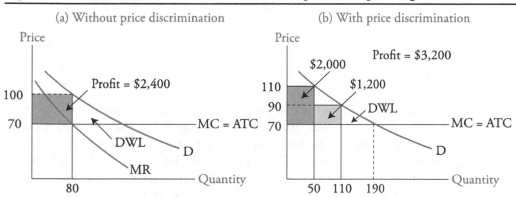

Figure 21 illustrates the difference in allocative efficiency between monopoly and perfect competition. Under perfect competition, the industry supply curve, S, is the sum of the supply curves of the many competing firms in the industry. The perfect competition equilibrium price and quantity are at the intersection of the industry supply curve and the market demand curve, D. The quantity produced is Q_{PC} at an equilibrium price P_{PC}. Because each firm is small relative to the industry, there is nothing to be gained by attempting to decrease output in an effort to increase price.

A monopolist facing the same demand curve, and with the same marginal cost curve, MC, will maximize profit by producing Q_{MON} (where MC = MR) and charging a price of P_{MON}.

The important thing to note here is that when compared to a perfectly competitive industry, the monopoly firm will produce less total output and charge a higher price.

Recall from our review of perfect competition that the efficient quantity is the one for which the sum of consumer surplus and producer surplus is maximized. In Figure 21, this quantity is where S = D, or equivalently, where marginal cost (MC) = marginal benefit (MB). *Monopoly creates a deadweight loss* relative to perfect competition because monopolies produce a quantity that does not maximize the sum of consumer surplus and producer surplus. A further loss of efficiency results from **rent seeking** when producers spend time and resources to try to acquire or establish a monopoly.

Figure 21: Perfect Competition vs. Monopoly

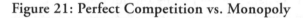

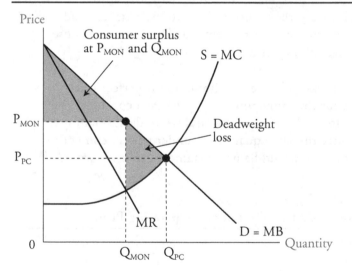

Natural Monopoly

In some industries, the economics of production lead to a single firm supplying the entire market demand for the product. When there are large economies of scale, it means that the average cost of production decreases as a single firm produces greater and greater output. An example is an electric utility. The fixed costs of producing electricity and building the power lines and related equipment to deliver it to homes are quite high. The marginal cost of providing electricity to an additional home or of providing more electricity to a home is, however, quite low. The more electricity provided, the lower the average cost per kilowatt hour. When the average cost of production for a single firm is falling throughout the relevant range of consumer demand, we say that the industry is a **natural monopoly**. The entry of another firm into the industry would divide the production between two firms and result in a higher average cost of production than for a single producer. Thus, large economies of scale in an industry present significant barriers to entry.

We illustrate the case of a natural monopoly in Figure 22. Left unregulated, a single-price monopolist will maximize profits by producing where MR = MC, producing quantity Q_U and charging P_U. Given the economies of scale, having another firm in the market would increase the ATC significantly. Note in Figure 22 that if two firms each produced approximately one-half of output Q_{AC}, average cost for each firm would be much higher than for a single producer producing Q_{AC}. Thus, there is a potential gain from monopoly because of lower average cost production when LRAC is decreasing so that economies of scale lead to a single supplier.

Figure 22: Natural Monopoly—Average Cost and Marginal Cost Pricing

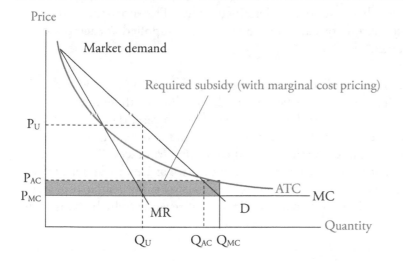

Regulators often attempt to increase competition and efficiency through efforts to reduce artificial barriers to trade, such as licensing requirements, quotas, and tariffs.

Because monopolists produce less than the optimal quantity (do not achieve efficient resource allocation), government regulation may be aimed at improving resource allocation by regulating the prices monopolies may charge. This may be done through average cost pricing or marginal cost pricing.

Average cost pricing is the most common form of regulation. This would result in a price of P_{AC} and an output of Q_{AC} as illustrated in Figure 22. It forces monopolists to reduce price to where the firm's ATC intersects the market demand curve. This will:

- Increase output and decrease price.
- Increase social welfare (allocative efficiency).
- Ensure the monopolist a *normal* profit because price = ATC.

Marginal cost pricing, which is also referred to as *efficient regulation*, forces the monopolist to reduce price to the point where the firm's MC curve intersects the market demand curve. This increases output and reduces price, but causes the monopolist to incur a loss because price is below ATC, as illustrated in Figure 22. Such a solution requires a government subsidy in order to provide the firm with a normal profit and prevent it from leaving the market entirely.

Another way of regulating a monopoly is for the government to sell the monopoly right to the highest bidder. The right to build a gasoline station and food court on a tollway is one example. In theory, the winning bidder will be an efficient supplier that bids an amount equal to the value of expected economic profit and sets prices equal to long-run average cost.

LOS 16.c: Describe a firm's supply function under each market structure.

CFA® Program Curriculum, Volume 2, page 173

The short-run supply function for a firm under perfect competition is its marginal cost curve above its average variable cost curve, as described earlier. The short-run market supply curve is constructed simply by summing the quantities supplied at each price across all firms in the market.

In markets characterized as monopolistic competition, oligopoly, and monopoly, there is no well-defined supply function. This is because under all three of these market structures, firms face downward-sloping demand curves. In each case, the quantity supplied is determined by the intersection of marginal cost and marginal revenue, and the price charged is then determined by the demand curve the firm faces. We cannot construct a function of quantity supplied as a function of price as we can under perfect competition, where price equals marginal revenue. The quantity supplied depends not only on a firm's marginal cost, but on demand and marginal revenue (which change with quantity) as well.

LOS 16.f: Describe pricing strategy under each market structure.

CFA® Program Curriculum, Volume 2, page 156

We have covered each market structure separately in detail, so we will simply summarize optimal pricing strategies.

Perfect competition: Profits are maximized by producing the quantity for which marginal cost equals marginal revenue. Note that marginal revenue and price are equal so price also equals marginal cost at the profit-maximizing quantity.

Monopoly: Profits are also maximized by producing the quantity for which marginal revenue equals marginal cost. Because the firm's demand curve is downward sloping, price is greater than marginal revenue and greater than marginal cost.

Monopolistic competition: Profits are maximized when a firm produces the quantity for which marginal revenue equals marginal cost. Similar to a monopoly structure, the firm faces a downward sloping demand curve and price will be greater than marginal cost and marginal revenue.

Oligopoly: Because one of the key characteristics of oligopoly is the interdependence of firms' pricing and output decisions, the optimal pricing strategy depends on our assumptions about the reactions of other firms to each firm's actions. Here we note different possible assumptions and the strategy that is implied by each.

1. Kinked demand curve: This assumes competitors will match a price decrease but not a price increase. Firms produce the quantity for which marginal revenue equals marginal cost. However, the marginal revenue curve is discontinuous (there's a gap in it), so for many cost structures the optimal quantity is the same, given they face the same kinked demand curve.

2. Collusion: If all producers agree to share the market to maximize total industry profits, they will produce a total quantity for which marginal cost equals marginal revenue and charge the price from the industry demand curve at which that quantity can be sold. This is the same overall price and quantity as for a profit maximizing monopoly firm, but the oligopoly firms must agree to share this total output among themselves and share the economic profits as a result.

3. Dominant firm model: In this case, we assume one firm has the lowest cost structure and a large market share as a result. The dominant firm will maximize profits by producing the quantity for which its marginal cost equals its marginal revenue and charge the price on its firm demand curve for that quantity. Other firms in the market will essentially take that price as given and produce the quantity for which their marginal cost equals that price.

4. Game theory: Because of the interdependence of oligopoly firms' decisions, assumptions about how a competitor will react to a particular price and output decision by a competitor can determine the optimal output and pricing strategy. Given the variety of models and assumptions about competitor reactions, the long-run outcome is indeterminate. We can only say that the price will be between the monopoly price (if firms successfully collude) and the perfect competition price which equals marginal cost (if potential competition rules out prices above that level).

LOS 16.g: Describe the use and limitations of concentration measures in identifying market structure.

CFA® Program Curriculum, Volume 2, page 193

When examining the pricing power of firms in an industry, we would like to be able to measure elasticity of demand directly, but that is very difficult. Regulators often use percentage of market sales (market share) to measure the degree of monopoly or market power of a firm. Often, mergers or acquisitions of companies in the same industry or market are not permitted by government authorities when they determine the market share of the combined firms will be too high and, therefore, detrimental to the economy.

Rather than estimate elasticity of demand, **concentration measures** for a market or industry are very often used as an indicator of market power. One concentration measure is the **N-firm concentration ratio**, which is calculated as the sum or the percentage market shares of the largest *N* firms in a market. While this measure is simple to calculate and understand, it does not directly measure market power or elasticity of demand.

One limitation of the N-firm concentration ratio is that it may be relatively insensitive to mergers of two firms with large market shares. This problem is reduced by using an alternative measure of market concentration, the **Herfindahl-Hirschman Index** (HHI). The HHI is calculated as the sum of the squares of the market shares of the largest firms in the market. The following example illustrates this difference between the two measures and their calculation.

Example: 4-firm concentration ratios

Given the market shares of the following firms, calculate the 4-firm concentration ratio and the 4-firm HHI, both before and after a merger of Acme and Blake.

Firm	Sales/Total Market Sales
Acme	25%
Blake	15%
Curtis	15%
Dent	10%
Erie	5%
Federal	5%

Answer:

Prior to the merger, the 4-firm concentration ratio for the market is 25 + 15 + 15 + 10 = 65%. After the merger, the Acme + Blake firm has 40% of the market, and the 4-firm concentration ratio is 40 + 15 + 10 + 5 = 70%. Although the 4-firm concentration ratio has only increased slightly, the market power of the largest firm in the industry has increased significantly from 25% to 40%.

Prior to the merger, the 4-firm HHI is $0.25^2 + 0.15^2 + 0.15^2 + 0.10^2 = 0.1175$.

After the merger, the 4-firm HHI is $0.40^2 + 0.15^2 + 0.10^2 + 0.05^2 = 0.1950$, a significant increase.

A second limitation that applies to both of our simple concentration measures is that barriers to entry are not considered in either case. Even a firm with high market share may not have much pricing power if barriers to entry are low and there is *potential competition*. With low barriers to entry, it may be the case that other firms stand ready to enter the market if firms currently in the market attempt to increase prices significantly. In this case, the elasticity of demand for existing firms may be high even though they have relatively high market shares and industry concentration measures.

LOS 16.h: Identify the type of market structure within which a firm operates.

CFA® Program Curriculum, Volume 2, page 193

The identification of the type of market structure within which a firm is operating is based on the characteristics we outlined earlier. Our earlier table is repeated here in Figure 23. Because the analyst is attempting to determine the degree of pricing power firms in the industry have, the focus is on number of firms in the industry, the importance of barriers to entry, the nature of substitute products, and the nature of industry competition. Significant interdependence among firm pricing and output decisions is always a characteristic of an oligopoly market, although some interdependence is present under monopolistic competition, even with many more firms than for an oligopoly structure.

The following table illustrates the differences in characteristics among the various market structures.

Figure 23: Characteristics of Market Structures

	Perfect Competition	Monopolistic Competition	Oligopoly	Monopoly
Number of sellers	Many firms	Many firms	Few firms	Single firm
Barriers to entry	Very low	Low	High	Very high
Nature of substitute products	Very good substitutes	Good substitutes but differentiated	Very good substitutes or differentiated	No good substitutes
Nature of competition	Price only	Price, marketing, features	Price, marketing, features	Advertising
Pricing power	None	Some	Some to significant	Significant

KEY CONCEPTS

LOS 16.a

Perfect competition is characterized by:
- Many firms, each small relative to the market.
- Very low barriers to entry into or exit from the industry.
- Homogeneous products that are perfect substitutes, no advertising or branding.
- No pricing power.

Monopolistic competition is characterized by:
- Many firms.
- Low barriers to entry into or exit from the industry.
- Differentiated products, heavy advertising and marketing expenditure.
- Some pricing power.

Oligopoly markets are characterized by:
- Few sellers.
- High barriers to entry into or exit from the industry.
- Products that may be homogeneous or differentiated by branding and advertising.
- Firms that may have significant pricing power.

Monopoly is characterized by:
- A single firm that comprises the whole market.
- Very high barriers to entry into or exit from the industry.
- Advertising used to compete with substitute products.
- Significant pricing power.

LOS 16.b

Perfect competition:
- Price = marginal revenue = marginal cost (in equilibrium).
- Perfectly elastic demand, zero economic profit in equilibrium.

Monopolistic competition:
- Price > marginal revenue = marginal cost (in equilibrium).
- Elasticity > 1 (elastic but not perfectly elastic), zero economic profit in long-run equilibrium.

Oligopoly:
- Price > marginal revenue = marginal cost (in equilibrium).
- Elasticity > 1 (elastic), may have positive economic profit in long-run equilibrium, but moves toward zero economic profit over time.

Monopoly:
- Price > marginal revenue = marginal cost (in equilibrium).
- Elasticity > 1 (elastic), may have positive economic profit in long-run equilibrium, profits may be zero because of expenditures to preserve monopoly.

LOS 16.c

Under perfect competition, a firm's short-run supply curve is the portion of the firm's short-run marginal cost curve above average variable cost. A firm's long-run supply curve is the portion of the firm's long-run marginal cost curve above average total cost.

Firms operating under monopolistic competition, oligopoly, and monopoly do not have well-defined supply functions, so neither marginal cost curves nor average cost curves are supply curves in these cases.

LOS 16.d

All firms maximize profits by producing the quantity of output for which marginal cost equals marginal revenue. Under perfect competition (perfectly elastic demand), marginal revenue also equals price.

Firms in monopolistic competition or that operate in oligopoly or monopoly markets all face downward-sloping demand curves. Selling price is determined from the price on the demand curve for the profit maximizing quantity of output.

LOS 16.e

An increase (decrease) in demand will increase (decrease) economic profits in the short run under all market structures. Positive economic profits result in entry of firms into the industry unless barriers to entry are high. Negative economic profits result in exit of firms from the industry unless barriers to exit are high. When firms enter (exit) an industry, market supply increases (decreases), resulting in a decrease (increase) in market price and an increase (decrease) in the equilibrium quantity traded in the market.

LOS 16.f

Whether a firm operates in perfect competition, monopolistic competition, or is a monopoly, profits are maximized by producing and selling the quantity for which marginal revenue equals marginal cost. Under perfect competition, price equals marginal revenue. Under monopolistic competition or monopoly, firms face downward-sloping demand curves so that marginal revenue is less than price, and the price charged at the profit-maximizing quantity is the price from the firm's demand curve at the optimal (profit-maximizing) level of output.

Under oligopoly, the pricing strategy is not clear. Because firm decisions are interdependent, the optimal pricing and output strategy depends on the assumptions made about other firms' cost structures and about competitors' responses to a firm's price changes.

LOS 16.g

A concentration ratio for N firms is calculated as the percentage of market sales accounted for by the N largest firms in the industry and is used as a simple measure of market structure and market power.

The Herfindahl-Hirschman Index measure of concentration is calculated as the sum of the squared market shares of the largest N firms in an industry and better reflects the effect of mergers on industry concentration.

Neither measure actually measures market power directly. Both can be misleading measures of market power when potential competition restricts pricing power.

LOS 16.h

To identify the market structure in which a firm is operating, we need to examine the number of firms in its industry, whether products are differentiated or other types of non-price competition exist, and barriers to entry, and compare these to the characteristics that define each market structure.

CONCEPT CHECKERS

1. The demand for products from monopolistic competitors is relatively elastic due to:
    A. high barriers to entry.
    B. the availability of many close substitutes.
    C. the availability of many complementary goods.

2. An oligopolistic industry has:
    A. few barriers to entry.
    B. few economies of scale.
    C. a great deal of interdependence among firms.

3. Which of the following statements *most accurately* describes a significant difference between a monopoly firm and a perfectly competitive firm? A perfectly competitive firm:
    A. minimizes costs; a monopolistic firm maximizes profit.
    B. maximizes profit; a monopolistic firm maximizes price.
    C. takes price as given; a monopolistic firm must search for the best price.

4. A monopolist will expand production until MR = MC and charge a price determined by the:
    A. demand curve.
    B. marginal cost curve.
    C. average total cost curve.

5. When a regulatory agency requires a monopolist to use average cost pricing, the intent is to price the product where the:
    A. ATC curve intersects the MR curve.
    B. MR curve intersects the demand curve.
    C. ATC curve intersects the demand curve.

6. When a firm operates under conditions of pure competition, marginal revenue always equals:
    A. price.
    B. average cost.
    C. marginal cost.

7. In which market structure(s) can a firm's supply function be described as its marginal cost curve above its average variable cost curve?
    A. Oligopoly or monopoly.
    B. Perfect competition only.
    C. Perfect competition or monopolistic competition.

8. In a purely competitive market, economic losses indicate that:
   A. price is below average total costs.
   B. collusion is occurring in the market place.
   C. firms need to expand output to reduce costs.

9. A purely competitive firm will tend to expand its output so long as:
   A. marginal revenue is positive.
   B. marginal revenue is greater than price.
   C. market price is greater than marginal cost.

10. Consider a firm in an oligopoly market that believes the demand curve for its product is more elastic above a certain price than below this price. This belief fits *most closely* to which of the following models?
    A. Cournot model.
    B. Dominant firm model.
    C. Kinked demand model.

11. Consider an agreement between France and Germany that will restrict wine production so that maximum economic profit can be realized. The possible outcomes of the agreement are presented in the table below.

	Germany complies	*Germany defaults*
France complies	France gets €8 billion Germany gets €8 billion	France gets €2 billion Germany gets €10 billion
France defaults	France gets €10 billion Germany gets €2 billion	France gets €4 billion Germany gets €4 billion

Based on the concept of a Nash equilibrium, the *most likely* strategy followed by the two countries with respect to whether they comply with or default on the agreement will be:
A. both countries will default.
B. both countries will comply.
C. one country will default and the other will comply.

12. A firm is likely to operate in the short run as long as price is at least as great as:
    A. marginal cost.
    B. average total cost.
    C. average variable cost.

13.   Which of the following is *most likely* an advantage of the Herfindahl-Hirschman
        Index relative to the *N*-firm concentration ratio? The Herfindahl-Hirschman
        Index:
        A. is simpler to calculate.
        B. considers barriers to entry.
        C. is more sensitive to mergers.

14.   A market characterized by low barriers to entry, good substitutes, limited pricing
        power, and marketing of product features is *best* characterized as:
        A. oligopoly.
        B. perfect competition.
        C. monopolistic competition.

ANSWERS – CONCEPT CHECKERS

1. **B** The demand for products from firms competing in monopolistic competition is relatively elastic due to the availability of many close substitutes. If a firm increases its product price, it will lose customers to firms selling substitute products at lower prices.

2. **C** An oligopolistic industry has a great deal of interdependence among firms. One firm's pricing decisions or advertising activities will affect the other firms.

3. **C** Monopolists must search for the profit maximizing price (and output) because they do not have perfect information regarding demand. Firms under perfect competition take the market price as given and only determine the profit maximizing quantity.

4. **A** A monopolist will expand production until MR = MC, and the price of the product will be determined by the demand curve.

5. **C** When a regulatory agency requires a monopolist to use average cost pricing, the intent is to price the product where the ATC curve intersects the market demand curve. A problem in using this method is actually determining exactly what the ATC is.

6. **A** When a firm operates under conditions of pure competition, MR always equals price. This is because, in pure competition, demand is perfectly elastic (a horizontal line), so MR is constant and equal to price.

7. **B** The supply function is not well-defined in markets other than those that can be characterized as perfect competition.

8. **A** In a purely competitive market, economic losses indicate that firms are overproducing, causing prices to fall below average total costs. This can occur in the short run. In the long run, however, market supply will decrease as firms exit the industry, and prices will rise to the point where economic profits are zero.

9. **C** A purely competitive firm will tend to expand its output so long as the market price is greater than MC. In the short run and long run, profit is maximized when P = MC.

10. **C** The kinked demand model assumes that each firm in a market believes that at some price, demand is more elastic for a price increase than for a price decrease.

11. **A** The Nash equilibrium results when each nation pursues the strategy that is best, given the strategy that is pursued by the other nation.
    - Given that Germany complies with the agreement: France will get €8 billion if it complies, but €10 billion if it defaults. Therefore, France should default.
    - Given that Germany defaults: France will get €2 billion if it complies, but €4 billion if it defaults. Therefore, France should default.
    - Because France is better off in either case by defaulting, France will default.
    - Germany will follow the same logic and reach the same conclusion.

12. **C** If price is greater than average variable cost, a firm will continue to operate in the short run because it is covering at least some of its fixed costs.

13. **C** Although the *N*-firm concentration ratio is simple to calculate, it can be relatively insensitive to mergers between companies with large market shares. Neither the HHI nor the *N*-firm concentration ratio consider barriers to entry.

14. **C** These characteristics are associated with a market structure of monopolistic competition. Firms in perfect competition do not compete on product features. Oligopolistic markets have high barriers to entry.

AGGREGATE OUTPUT, PRICES, AND ECONOMIC GROWTH

EXAM FOCUS

This topic review introduces macroeconomics and the measurement of aggregate economic output. The crucial concepts to grasp here are aggregate demand, short-run aggregate supply, and long-run aggregate supply. Know the factors that cause the aggregate demand and supply curves to shift and the sources of long-run economic growth. Understand the various measures of aggregate income (nominal and real GDP, national income, personal income, and personal disposable income). The interaction among saving, investment, the fiscal balance, and the trade balance will be built on in the next Study Session on international trade and foreign exchange.

LOS 17.a: Calculate and explain gross domestic product (GDP) using expenditure and income approaches.

CFA® Program Curriculum, Volume 2, page 210

Gross domestic product (GDP) is the total market value of the goods and services produced in a country within a certain time period. GDP is the most widely used measure of the size of a nation's economy. GDP includes only purchases of newly produced goods and services. The sale or resale of goods produced in previous periods is excluded. Transfer payments made by the government (e.g., unemployment, retirement, and welfare benefits) are not economic output and are not included in the calculation of GDP.

The values used in calculating GDP are *market values* of *final goods* and services—that is, goods and services that will not be resold or used in the production of other goods and services. The value of the computer chips that Intel makes is not explicitly included in GDP; their value is included in the final prices of computers that use the chips. The value of a Rembrandt painting that sells for 10 million euros is not included in the calculation of GDP, as it was not produced during the period.

Goods and services provided by government are included in GDP even though they are not explicitly priced in markets. For example, the services provided by police and the judiciary, and goods such as roads and infrastructure improvements, are included. Because these goods and services are not sold at market prices, they are valued at their cost to the government.

GDP also includes the value of owner-occupied housing, just as it includes the value of rental housing services. Because the value of owner-occupied housing is not revealed in market transactions, the value is estimated for inclusion in GDP. The value of labor not sold, such as a homeowner's repairs to his own home, is not included in GDP. By-products of production, such as environmental damage, are not included in GDP.

GDP can be calculated as the sum of all the spending on newly produced goods and services, or as the sum of the income received as a result of producing these goods and services. Under the **expenditure approach**, GDP is calculated by summing the amounts spent on goods and services produced during the period. Under the **income approach**, GDP is calculated by summing the amounts earned by households and companies during the period, including wage income, interest income, and business profits.

For the whole economy, total expenditures and total income must be equal, so the two approaches should produce the same result. In practice, measurement issues result in different values under the two methods.

LOS 17.b: Compare the sum-of-value-added and value-of-final-output methods of calculating GDP.

CFA® Program Curriculum, Volume 2, page 211

So far, we have described the calculation of GDP under the expenditure approach as summing the values of all final goods and services produced. This expenditure method is termed the **value-of-final-output method**.

Under the **sum-of-value-added method**, GDP is calculated by summing the additions to value created at each stage of production and distribution. An example of the calculation for a specific product is presented in Figure 1.

Figure 1: Value Added at Stages of Production

Stage of Production	Sales Value ($)	Value Added ($)
Raw materials/components	$100	$100
Manufacturing	$350	$250
Retail	**$400**	$50
Sum of value added		**$400**

The intuition is clear. The prices of final goods and services include, and are equal to, the additions to value at each stage of production (e.g., from mining iron ore and making steel to assembling an automobile that contains machined steel parts).

LOS 17.c: Compare nominal and real GDP and calculate and interpret the GDP deflator.

CFA® Program Curriculum, Volume 2, page 214

Nominal GDP is simply GDP as we have described it under the expenditures approach: the total value of all goods and services produced by an economy, valued at current

Study Session 5
Cross-Reference to CFA Institute Assigned Reading #17 – Aggregate Output, Prices, and Economic Growth

Study Session 5

market prices. For an economy with N different goods and services, we can express nominal GDP as:

$$\text{nominal GDP}_t = \sum_{i=1}^{N} P_{i,t} Q_{i,t}$$

$$= \sum_{i=1}^{N} (\text{price of good } i \text{ in year } t) \times (\text{quantity of good } i \text{ produced in year } t)$$

Because nominal GDP is based on current prices, inflation will increase nominal GDP even if the physical output of goods and services remains constant from one year to the next. **Real GDP** measures the output of the economy using prices from a base year, removing the effect of changes in prices so that inflation is not counted as economic growth.

Real GDP is calculated relative to a *base year*. By using base-year prices and current-year output quantities, real GDP growth reflects only increases in total output, not simply increases (or decreases) in the money value of total output.

Assuming the base year prices are those for five years ago, real GDP can be calculated as:

$$\text{real GDP}_t = \sum_{i=1}^{N} P_{i,t-5} Q_{i,t}$$

$$= \sum_{i=1}^{N} (\text{price of good } i \text{ in year } t-5) \times (\text{quantity of good } i \text{ produced in year } t)$$

The **GDP deflator** is a price index that can be used to convert nominal GDP into real GDP, taking out the effects of changes in the overall price level. The GDP deflator is based on the current mix of goods and services, using prices at the beginning and end of the period. The GDP deflator is calculated as:

$$\text{GDP deflator for year } t = \frac{\sum_{i=1}^{N} P_{i,t} Q_{i,t}}{\sum_{i=1}^{N} P_{i,t-5} Q_{i,t}} \times 100 = \frac{\text{nominal GDP in year } t}{\text{value of year } t \text{ output at year } t-5 \text{ prices}} \times 100$$

Example: Calculating and using the GDP deflator

1. GDP in 20X2 is $1.80 billion at 20X2 prices and $1.65 billion when calculated using 20X1 prices. Calculate the GDP deflator using 20X1 as the base period.

2. Nominal GDP was $213 billion in 20X6 and $150 billion in 20X1. The 20X6 GDP deflator relative to the base year 20X1 is 122.3. Calculate real GDP for 20X6 and the compound annual real growth rate of economic output from 20X1 to 20X6.

Answer:

1. GDP deflator = 1.80 / 1.65 × 100 = 109.1, reflecting a 9.1% increase in the price level.

2. Real GDP 20X6 = $213 / 1.223 = $174.16.

   Noting that real and nominal GDP are the same for the base year, the compound real annual growth rate of economic output over the 5-year period is:

   $$\left(\frac{174.16}{150}\right)^{\frac{1}{5}} - 1 = 3.03\%$$

Per-capita real GDP is defined as real GDP divided by population and is often used as a measure of the economic well-being of a country's residents.

LOS 17.d: Compare GDP, national income, personal income, and personal disposable income.

CFA® Program Curriculum, Volume 2, page 221

Using the expenditure approach, the major components of real GDP are consumption, investment, government spending, and **net exports** (exports minus imports). These components are summarized in the equation:

GDP = C + I + G + (X – M)

where:
C = consumption spending
I = business investment (capital equipment, inventories)
G = government purchases
X = exports
M = imports

Under the income approach, we have the following equation for GDP:

GDP = national income + capital consumption allowance + statistical discrepancy

A **capital consumption allowance** (CCA) measures the depreciation (i.e., wear) of physical capital from the production of goods and services over a period. CCA can be thought of as the amount that would have to be reinvested to maintain the productivity of physical capital from one period to the next. The *statistical discrepancy* is an adjustment for the difference between GDP measured under the income approach and the expenditure approach because they use different data.

National income is the sum of the income received by all factors of production that go into the creation of final output:

national income = compensation of employees (wages and benefits)
+ corporate and government enterprise profits before taxes
+ interest income
+ unincorporated business net income (business owners' incomes)
+ rent
+ indirect business taxes − subsidies (taxes and subsidies that are included in final prices)

Personal income is a measure of the pretax income received by households and is one determinant of consumer purchasing power and consumption. Personal income differs from national income in that personal income includes all income that households receive, including government transfer payments such as unemployment or disability benefits, and excludes business taxes and profits that go to the government or business sector rather than directly to households.

personal income = national income
+ transfer payments to households
− indirect business taxes
− corporate income taxes
− undistributed corporate profits

Personal disposable income (PDI) is personal income after taxes. PDI measures the amount that households have available to either save or spend on goods and services and is an important economic indicator of the ability of consumers to spend and save.

personal disposable income = personal income − personal taxes

---

LOS 17.e: Explain the fundamental relationship among saving, investment, the fiscal balance, and the trade balance.

CFA® Program Curriculum, Volume 2, page 227

To show how private savings are related to investment, the government sector, and foreign trade, we will combine the income and expenditure approaches to measuring GDP.

As we have seen, total expenditures can be stated as GDP = C + I + G + (X − M). Total income, which must equal total expenditures, can be stated as:

GDP = C + S + T

where:
C = consumption spending
S = household and business savings
T = net taxes (taxes paid minus transfer payments received)

Because total income equals total expenditures, we have the equality:

$$C + I + G + (X - M) = C + S + T$$

Rearranging this equation and solving for S (household and business savings), we get the following fundamental relationship:

$$S = I + (G - T) + (X - M)$$

Note that $(G - T)$ is the **fiscal balance**, or the difference between government spending and tax receipts. Recall that $(X - M)$ is net exports, or the **trade balance**. This equation shows that private savings must equal private investment, plus government borrowing or minus government savings, and minus the trade deficit or plus the trade surplus.

 Professor's Note: In this equation and the ones we will derive from it, a positive value for $(G - T)$ is a government budget deficit and a negative value for $(G - T)$ is a budget surplus. On the other hand, a positive value for $(X - M)$ is a trade surplus and a negative value for $(X - M)$ is a trade deficit.

If we solve this equation for the fiscal balance, we get:

$$(G - T) = (S - I) - (X - M)$$

From this equation, we can see that a government deficit $(G - T > 0)$ must be financed by some combination of a trade deficit $(X - M < 0)$ or an excess of private saving over private investment $(S - I > 0)$.

 Professor's Note: In the topic review of International Trade and Capital Flows, we will see that a trade deficit (current account deficit) must be associated with an inflow of foreign investment (capital account surplus). So we can interpret this equation as saying a fiscal deficit must be financed by a combination of domestic and foreign capital.

LOS 17.f: Explain the IS and LM curves and how they combine to generate the aggregate demand curve.

CFA® Program Curriculum, Volume 2, page 227

To derive the aggregate demand curve, we need to understand the factors that determine each of the components of GDP:

- *Consumption* is a function of disposable income. An increase in personal income or a decrease in taxes will increase both consumption and saving. Additional disposable income will be consumed or saved. The proportion of additional income spent on consumption is called the **marginal propensity to consume** (MPC), and the proportion saved is the **marginal propensity to save** (MPS). MPC + MPS must equal 100%.

- *Investment* is a function of expected profitability and the cost of financing. Expected profitability depends on the overall level of economic output. Financing costs are reflected in **real interest rates**, which are approximated by nominal interest rates minus the expected inflation rate.
- *Government purchases* may be viewed as independent of economic activity to a degree, but tax revenue to the government, and therefore the fiscal balance, is clearly a function of economic output.
- *Net exports* are a function of domestic disposable incomes (which affect imports), foreign disposable incomes (which affect exports), and relative prices of goods in foreign and domestic markets.

The **IS curve** (income-savings) in Figure 2 illustrates the negative relationship between real interest rates and real income for equilibrium in the goods market. Points on the IS curve are the combinations of real interest rates and income consistent with equilibrium in the goods market (i.e., those combinations of real interest rates and income for which planned expenditures equal income).

Figure 2: The IS Curve

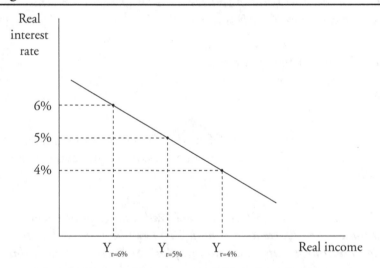

Lower interest rates tend to decrease savings (in favor of current consumption) and tend to increase investment by firms because more investments will have positive NPVs when firms' cost of capital is lower. Therefore, a decrease in interest rates decreases S – I, so that (S – I) < (G – T) + (X – M). In order to satisfy this fundamental relationship, income must increase. Greater income can restore equilibrium in the goods market by increasing savings (which increases S – I), increasing tax receipts (which decreases G – T), and increasing imports (which decreases X – M).

The **LM curve** (liquidity-money) in Figure 3 illustrates the positive relationship between real interest rates and income consistent with equilibrium in the money market. Higher real interest rates decrease the quantity of real money balances individuals want to hold, so for a given real money supply (M/P constant), equilibrium in the money market requires that an increase in real interest rates be accompanied by an increase in income. The increase in the demand for money from an increase in income can offset the decrease in demand for money from higher real interest rates and restore equilibrium in the money market.

Figure 3: The LM Curve

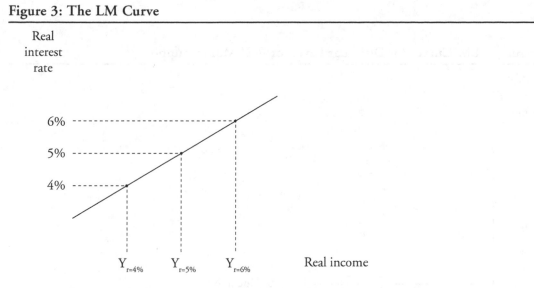

For overall equilibrium, the values of real interest rates and income must be consistent with equilibrium in both the goods market and the money market. We illustrate this simultaneous equilibrium as the intersection of the IS and LM curves in Figure 4.

Figure 4: Simultaneous Equilibrium in the Goods Market and the Money Market

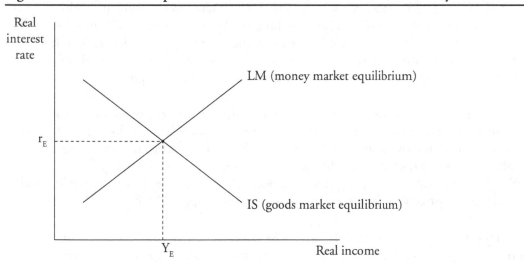

The LM curve is drawn for a given level of the real money supply, M/P. Holding the nominal money supply, M, constant, an increase in the price level decreases the real money supply and a decrease in the price level increases the real money supply. Because an increase (decrease) in the real money supply shifts the LM curve downward (upward), we can identify the different combinations of income and real interest rates consistent with equilibrium for different price levels. The intuition here is that a greater real money supply reduces equilibrium real interest rates and shifts the LM curve, as illustrated in Figure 5.

Figure 5: LM Curves for Different Levels of Real Money Supply

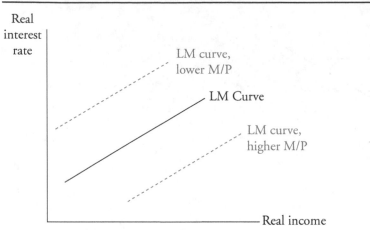

The Aggregate Demand Curve

When the IS and LM curves are combined, the point at which they intersect represents the levels of the real interest rate and income that are consistent with equilibrium between income and expenditure (points along the IS curve) and equilibrium between the real money supply and the real interest rate (points along the LM curve). The intersection between the IS and LM curves determines the equilibrium levels of prices and real income (real GDP) for a given level of the real money supply.

The **aggregate demand curve** shows the relationship between the quantity of real output demanded (which equals real income) and the price level. When we drew the LM curve, we held the real money supply (M/P) constant. Now, if we hold the nominal money supply (*M*) constant, changes in the real money supply are due to changes in the price level (*P*). An increase in the price level will decrease the real money supply (M/P), and a decrease in the price level will increase the real money supply (M/P).

In Panel (a) of Figure 6, Point A is on an LM curve for a lower real money supply (and therefore a higher price level) than Point B. Point C is on an LM curve for a higher real money supply (and therefore a lower price level) then Point B. As a result, the relationship between the price level and real income, given that income is equal to planned expenditures (the IS curve) and money demand is equal to money supply (the LM curve), must be downward sloping. This is the aggregate demand curve [Panel (b) in Figure 6].

The aggregate demand curve slopes downward because higher price levels (holding the money supply constant) reduce real wealth, increase real interest rates, and make domestically produced goods more expensive compared to goods produced abroad, all of which reduce the quantity of domestic output demanded.

Figure 6: Deriving the Aggregate Demand Curve

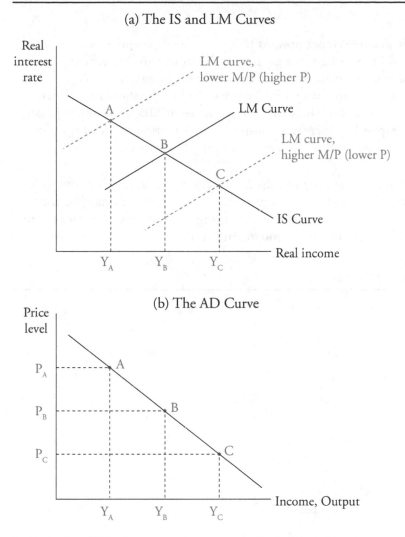

(a) The IS and LM Curves

(b) The AD Curve

LOS 17.g: Explain the aggregate supply curve in the short run and long run.

CFA® Program Curriculum, Volume 2, page 238

The Aggregate Supply Curve

The **aggregate supply** (AS) curve describes the relationship between the price level and the quantity of real GDP supplied, when all other factors are kept constant. That is, it represents the amount of output that firms will produce at different price levels.

We need to consider three aggregate supply curves with different time frames: the very short-run aggregate supply (VSRAS) curve, the short-run aggregate supply (SRAS) curve, and the long-run aggregate supply (LRAS) curve.

In the very short run, firms will adjust output without changing price by adjusting labor hours and intensity of use of plant and equipment in response to changes in demand.

We represent this with the perfectly elastic very short run aggregate supply (VSRAS) curve in Figure 7.

In the short run, the SRAS curve slopes upward because some input prices will change as production is increased or decreased. We assume in the short run that *output prices* will change proportionally to the price level but that at least some *input prices* are sticky, meaning that they do not adjust to changes in the price level in the short run. When output prices increase, the price level increases, but firms see no change in input prices in the short run. Firms respond by increasing output in anticipation of greater profits from higher output prices. The result is an upward-sloping SRAS curve.

All input costs can vary in the long run, and the LRAS curve in Figure 7 is perfectly inelastic. In the long run, wages and other input prices change proportionally to the price level, so the price level has no long-run effect on aggregate supply. We refer to this level of output as **potential GDP** or **full-employment GDP**.

Figure 7: Aggregate Supply Curves

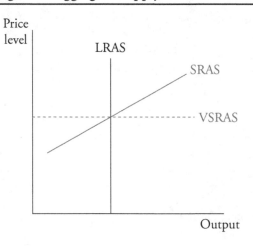

LOS 17.h: Explain causes of movements along and shifts in aggregate demand and supply curves.

CFA® Program Curriculum, Volume 2, page 240

Shifts in the Aggregate Demand Curve

The aggregate demand (AD) curve reflects the total level of expenditures in an economy by consumers, businesses, governments, and foreigners. A number of factors can affect this level of expenditures and cause the AD curve to shift. Note that a *change in the price level* is represented as a *movement along the AD curve,* not a shift in the AD curve. In Figure 8, an increase in aggregate demand is shown by a shift to the right, indicating that the quantity of goods and services demanded is greater at any given price level.

Figure 8: Increase in Aggregate Demand

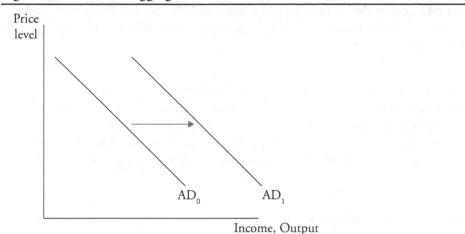

In trying to understand and remember the factors that affect aggregate demand, it may help to recall that, from the expenditure point of view, GDP = C + I + G + net X. For changes in each of the following factors that increase aggregate demand (shift AD to the right), we identify which component of expenditures is increased.

1. **Increase in consumers' wealth:** As the value of households' wealth increases (real estate, stocks, and other financial securities), the proportion of income saved decreases and spending increases, increasing aggregate demand (*C* increases).

2. **Business expectations:** When businesses are more optimistic about future sales, they tend to increase their investment in plant, equipment, and inventory, which increases aggregate demand (*I* increases).

3. **Consumer expectations of future income:** When consumers expect higher future incomes, due to a belief in greater job stability or expectations of rising wage income, they save less for the future and increase spending now, increasing aggregate demand (*C* increases).

4. **High capacity utilization:** When companies produce at a high percentage[1] of their capacity, they tend to invest in more plant and equipment, increasing aggregate demand (*I* increases).

5. **Expansionary monetary policy:** When the rate of growth of the money supply is increased, banks have more funds to lend, which puts downward pressure on interest rates. Lower interest rates increase investment in plant and equipment because the cost of financing these investments declines. Lower interest rates and greater availability of credit will also increase consumers' spending on consumer durables (e.g., automobiles, large appliances) that are typically purchased on credit. Thus, the effect of expansionary monetary policy is to increase aggregate demand (*C* and *I* increase).

---

1. According to the Federal Reserve, "Industrial plants usually operate at capacity utilization rates that are well below 100 percent... For total industry and total manufacturing, utilization rates have exceeded 90 percent only in wartime." (Federal Reserve Statistical Release G.17, "Industrial Production and Capacity Utilization," *www.federalreserve.gov/ releases/g17/current/g17.pdf*)

Note that if the economy is operating at potential GDP (LRAS) when the monetary expansion takes place, the increase in real output will be only for the short run. In the long run, subsequent increases in input prices decrease SRAS and return output to potential GDP.

6. **Expansionary fiscal policy:** Expansionary fiscal policy refers to a decreasing government budget surplus (or an increasing budget deficit) from decreasing taxes, increasing government expenditures, or both. A decrease in taxes increases disposable income and consumption, while an increase in government spending increases aggregate demand directly (*C* increases for tax cut, *G* increases for spending increase).

> *Professor's Note: A complete analysis of monetary and fiscal policy as they relate to overall expenditures and GDP is presented in our topic review of Monetary and Fiscal Policy.*

7. **Exchange rates:** A decrease in the relative value of a country's currency will increase exports and decrease imports. Both of these effects tend to increase domestic aggregate demand (net *X* increases).

> *Professor's Note: We will analyze the effect of exchange rates on exports and imports in our topic review of Currency Exchange Rates.*

8. **Global economic growth:** GDP growth in foreign economies tends to increase the quantity of imports (domestic exports) foreigners demand. By increasing domestic export demand, this will increase aggregate demand (net *X* increases).

Note that for each factor, a change in the opposite direction will tend to decrease aggregate demand.

Shifts in the Short-Run Aggregate Supply Curve

The **short-run aggregate supply** (SRAS) **curve** reflects the relationship between output and the price level when wages and other input prices are held constant (or are slow to adjust to higher output prices). The curve shows the total level of output that businesses are willing to supply at different price levels. A number of factors can affect this level of output and cause the SRAS curve to shift. In Figure 9, an increase in aggregate supply is shown by a shift to the right, as the quantity supplied at each price level increases.

Figure 9: Increase in Aggregate Supply

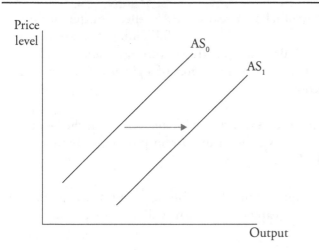

In addition to changes in potential GDP (shifts in long-run aggregate supply), a number of factors can cause the SRAS curve to shift to the right:

1. **Labor productivity:** Holding the wage rate constant, an increase in labor productivity (output per hour worked) will decrease unit costs to producers. Producers will increase output as a result, increasing SRAS (shifting it to the right).

2. **Input prices:** A decrease in nominal wages or the prices of other important productive inputs will decrease production costs and cause firms to increase production, increasing SRAS. Wages are often the largest contributor to a producer's costs and have the greatest impact on SRAS.

3. **Expectations of future output prices:** When businesses expect the price of their output to increase in the future, they will expand production, increasing SRAS.

4. **Taxes and government subsidies:** Either a decrease in business taxes or an increase in government subsidies for a product will decrease the costs of production. Firms will increase output as a result, increasing SRAS.

5. **Exchange rates:** Appreciation of a country's currency in the foreign exchange market will decrease the cost of imports. To the extent that productive inputs are purchased from foreign countries, the resulting decrease in production costs will cause firms to increase output, increasing SRAS.

Again, an opposite change in any of these factors will tend to decrease SRAS.

Shifts in the Long-Run Aggregate Supply Curve

The **long-run aggregate supply** (LRAS) **curve** is vertical (perfectly inelastic) at the potential (full-employment) level of real GDP. Changes in factors that affect the real output that an economy can produce at full employment will shift the LRAS curve.

Factors that will shift the LRAS curve are:

1. **Increase in the supply and quality of labor:** Because LRAS reflects output at full employment, an increase in the labor force will increase full-employment output and the LRAS. An increase in the skills of the workforce, through training and education, will increase the productivity of a labor force of a given size, increasing potential real output and increasing LRAS.

2. **Increase in the supply of natural resources:** Just as with an increase in the labor force, increases in the available amounts of other important productive inputs will increase potential real GDP and LRAS.

3. **Increase in the stock of physical capital:** For a labor force of a given size, an increase in an economy's accumulated stock of capital equipment will increase potential output and LRAS.

4. **Technology:** In general, improvements in technology increase labor productivity (output per unit of labor) and thereby increase the real output that can be produced from a given amount of productive inputs, increasing LRAS.

Decreases in labor quality, labor supply, the supply of natural resources, or the stock of physical capital will all decrease LRAS (move the curve to the left). Technology does not really retreat, but a law prohibiting the use of an improved technology could decrease LRAS.

Movement Along Aggregate Demand and Supply Curves

In contrast with *shifts* in the aggregate demand and aggregate supply curves, *movements along* these curves reflect the impact of a change in the price level on the quantity demanded and the quantity supplied. Changes in the price level alone do not cause shifts in the AD and AS curves, although we have allowed that changes in expected future prices can.

LOS 17.i: Describe how fluctuations in aggregate demand and aggregate supply cause short-run changes in the economy and the business cycle.

LOS 17.j: Distinguish between the following types of macroeconomic equilibria: long-run full employment, short-run recessionary gap, short-run inflationary gap, and short-run stagflation.

LOS 17.k: Explain how a short-run macroeconomic equilibrium may occur at a level above or below full employment.

CFA® Program Curriculum, Volume 2, page 253

Having explained the factors that cause shifts in the aggregate demand and aggregate supply curves, we now turn our attention to the effects of fluctuations in aggregate supply and demand on real GDP and the business cycle. Our starting point is an economy that is in *long-run full-employment equilibrium*, as illustrated in Figure 10.

Figure 10: Long-Run Equilibrium Real Output

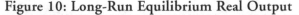

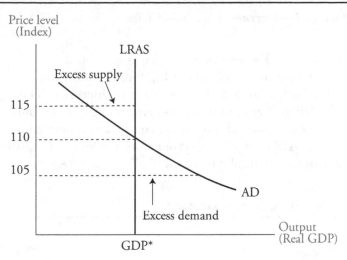

First consider a decrease in aggregate demand, which can result from a decrease in the growth rate of the money supply, an increase in taxes, a decrease in government spending, lower equity and house prices, or a decrease in the expectations of consumers and businesses for future economic growth. As illustrated in Figure 11, a decrease in aggregate demand will reduce both real output and the price level in the short run. The new short-run equilibrium output, GDP_1, is less than full employment (potential) GDP. The decrease in aggregate demand has resulted in both lower real output and a lower price level.

Figure 11: Adjustment to a Decrease in Aggregate Demand

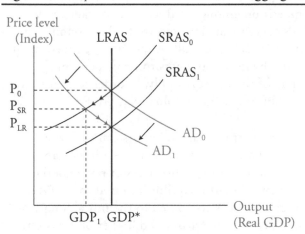

Because real GDP is less than full employment GDP, we say there is a **recessionary gap**. A recession is a period of declining GDP and rising unemployment. Classical economists believed that unemployment would drive down wages, as workers compete for available jobs, which in turn would increase SRAS and return the economy to its full employment level of real GDP. Keynesian economists, on the other hand, believe that this might be a slow and economically painful process and that increasing aggregate demand through government action is the preferred alternative. Both expansionary fiscal policy (increasing government spending or decreasing taxes) and expansionary monetary policy (increasing the growth rate of the money supply to reduce interest rates) are methods to increase aggregate demand and return real GDP to its full employment (potential) level.

Professor's Note: We will describe Classical, Keynesian, and other business cycle theories in the topic review of Understanding Business Cycles.

A second case to consider is an increase in aggregate demand that results in an equilibrium at a level of GDP greater than full-employment GDP in the short run, as illustrated in Figure 12. Note that both GDP and the price level are increased. The economy can operate at a level of GDP greater than full-employment GDP in the short run, as workers work overtime and maintenance of productive equipment is delayed, but output greater than full-employment GDP cannot be maintained in the long run. In the long run, the economy always returns to full-employment GDP along the LRAS curve.

Figure 12: Adjustment to an Increase in Aggregate Demand

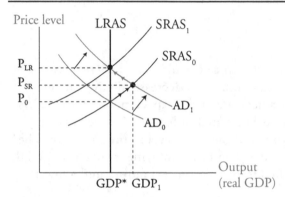

We term the difference between GDP_1 and full-employment GDP in Figure 12 an **inflationary gap** because the increase in aggregate demand from its previous level causes upward pressure on the price level. Competition among producers for workers, raw materials, and energy may shift the SRAS curve to the left, returning the economy to full-employment GDP but at a price level that is higher still. Alternatively, government policy makers can reduce aggregate demand by decreasing government spending, increasing taxes, or slowing the growth rate of the money supply, in order to move the economy back to the initial long run equilibrium at full-employment GDP.

Changes in wages or the prices of other important productive inputs can shift the SRAS curve, affecting real GDP and the price level in the short run. An important case to consider is a decrease in SRAS caused by an increase in the prices of raw materials or energy. As illustrated in Figure 13, the new short-run equilibrium is at lower GDP and a higher overall price level for goods and services compared to the initial long-run equilibrium. This combination of declining economic output and higher prices is termed **stagflation** (stagnant economy with inflation).

Figure 13: Stagflation

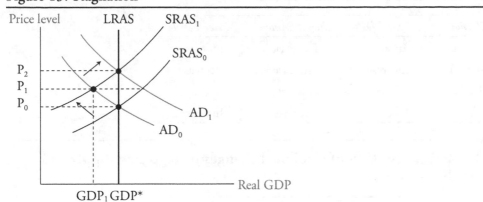

A subsequent decrease in input prices can return the economy to its long-run equilibrium output. An increase in aggregate demand from either expansionary fiscal or monetary policy can also return the economy to its full employment level, but at a price level that is higher still compared to the initial equilibrium.

Stagflation is an especially difficult situation for policy makers because actions to increase aggregate demand to restore full employment will also increase the price level even more. Conversely, a decision by policy makers to fight inflation by decreasing aggregate demand will decrease GDP even further. A decrease in wages and the prices of other productive inputs may be expected to increase SRAS and restore full-employment equilibrium. However, this process may be quite slow and doing nothing may be a very risky strategy for a government when voters expect action to restore economic growth or stem inflationary pressures.

The fourth case to consider is an increase in SRAS due to a decrease in the price of important productive inputs. As illustrated in Figure 14, the resulting new short-run equilibrium is at a level of GDP greater than full-employment GDP and a lower overall price level.

Figure 14: Decrease in Input Prices

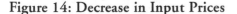

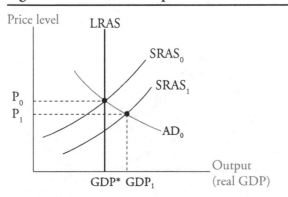

In Figure 15, we present a summary of the short-run effects of shifts in aggregate demand and in aggregate supply on real GDP, unemployment, and the price level.

Figure 15: Short-Run Macroeconomic Effects

Type of Change	Real GDP	Unemployment	Price Level
Increase in AD	Increase	Decrease	Increase
Decrease in AD	Decrease	Increase	Decrease
Increase in AS	Increase	Decrease	Decrease
Decrease in AS	Decrease	Increase	Increase

LOS 17.l: Analyze the effect of combined changes in aggregate supply and demand on the economy.

CFA® Program Curriculum, Volume 2, page 260

When both aggregate supply and aggregate demand change, the effects on equilibrium output and the price level may be clear when the effects on the variable are in the same direction (or ambiguous when the effects on the variable are in opposite directions). We summarize the effects of combined changes in demand and supply in Figure 16.

- When *aggregate demand and aggregate supply both increase*, real GDP increases but the effect on the price level depends on the relative magnitudes of the changes because their price effects are in opposite directions (Panel a of Figure 16).
- When *aggregate demand and aggregate supply both decrease*, real GDP decreases but the effect on the price level depends on the relative magnitudes of the changes because their price effects are in opposite directions (Panel b of Figure 16).
- When *aggregate demand increases and aggregate supply decreases*, the price level will increase but the effect on real GDP depends on the relative magnitudes of the changes because their effects on economic output are in opposite directions (Panel c of Figure 16).
- When *aggregate demand decreases and aggregate supply increases*, the price level will decrease but the effect on real GDP depends on the relative magnitudes of the changes because their effects on economic output are in opposite directions (Panel d of Figure 16).

Figure 16: Changes in Aggregate Supply and Aggregate Demand

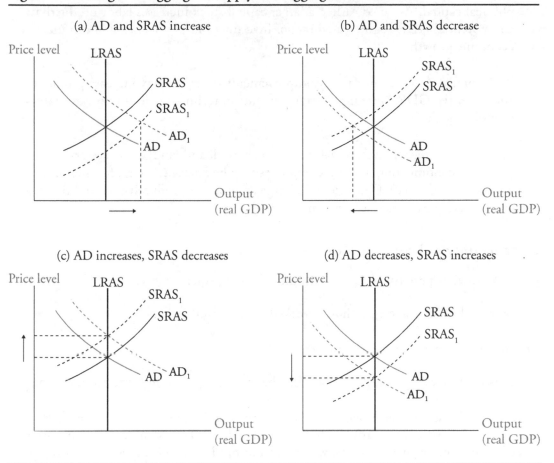

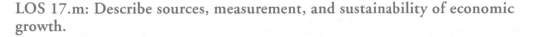

LOS 17.m: Describe sources, measurement, and sustainability of economic growth.

CFA® Program Curriculum, Volume 2, page 263

Economic growth can best be explained by examining five important **sources of economic growth**:

1. **Labor supply**. The **labor force** is the number of people over the age of 16 who are either working or available for work but currently unemployed. It is affected by population growth, net immigration, and the labor force participation rate (described in our topic review of Understanding Business Cycles). Growth of the labor force is an important source of economic growth.

2. **Human capital**. The education and skill level of a country's labor force can be just as important a determinant of economic output as the size of the labor force. Because workers who are skilled and well-educated (possess more human capital) are more productive and better able to take advantage of advances in technology, investment in human capital leads to greater economic growth.

3. **Physical capital stock.** A high rate of investment increases a country's stock of physical capital. As noted earlier, a larger capital stock increases labor productivity and potential GDP. An increased rate of investment in physical capital can increase economic growth.

4. **Technology.** As noted previously, improvements in technology increase productivity and potential GDP. More rapid improvements in technology lead to greater rates of economic growth.

5. **Natural resources.** Raw material inputs, such as oil and land, are necessary to produce economic output. These resources may be *renewable* (e.g., forests) or *non-renewable* (e.g., coal). Countries with large amounts of productive natural resources can achieve greater rates of economic growth.

Sustainability of Economic Growth

One way to view potential GDP is with the following equation:

potential GDP = aggregate hours worked × labor productivity

Or, stated in terms of economic growth:

growth in potential GDP = growth in labor force + growth in labor productivity

An economy's sustainable growth rate can be estimated by estimating the growth rate of labor productivity and the growth rate of the labor force. For example, if Japan's labor force is projected to shrink by 1%, while its labor productivity is expected to grow by 2%, then we would estimate the growth in potential GDP as: –1% + 2% = 1%.

The **sustainable rate of economic growth** is important because long-term equity returns are highly dependent on economic growth over time. A country's sustainable rate of economic growth is the rate of increase in the economy's productive capacity (potential GDP).

LOS 17.n: Describe the production function approach to analyzing the sources of economic growth.

CFA® Program Curriculum, Volume 2, page 264

A **production function** describes the relationship between output and labor, the capital stock, and productivity.

Economic output can be thought of as a function of the amounts of labor and capital that are available and their productivity, which depends on the level of technology available. That is:

$$Y = A \times f(L, K)$$

where:
Y = aggregate economic output
L = size of labor force
K = amount of capital available
A = total factor productivity

Total factor productivity is a multiplier that quantifies the amount of output growth that cannot be explained by the increases in labor and capital. Total factor productivity is closely related to technological advances. Generally, total factor productivity cannot be observed directly and must be inferred based on the other factors.

The production function can be stated on a per-worker basis by dividing by *L*:

$$Y/L = A \times f\left(K/L\right)$$

where:
Y/L = output per worker (labor productivity)
K/L = physical capital per worker

This relationship suggests that labor productivity can be increased by either improving technology or increasing physical capital per worker.

We assume that the production function exhibits **diminishing marginal productivity** for each individual input, meaning the amount of additional output produced by each additional unit of input declines (holding the quantities of other inputs constant). For this reason, sustainable long-term growth cannot necessarily be achieved simply by **capital deepening investment**—that is to say, increasing physical capital per worker over time. Productivity gains and growth of the labor force are also necessary for long-term sustainable growth.

LOS 17.o: Distinguish between input growth and growth of total factor productivity as components of economic growth.

CFA® Program Curriculum, Volume 2, page 266

A well-known model (the *Solow model* or *neoclassical model*) of the contributions of technology, labor, and capital to economic growth is:

growth in potential GDP = growth in technology + W_L(growth in labor) + W_C(growth in capital)

where W_L and W_C are labor's percentage share of national income and capital's percentage share of national income.

Consider a developed country where $W_L = 0.7$ and $W_C = 0.3$. For that country, a 1% increase in the labor force will lead to a much greater increase in economic output than a 1% increase in the capital stock. Similarly, sustained growth of the labor force will result in greater economic growth over time than sustained growth of the capital stock of an equal magnitude.

Growth in total factor productivity is driven by improvements in technology. Sometimes, the relationship between potential GDP, technology improvements, and capital growth is written on a per-capita basis[2] as:

$$\text{growth in per-capita potential GDP} = \text{growth in technology} + W_C \, (\text{growth in the capital-to-labor ratio})$$

With $W_C = 0.25$, for example, each 1% increase in capital per worker will increase GDP per worker by 0.25%. In developed economies, where capital per worker is already relatively high, growth of technology will be the primary source of growth in GDP per worker. At higher levels of capital per worker, an economy will experience diminishing marginal productivity of capital and must look to advances in technology for strong economic growth.

---

2. Paul R. Kutasovic, CFA, and Richard G. Fritz, *Aggregate Output, Prices, and Economic Growth*, CFA® Program Level I 2015 Curriculum, Volume 2, 2014.

KEY CONCEPTS

LOS 17.a
Gross domestic product (GDP) is the market value of all final goods and services produced within a country during a certain time period.

Using the expenditure approach, GDP is calculated as the total amount spent on goods and services produced in the country during a time period.

Using the income approach, GDP is calculated as the total income earned by households and businesses in the country during a time period.

LOS 17.b
The expenditure approach to measuring GDP can use the sum-of-value-added method or the value-of-final-output method.
- Sum-of-value-added: GDP is calculated by summing the additions to value created at each stage of production and distribution.
- Value-of-final-output: GDP is calculated by summing the values of all final goods and services produced during the period.

LOS 17.c
Nominal GDP values goods and services at their current prices. Real GDP measures current year output using prices from a base year.

The GDP deflator is a price index that can be used to convert nominal GDP into real GDP by removing the effects of changes in prices.

LOS 17.d
The four components of gross domestic product are consumption spending, business investment, government spending, and net exports. GDP = C + I + G + (X − M).

National income is the income received by all factors of production used in the creation of final output.

Personal income is the pretax income received by households.

Personal disposable income is personal income after taxes.

LOS 17.e
Private saving and investment are related to the fiscal balance and the trade balance. A fiscal deficit must be financed by some combination of a trade deficit or an excess of private saving over private investment. (G − T) = (S − I) − (X − M).

LOS 17.f

The IS curve shows the negative relationship between the real interest rate and levels of aggregate income that are equal to planned expenditures at each real interest rate.

The LM curve shows, for a given level of the real money supply, a positive relationship between the real interest rate and levels of aggregate income at which demand and supply of real money balances are equal.

The points at which the IS curve intersects LM curves for different levels of the real money supply (i.e., for different price levels, holding the nominal money supply constant) form the aggregate demand curve. The aggregate demand curve shows the negative relationship between GDP (real output demanded) and the price level, when other factors are held constant.

LOS 17.g

The short-run aggregate supply curve shows the positive relationship between real GDP supplied and the price level, when other factors are held constant. Holding some input costs such as wages fixed in the short run, the curve slopes upward because higher output prices result in greater output (real wages fall).

Because all input prices are assumed to be flexible in the long run, the long-run aggregate supply curve is perfectly inelastic (vertical). Long-run aggregate supply represents potential GDP, the full employment level of economic output.

LOS 17.h

Changes in the price level cause movement along the aggregate demand or aggregate supply curves.

Shifts in the aggregate demand curve are caused by changes in household wealth, business and consumer expectations, capacity utilization, fiscal policy, monetary policy, currency exchange rates, and global economic growth rates.

Shifts in the short-run aggregate supply curve are caused by changes in nominal wages or other input prices, expectations of future prices, business taxes, business subsidies, and currency exchange rates, as well as by the factors that affect long-run aggregate supply.

Shifts in the long-run aggregate supply curve are caused by changes in labor supply and quality, the supply of physical capital, the availability of natural resources, and the level of technology.

LOS 17.i

The short-run effects of changes in aggregate demand and in aggregate supply are summarized in the following table:

Type of Change	Real GDP	Unemployment	Price Level
Increase in AD	Increase	Decrease	Increase
Decrease in AD	Decrease	Increase	Decrease
Increase in AS	Increase	Decrease	Decrease
Decrease in AS	Decrease	Increase	Increase

LOS 17.j

In long-run equilibrium, real GDP is equal to full-employment (potential) GDP. An increase in aggregate demand can result in a short-run equilibrium with GDP greater than full-employment GDP, termed an inflationary gap. A decrease in aggregate demand can result in a short-run equilibrium with GDP less than full-employment, termed a recessionary gap. When short-run aggregate supply decreases, the resulting short-run equilibrium is with GDP reduced to less than full-employment GDP but with an increase in the price level, termed stagflation.

LOS 17.k

From a situation of long-run equilibrium: an increase in either aggregate demand or aggregate supply can result in a short-run equilibrium with real GDP greater than full employment GDP; a decrease in either aggregate demand or aggregate supply can result in a short-run equilibrium with real GDP less than full-employment GDP.

LOS 17.l

Short-run effects of shifts in both aggregate demand and aggregate supply on the price level and real GDP:

Aggregate Demand	Aggregate Supply	Change in Real GDP	Change in Price Level
Increase	Increase	Increase	May increase or decrease
Decrease	Decrease	Decrease	May increase or decrease
Increase	Decrease	May increase or decrease	Increase
Decrease	Increase	May increase or decrease	Decrease

LOS 17.m

Sources of economic growth include increases in the supply of labor, increases in human capital, increases in the supply of physical capital, increasing availability of natural resources, and advances in technology.

The sustainable rate of economic growth is determined by the rate of increase in the labor force and the rate of increase in labor productivity.

LOS 17.n

A production function relates economic output to the supply of labor, the supply of capital, and total factor productivity. Total factor productivity is a residual factor, which represents that part of economic growth not accounted for by increases in the supply of labor and capital. Increases in total factor productivity can be attributed to advances in technology.

LOS 17.o

In developed countries, where a high level of capital per worker is available and capital inputs experience diminishing marginal productivity, technological advances that increase total factor productivity are the main source of sustainable economic growth.

CONCEPT CHECKERS

1. The *least appropriate* approach to calculating a country's gross domestic product (GDP) is summing for a given time period the:
   A. value of all purchases and sales that took place within the country.
   B. amount spent on final goods and services produced within the country.
   C. income generated in producing all final goods and services produced within the country.

2. Gross domestic product does not include the value of:
   A. transfer payments.
   B. government services.
   C. owner-occupied housing.

3. When GDP is calculated by the sum-of-value-added method, what is the value of a manufactured product in GDP?
   A. The sum of the product's value at each stage of production and distribution.
   B. The sum of the increases in the product's value at each stage of production and distribution.
   C. The product's retail price less the value added at each stage of production and distribution.

4. Real GDP is *best* described as the value of:
   A. current output measured at current prices.
   B. current output measured at base-year prices.
   C. base-year output measured at current prices.

5. The GDP deflator is calculated as 100 times the ratio of:
   A. nominal GDP to real GDP.
   B. base year prices to current year prices.
   C. current year nominal GDP to base year nominal GDP.

6. Which of the following measures of income is the sum of wages and benefits, pretax profits, interest income, owners' income from unincorporated businesses, rent, and taxes net of subsidies?
   A. Personal income.
   B. National income.
   C. Personal disposable income.

7. Which of the following statements *most accurately* describes personal income? Personal income:
   A. includes unearned income from governments, such as transfer payments.
   B. measures the amount of after-tax income that households can spend or save.
   C. includes indirect business taxes, corporate income taxes, and retained earnings.

8. If a government budget deficit increases, net exports must:
    A. increase, or the excess of private saving over private investment must decrease.
    B. decrease, or the excess of private saving over private investment must increase.
    C. decrease, or the excess of private saving over private investment must decrease.

9. The IS curve illustrates which of the following relationships?
    A. Direct relationship between aggregate income and the price level.
    B. Inverse relationship between aggregate income and the price level.
    C. Inverse relationship between aggregate income and the real interest rate.

10. An economy's potential output is *best* represented by:
    A. long-run aggregate supply.
    B. short-run aggregate supply.
    C. long-run aggregate demand.

11. A stronger domestic currency relative to foreign currencies is *most likely* to result in a:
    A. shift in the aggregate supply curve toward lower supply.
    B. shift in the aggregate demand curve toward lower demand.
    C. movement along the aggregate demand curve towards higher prices.

12. Which of the following factors would be *least likely* to shift the aggregate demand curve?
    A. The price level increases.
    B. The federal deficit expands.
    C. Expected inflation decreases.

13. In short-run equilibrium, if aggregate demand is increasing faster than long-run aggregate supply:
    A. the price level is likely to increase.
    B. downward pressure on wages should ensue.
    C. supply will increase to meet the additional demand.

14. Labor productivity is *most likely* to increase as a result of a(n):
    A. increase in physical capital.
    B. decrease in net immigration.
    C. increase in the labor force participation rate.

15. Long-term sustainable growth of an economy is *least likely* to result from growth in:
   A. the supply of labor.
   B. capital per unit of labor.
   C. output per unit of labor.

16. In a developed economy, the primary source of growth in potential GDP is:
   A. capital investment.
   B. labor supply growth.
   C. technology advances.

ANSWERS – CONCEPT CHECKERS

1. **A**   Adding all purchases and sales is not appropriate because these would include goods that were produced before the time period in question. All purchases and sales could also result in double-counting intermediate goods. GDP is the market value of all final goods and services produced in a country in a certain period of time. GDP can be calculated either by totaling the amount spent on goods and services produced in the economy (the expenditure approach), or the income generated in producing these goods and services (the income approach).

2. **A**   Owner-occupied housing and government services are included in GDP at imputed (estimated) values. Transfer payments are excluded from the calculation of GDP.

3. **B**   Using the sum-of-value-added method, GDP can be calculated by summing the value added at each stage in the production and distribution process. Summing the value of the product at each stage of production would count the value added at earlier stages multiple times. The value added at earlier stages would not be included in GDP if it was deducted from the retail price.

4. **B**   Real GDP is the value of current period output calculated using prices from a base year.

5. **A**   The GDP deflator is the ratio of nominal GDP to real GDP, or equivalently the ratio of current year prices to base year prices.

6. **B**   National income is the income received by all factors of production used in the generation of final output. Personal income measures the pretax income that households receive. Personal disposable income is personal income after taxes.

7. **A**   Personal income reflects the pretax income received by households and includes government transfer payments. Personal income does not include components of national income such as undistributed corporate profits, corporate income taxes, and indirect business taxes. The amount of after-tax income that households have available to spend or save is disposable personal income.

8. **B**   The fundamental relationship among saving, investment, the fiscal balance, and the trade balance is described by the following equation: $(G − T) = (S − I) − (X − M)$. If the government budget deficit $(G − T)$ increases, the larger budget deficit must be financed by some combination of an increase in the excess of private saving over private investment $(S − I)$ or a decrease in net exports $(X − M)$.

9. **C**   The IS curve shows an inverse relationship between aggregate income and the real interest rate. The inverse relationship between aggregate income and the price level is the aggregate demand curve.

10. **A**   The LRAS curve is vertical at the level of potential GDP.

11. **B**   Strengthening of the domestic currency should cause exports to decrease and imports to increase, causing the AD curve to shift to the left (lower demand). At the same time, the cost of raw material inputs should decrease in domestic currency terms, causing the SRAS curve to shift to the right (greater supply). Changes in the price level cause movement along the AD and AS curves; in this case, any shifts along these curves will be towards lower prices.

12. **A** Since the y-axis of the aggregate supply/demand model is the price level, a change in the price level is a movement along the AD curve. As long as inflation expectations are unchanged, an increase in the price level will not shift the aggregate demand curve.

13. **A** If AD is increasing faster than LRAS, the economy is expanding faster than its full-employment rate of output. This will cause pressure on wages and resource prices and lead to an increase in the price level. The SRAS curve will shift to the left—a decrease in supply for any given price level—until the rate of output growth slows to its full-employment potential.

14. **A** Increased investment in physical capital can increase labor productivity. Labor force participation rates and net immigration affect the size of the labor force and the aggregate number of hours worked, but do not necessarily affect labor productivity.

15. **B** The sustainable rate of economic growth is a measurement of the rate of increase in the economy's productive capacity. An economy's sustainable rate of growth depends on the growth rate of the labor supply and the growth rate of labor productivity. Due to diminishing marginal productivity, an economy generally cannot achieve long-term sustainable growth through continually increasing the stock of capital relative to labor (i.e., capital deepening).

16. **C** For developed economies, advances in technology are likely to be the primary source of growth in potential GDP because capital per worker is already high enough to experience diminishing marginal productivity of capital.

The following is a review of the Economics: Macroeconomic Analysis principles designed to address the learning outcome statements set forth by CFA Institute. This topic is also covered in:

UNDERSTANDING BUSINESS CYCLES

Study Session 5

EXAM FOCUS

The phase of the business cycle is the starting point for top-down financial analysis. Candidates need to know how to interpret the many economic indicators that are available and why various indicators tend to lead, coincide with, or lag behind changes in economic activity. Indicators of unemployment and inflation are crucial for understanding fiscal and monetary policy actions.

LOS 18.a: Describe the business cycle and its phases.

CFA® Program Curriculum, Volume 2, page 290

The **business cycle** is characterized by fluctuations in economic activity. Real gross domestic product (GDP) and the rate of unemployment are the key variables used to determine the current phase of the cycle.

The business cycle has four phases: **expansion** (real GDP is increasing), **peak** (real GDP stops increasing and begins decreasing), **contraction** or **recession** (real GDP is decreasing), and **trough** (real GDP stops decreasing and begins increasing). The phases are illustrated in Figure 1.

Figure 1: Business Cycle

Real GDP

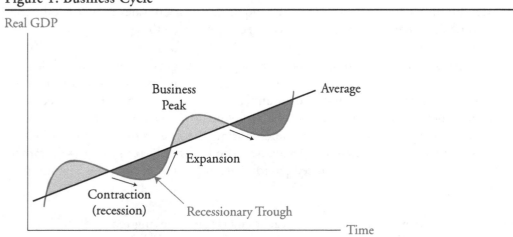

An expansion features growth in most sectors of the economy, with increasing employment, consumer spending, and business investment. As an expansion approaches its peak, the rates of increase in spending, investment, and employment slow but remains positive, while inflation accelerates.

A contraction or recession is associated with declines in most sectors, with inflation typically decreasing. When the contraction reaches a trough and the economy begins a new expansion or **recovery**, economic growth becomes positive again and inflation is typically moderate, but employment growth may not start to increase until the expansion has taken hold convincingly.

A common rule of thumb is to consider two consecutive quarters of growth in real GDP as the beginning of an expansion and two consecutive quarters of declining real GDP as indicating the beginning of a contraction. Statistical agencies that date expansions and recessions, such as the National Bureau of Economic Research in the United States, look at a wider variety of economic data such as employment, industrial production, and real personal income to identify turning points in the business cycle.

A key aspect of business cycles is that they recur, but not at regular intervals. Past business cycles have been as short as a year or longer than a decade.

The idea of a business cycle applies to economies that consist mainly of businesses. For economies that are mostly subsistence agriculture or dominated by state planning, fluctuations in activity are not really "business cycles" in the sense we are discussing here.

LOS 18.b: Describe how resource use, housing sector activity, and external trade sector activity vary as an economy moves through the business cycle.

CFA® Program Curriculum, Volume 2, page 294

Resource Use Fluctuation

Inventories are an important business cycle indicator. Firms try to keep enough inventory on hand to meet sales demand but do not want to keep too much of their capital tied up in inventory. As a result, the ratio of inventory to sales in many industries trends toward a normal level in times of steady economic growth.

When an expansion is approaching its peak, sales growth begins to slow, and unsold inventories accumulate. This can be seen in an increase in the **inventory-sales ratio** above its normal level. Firms respond to an unplanned increase in inventory by reducing production, which is one of the causes of the subsequent contraction in the economy. An increase in inventories is counted in the GDP statistics as economic output, whether the increase is planned or unplanned. An analyst who looks only at GDP growth, rather than the inventory-sales ratio, might see economic strength rather than the beginning of weakness.

The opposite occurs when a contraction reaches its trough. Having reduced their production levels to adjust for lower sales demand, firms find their inventories becoming depleted more quickly once sales growth begins to accelerate. This causes the inventory-sales ratio to decrease below its normal level. To meet the increase in demand, firms will increase output, and the inventory-sales ratio will increase toward normal levels.

One of the ways firms react to fluctuations in business activity is by adjusting their utilization of labor and physical capital. Adding and subtracting workers in lockstep with changes in economic growth would be costly for firms, in terms of both direct expenses and the damage it would do to employee morale and loyalty. Instead, firms typically begin by changing how they utilize their current workers, producing less or more output per hour or adjusting the hours they work by adding or removing overtime. Only when an expansion or contraction appears likely to persist will they hire or lay off workers.

Similarly, because it is costly to adjust production levels by frequently buying and selling plant and equipment, firms first adjust their production levels by using their existing physical capital more or less intensively. As an expansion persists, firms will increase their production capacity by investing more in plant and equipment. During contractions, however, firms will not necessarily sell plant and equipment outright. They can reduce their physical capacity by spending less on maintenance or by delaying the replacement of equipment that is near the end of its useful life.

Housing Sector Activity

Although the housing sector is a small part of the economy relative to overall consumer spending, cyclical swings in activity in the housing market can be large so that the effect on overall economic activity is greater than it otherwise would be. Important determinants of the level of economic activity in the housing sector are:

1. **Mortgage rates:** Low interest rates tend to increase home buying and construction while high interest rates tend to reduce home buying and construction.

2. **Housing costs relative to income:** When incomes are cyclically high (low) relative to home costs, including mortgage financing costs, home buying and construction tend to increase (decrease). Housing activity can decrease even when incomes are rising late in a cycle if home prices are rising faster than incomes, leading to decreases in purchase and construction activity in the housing sector.

3. **Speculative activity:** As we saw in the housing sector in 2007 and 2008 in many economies, rising home prices can lead to purchases based on expectations of further gains. Higher prices led to more construction and eventually excess building. This resulted in falling prices that decreased or eliminated speculative demand and led to dramatic decreases in housing activity overall.

4. **Demographic factors:** The proportion of the population in the 25- to 40-year-old segment is positively related to activity in the housing sector because these are the ages of greatest household formation. In China, a strong population shift from rural areas to cities as manufacturing activity has grown has required large increases in construction of new housing to accommodate those needs.

External Trade Sector Activity

The most important factors determining the level of a country's imports and exports are domestic GDP growth, GDP growth of trading partners, and currency exchange rates. Increasing growth of domestic GDP leads to increases in purchases of foreign goods (imports), while decreasing domestic GDP growth reduces imports. Exports depend on the growth rates of GDP of other economies (especially those of important trading partners). Increasing foreign incomes increase sales to foreigners (exports) and decreasing economic growth in foreign countries decreases domestic exports.

An increase in the value of a country's currency makes its goods more expensive to foreign buyers and foreign goods less expensive to domestic buyers, which tends to decrease exports and increase imports. A decrease in the value of a country's currency has the opposite effect, increasing exports and decreasing imports. Currencies affect import and export volumes over time in response to persistent trends in foreign exchange rates, rather than in response to short-term changes which can be quite volatile.

Currency effects can differ in direction from GDP growth effects and change in response to a complex set of variables. The effects of changes in GDP levels and growth rates are more direct and immediate.

Typical business cycle characteristics may be summarized as follows:

Trough:

- GDP growth rate changes from negative to positive.
- High unemployment rate, increasing use of overtime and temporary workers.
- Spending on consumer durable goods and housing may increase.
- Moderate or decreasing inflation rate.

Expansion:

- GDP growth rate increases.
- Unemployment rate decreases as hiring accelerates.
- Investment increases in producers' equipment and home construction.
- Inflation rate may increase.
- Imports increase as domestic income growth accelerates.

Peak:

- GDP growth rate decreases.
- Unemployment rate decreases but hiring slows.
- Consumer spending and business investment grow at slower rates.
- Inflation rate increases.

Contraction/recession:

- GDP growth rate is negative.
- Hours worked decrease, unemployment rate increases.
- Consumer spending, home construction, and business investment decrease.
- Inflation rate decreases with a lag.
- Imports decrease as domestic income growth slows.

LOS 18.c: Describe theories of the business cycle.

CFA® Program Curriculum, Volume 2, page 305

The causes of business cycles are a subject of considerable debate among economists.

Neoclassical school economists believe shifts in both aggregate demand and aggregate supply are primarily *driven by changes in technology* over time. They also believe that the economy has a strong tendency toward full-employment equilibrium, as recession puts downward pressure on the money wage rate, or as over-full employment puts upward pressure on the money wage rate. They conclude that business cycles result from *temporary deviations from long-run equilibrium*.

The Great Depression of the 1930s did not support the beliefs of the neoclassical economists. The economy in the United States operated significantly below its full-employment level for many years. Additionally, business cycles in general have been more severe and more prolonged than the neoclassical model would suggest.

British economist John Maynard Keynes attempted to explain the Depression and the nature of business cycles. He provided policy recommendations for moving the economy toward full-employment GDP and reducing the severity and duration of business cycles. Keynes believed that *shifts in aggregate demand due to changes in expectations* were the primary cause of business cycles. **Keynesian school** economists believe these fluctuations are primarily due to swings in the level of optimism of those who run businesses. They overinvest and overproduce when they are too optimistic about future growth in potential GDP, and they underinvest and underproduce when they are too pessimistic or fearful about the future growth in potential GDP.

Keynesians argue that wages are "downward sticky," reducing the ability of a decrease in money wages to increase short-run aggregate supply and move the economy from recession (or depression) back toward full employment. The policy prescription of Keynesian economists is to increase aggregate demand directly, through monetary policy (increasing the money supply) or through fiscal policy (increasing government spending, decreasing taxes, or both).

The **New Keynesian school** added the assertion that the prices of productive inputs other than labor are also "downward sticky," presenting additional barriers to the restoration of full-employment equilibrium.

A third view of macroeconomic equilibrium is that held by the **Monetarist school**. Monetarists believe the variations in aggregate demand that cause business cycles are due to variations in the rate of growth of the money supply, likely from *inappropriate decisions by the monetary authorities*. Monetarists believe that recessions can be caused by external shocks or by inappropriate decreases in the money supply. They suggest that to keep aggregate demand stable and growing, the central bank should follow a policy of steady and predictable increases in the money supply.

Economists of the **Austrian school** believe business cycles are caused by *government intervention in the economy*. When policymakers force interest rates down to artificially low levels, firms invest too much capital in long-term and speculative lines of production, compared to actual consumer demand. When these investments turn out poorly, firms must decrease output in those lines, which causes a contraction.

New Classical school economists introduced **real business cycle theory** (RBC). RBC emphasizes the effect of real economic variables such as *changes in technology and external shocks*, as opposed to monetary variables, as the cause of business cycles. RBC applies utility theory, which we described in the Study Session on microeconomic analysis, to macroeconomics. Based on a model in which individuals and firms maximize expected utility, New Classical economists argue that policymakers should not try to counteract business cycles because expansions and contractions are efficient market responses to real external shocks.

LOS 18.d: Describe types of unemployment and measures of unemployment.

CFA® Program Curriculum, Volume 2, page 313

Unemployment can be divided into three categories:

1. **Frictional unemployment** results from the time lag necessary to match employees who seek work with employers needing their skills. Frictional unemployment is always with us as employers expand or contract their businesses and workers move, are fired, or quit to seek other opportunities.

2. **Structural unemployment** is caused by long-run changes in the economy that eliminate some jobs while generating others for which unemployed workers are not qualified. Structural unemployment differs from frictional unemployment in that the unemployed workers do not currently have the skills needed to perform the jobs that are available.

3. **Cyclical unemployment** is caused by changes in the general level of economic activity. Cyclical unemployment is positive when the economy is operating at less than full capacity and can be negative when an expansion leads to employment temporarily over the full employment level.

A person who is not working is considered to be **unemployed** if he is actively searching for work.[1] One who has been seeking work unsuccessfully for several months is referred to as *long-term unemployed*.

The **unemployment rate** is the percentage of people in the labor force who are unemployed. The **labor force** includes all people who are either employed or unemployed. People who choose not to be in the labor force are said to be *voluntarily unemployed* and are not included in the calculation of the unemployment rate.

---

1. In the United States, the Bureau of Labor Statistics counts people as unemployed "if they do not have a job, have actively looked for work in the prior 4 weeks, and are currently available for work. Persons who were not working and were waiting to be recalled to a job from which they had been temporarily laid off are also included as unemployed." (*http://www.bls.gov/cps/lfcharacteristics.htm#unemp*)

A person who is employed part time but would prefer to work full time or is employed at a low-paying job despite being qualified for a significantly higher-paying one is said to be **underemployed**. Identification of the number of underemployed is somewhat subjective and not easily discernible from employment statistics.

The **participation ratio** (also referred to as the *activity ratio* or *labor force participation rate*) is the percentage of the working-age population who are either employed or actively seeking employment.

Short-term fluctuations in the participation ratio can occur because of changes in the number of **discouraged workers**, those who are available for work but are neither employed nor actively seeking employment. The participation rate tends to increase when the economy expands and decrease during recessions. Discouraged workers who stopped seeking jobs during a recession are motivated to seek work again once the expansion takes hold and they believe their prospects of finding work are better.

This movement of discouraged workers out of and back into the labor force causes the unemployment rate to be a lagging indicator of the business cycle. Early in an expansion when hiring prospects begin to improve, the number of discouraged workers who re-enter the labor force is greater than the number who are hired immediately. This causes the unemployment rate to increase even though employment is expanding. To gauge the current state of the labor market, analysts should include other widely available indicators such as the number of employees on payrolls.

Earlier, we noted that firms tend to be slow to hire or lay off workers at business cycle turning points. This also causes the unemployment rate to lag the business cycle. The effect can also be seen in data on **productivity**, or output per hour worked. Productivity declines early in contractions as firms try to keep employees on despite producing less output. Productivity increases early in expansions as firms try to produce more output but are not yet ready to hire new workers.

When comparing unemployment rates across countries, analysts should note that different reporting agencies may use somewhat dissimilar methods for calculating the statistics. Also, all of the employment indicators mentioned here apply only to legal employment. Participants in illegal sectors of the economy are not reflected in employment data.

LOS 18.e: Explain inflation, hyperinflation, disinflation, and deflation.

CFA® Program Curriculum, Volume 2, page 317

Inflation is a persistent increase in the price level over time. If the price level increases in a single jump but does not continue rising, the economy is not experiencing inflation. An increase in the price of a single good, or in relative prices of some goods, is not inflation. If inflation is present, the prices of almost all goods and services are increasing.

Inflation erodes the purchasing power of a currency. Inflation favors borrowers at the expense of lenders because when the borrower returns the principal to the lender, it is worth less in terms of goods and services (in real terms) than it was worth when it was borrowed. Inflation that accelerates out of control is referred to as **hyperinflation**, which can destroy a country's monetary system and bring about social and political upheavals.

The **inflation rate** is the percentage increase in the price level, typically compared to the prior year. Analysts can use the inflation rate as a business cycle indicator and to anticipate changes in central bank monetary policy. As we will see in the topic review on fiscal and monetary policy, an objective of central banks is to keep inflation within some target range. **Disinflation** refers to an inflation rate that is decreasing over time but remains greater than zero.

A persistently decreasing price level (i.e., a negative inflation rate) is called **deflation**. Deflation is commonly associated with deep recessions. When most prices are decreasing, consumers delay purchases because they believe they can buy the same goods more cheaply in the future. For firms, deflation results in decreasing revenue and increasing real fixed costs.

Professor's Note: Values stated as "real" are adjusted for inflation over some defined period. This makes values at different points in time comparable in terms of purchasing power.

LOS 18.f: Explain the construction of indices used to measure inflation.

CFA® Program Curriculum, Volume 2, page 319

To calculate a rate of inflation, we need to use a **price index** as a proxy for the price level. A price index measures the average price for a defined basket of goods and services. The **consumer price index** (CPI) is the best-known indicator of U.S. inflation. Many countries use indexes similar to the CPI.

The CPI basket represents the purchasing patterns of a typical urban household. Weights for the major categories in the CPI are shown in Figure 2.

Figure 2: Relative Importance in the CPI as of May 2014

Category	Percent of Index
Food	13.9%
Energy	9.7%
All items less food and energy	76.5%
Commodities less food and energy commodities:	
Apparel	3.4%
New vehicles	3.5%
Used cars and trucks	1.7%
Medical care commodities	1.7%
Alcoholic beverages	1.0%
Tobacco and smoking products	0.7%
Services less energy services:	
Shelter	31.8%
Medical care services	5.8%
Transportation services	5.6%

Source: Bureau of Labor Statistics, U.S. Department of Labor (stats.bls.gov)

To calculate the CPI, the Bureau of Labor Statistics compares the cost of the CPI basket today with the cost of the basket in an earlier *base period*. The value of the index is as follows:

$$CPI = \frac{\text{cost of basket at current prices}}{\text{cost of basket at base period prices}} \times 100$$

Example: Calculating a price index

The following table shows price information for a simplified basket of goods:

Item	Quantity	Price in Base Period	Current Price
Cheeseburgers	200	2.50	3.00
Movie tickets	50	7.00	10.00
Gasoline (in gallons)	300	1.50	3.00
Digital watches	100	12.00	9.00

Calculate the change in the price index for this basket from the base period to the current period.

Answer:

Reference base period:

Cheeseburgers	200 × 2.50 =	500
Movie tickets	50 × 7.00 =	350
Gasoline	300 × 1.50 =	450
Watches	100 × 12.00 =	1,200
Cost of basket		2,500

Current period:

Cheeseburgers	200 × 3.00 =	600
Movie tickets	50 × 10.00 =	500
Gasoline	300 × 3.00 =	900
Watches	100 × 9.00 =	900
Cost of basket		2,900

$$\text{price index} = \frac{2,900}{2,500} \times 100 = 116$$

The price index is up $\frac{116}{100} - 1 = 16\%$ over the period.

Professor's Note: The LOS requires you to "explain the construction of" price indexes but does not require you to calculate them.

Analysts who compare price indexes for different countries should be aware of differences in their composition. The weights assigned to each good and service reflect the typical consumer's purchasing patterns, which are likely to be significantly different across countries and regions. There can also be differences in how the data are collected. In the United States, for example, the most frequently cited CPI measure is based on the purchases typical of "all urban consumers." Other countries may survey a different set of consumers and consequently use different baskets of goods.

An alternative measure of consumer price inflation is the *price index for personal consumption expenditures*. In the United States, this index is created by surveying businesses rather than consumers. The *GDP deflator*, which we described in an earlier topic review, is another widely used inflation measure.

Analysts who look for emerging trends in consumer prices are often interested in the prices of goods in process. Widespread price increases for producers' goods may be passed along to consumers. For most major economies, a **producer price index** (PPI) or **wholesale price index** (WPI) is available. Analysts can observe the PPI for different stages of processing (raw materials, intermediate goods, and finished goods) to watch for emerging price pressure. Sub-indexes of the PPI are also useful for identifying changes in relative prices of producers' inputs, which may indicate shifts in demand among industries.

For both consumer and producer prices, analysts and policymakers often distinguish between **headline inflation** and **core inflation**. Headline inflation refers to price indexes for all goods. Core inflation refers to price indexes that exclude food and energy. Food and energy prices are typically more volatile than those of most other goods. Thus, core inflation can sometimes be a more useful measure of the underlying trend in prices.

LOS 18.g: Compare inflation measures, including their uses and limitations.

CFA® Program Curriculum, Volume 2, page 320

The price index we calculated in our example is a **Laspeyres index**, which uses a constant basket of goods and services. Most countries calculate consumer price inflation this way.

Three factors cause a Laspeyres index of consumer prices to be biased upward as a measure of the cost of living:

* *New goods.* Older products are often replaced by newer, but initially more expensive, products. New goods are periodically added to the market basket, and the older goods they replace are reduced in weight in the index. This biases the index upward.
* *Quality changes.* If the price of a product increases because the product has improved, the price increase is not due to inflation but still increases the price index.
* *Substitution.* Even in an inflation-free economy, prices of goods relative to each other change all the time. When two goods are substitutes for each other, consumers increase their purchases of the relatively cheaper good and buy less of the relatively more expensive good. Over time, such changes can make a Laspeyres index's fixed basket of goods a less accurate measure of typical household spending.

A technique known as **hedonic pricing** can be used to adjust a price index for product quality. To address the bias from substitution, reporting agencies can use a *chained* or *chain-weighted* price index such as a **Fisher index**. A Fisher index is the geometric mean of a Laspeyres index and a **Paasche index**. A Paasche index uses the current consumption weights, prices from the base period, and prices in the current period.

Example: Paasche index

Continuing the example we presented earlier, assume the basket of goods has changed as follows:

Item	Quantity in base period	Price in base period	Quantity in current period	Current price
Cheeseburgers	200	2.50	205	3.00
Movie tickets	50	7.00	45	10.00
Gasoline (in gallons)	300	1.50	295	3.00
Digital watches	100	12.00	105	9.00

Calculate a Paasche index for the current period, compare it to the Laspeyres index (previously calculated as 116), and explain the difference.

Answer:

Reference base period:

Cheeseburgers	205 × 2.50 =	512.50
Movie tickets	45 × 7.00 =	315.00
Gasoline	295 × 1.50 =	442.50
Watches	105 × 12.00 =	<u>1,260.00</u>
Cost of basket		2,530.00

Current period:

Cheeseburgers	205 × 3.00 =	615.00
Movie tickets	45 × 10.00 =	450.00
Gasoline	295 × 3.00 =	885.00
Watches	105 × 9.00 =	<u>945.00</u>
Cost of basket		2,895.00

$$\text{Paasche index} = \frac{2,895}{2,530} \times 100 = 114.43$$

The Paasche index is less than 116 because, compared to the base period, consumers have substituted away from the two goods with the largest percentage price increases (gasoline and movie tickets).

Professor's Note: The LOS does not require you to calculate these indexes. We show these examples to illustrate how substitution of goods by consumers can affect index values.

LOS 18.h: Distinguish between cost-push and demand-pull inflation.

CFA® Program Curriculum, Volume 2, page 323

The two types of inflation are cost-push and demand-pull. **Cost-push inflation** results from a decrease in aggregate supply, while **demand-pull inflation** results from an increase in aggregate demand.

Cost-Push Inflation

Inflation can result from an initial decrease in aggregate supply caused by an increase in the real price of an important factor of production, such as wages or energy. Figure 3 illustrates the effect on output and the price level of a decrease in aggregate supply. The reduction from $SRAS_0$ to $SRAS_1$ increases the price level to P_1, and with no initial change in aggregate demand, reduces output to GDP_1.

If the decline in GDP brings a policy response that stimulates aggregate demand so output returns to its long-run potential, the result would be a further increase in the price level to P_2.

Figure 3: Cost-Push Inflation

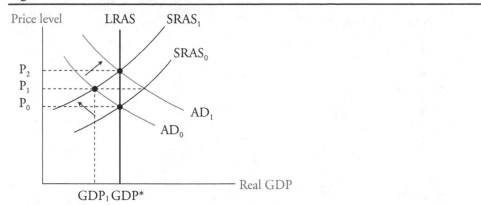

Because labor is the most important cost of production, wage pressure can be a source of cost-push inflation (sometimes called *wage-push inflation* when it occurs). Upward pressure on wages is more likely to emerge when cyclical unemployment is low, but it can occur even when cyclical unemployment is present. Because every individual provides a different type and quality of labor, some segments of the economy may have trouble finding enough qualified workers even during a contraction. As a result, the **non-accelerating inflation rate of unemployment** (NAIRU), also called the **natural rate of unemployment** (NARU), can be higher than the rate associated with the absence of cyclical unemployment. NARU or NAIRU can vary over time and is likely different across countries.

Analysts can use publicly available data on hourly and weekly earnings and labor productivity to identify signs of potential wage pressure. Wage increases are not inflationary as long as they remain in line with gains in productivity. A useful indicator of wages and benefits in terms of productivity is **unit labor costs**, the ratio of total labor compensation per hour to output units per hour.

An additional source of wage pressure is **expected inflation**. If workers expect inflation to increase, they will increase their wage demands accordingly. One indicator analysts use to gauge expected inflation is the difference in yield between inflation-indexed bonds, such as Treasury Inflation-Protected Securities, and otherwise similar non-indexed Treasury bonds.

Demand-Pull Inflation

Demand-pull inflation can result from an increase in the money supply, increased government spending, or any other change that increases aggregate demand. Figure 4 shows the effect on the price level when the economy is at full employment and aggregate demand increases (shifts to the right). In Figure 4, the economy is initially at full-employment equilibrium, with output at GDP^* and the price level at P_0, so that the aggregate demand and short-run aggregate supply curves are AD_0 and $SRAS_0$. Real GDP is equal to potential GDP, which is represented by the long-run aggregate supply curve LRAS.

Figure 4: Demand-Pull Inflation

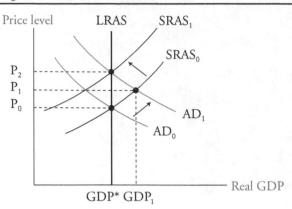

Now suppose the central bank increases the money supply, which increases aggregate demand to AD_1. With no initial change in aggregate supply, output increases to GDP_1, and the price level increases to P_1. Prices rise, and real GDP is above potential (full-employment) GDP.

With real GDP above its full-employment level, the increase in GDP is not sustainable. Unemployment falls below its natural rate, which puts upward pressure on real wages. Rising real wages result in a decrease in short-run aggregate supply (the curve shifts left to $SRAS_1$) until real GDP reverts back to full-employment GDP. Output falls back to GDP^*, and the price level increases further to P_2.

In the absence of other changes, the economy would reach a new equilibrium price level at P_2. But what would happen if the central bank tried to keep GDP above the full-employment level with further increases in the money supply? The same results would occur repeatedly. Output cannot remain above its potential in the long run, but the induced increase in aggregate demand and the resulting pressure on wages would keep the price level rising even higher. Demand-pull inflation would persist until the central bank reduced the growth rate of the money supply and allowed the economy to return to full-employment equilibrium at a level of real GDP equal to potential GDP.

Economists often use the capacity utilization rate of industry to indicate the potential for demand-pull inflation. High rates of capacity utilization suggest the economy is producing at or above potential GDP and may experience inflationary pressure.

The impact on output is the key difference between the demand-pull and cost-push effects. The demand-pull effect increases GDP above full-employment GDP, while with cost-push inflation, a decrease in aggregate supply initially decreases GDP.

LOS 18.i: Describe economic indicators, including their uses and limitations.

CFA® Program Curriculum, Volume 2, page 328

Earlier in this topic review, we described the unemployment rate as a *lagging indicator*. Economic indicators can be classified into three categories: **leading indicators** that have been known to change direction before peaks or troughs in the business cycle,

©2014 Kaplan, Inc.

coincident indicators that change direction at roughly the same time as peaks or troughs, and **lagging indicators** that don't tend to change direction until after expansions or contractions are already underway.

Organizations such as The Conference Board and the Organization for Economic Co-Operation and Development compile indexes of leading, coincident, and lagging indicators for the world's major economies. Figure 5 lists the components of The Conference Board's indexes for the United States. Indexes for other economies are similar to those for the United States but reflect differences among countries in the economic indicators that are available.

Figure 5: Leading, Coincident, and Lagging Economic Indicators, United States, as of January 2013

Leading Economic Index
Average weekly hours, manufacturing
Average weekly initial claims for unemployment insurance
Manufacturers' new orders, consumer goods and materials
Institute for Supply Management new orders index
Manufacturers' new orders, nondefense capital goods excluding aircraft
Building permits, new private housing units
Stock prices, 500 common stocks
Leading Credit Index™
Interest rate spread, 10-year Treasury bonds less federal funds
Index of consumer expectations
Coincident Economic Index
Employees on nonagricultural payrolls
Personal income less transfer payments
Industrial production
Manufacturing and trade sales
Lagging Economic Index
Average duration of unemployment
Inventories to sales ratio, manufacturing and trade
Labor cost per unit of output, manufacturing
Average prime rate
Commercial and industrial loans
Consumer installment credit to personal income ratio
Consumer price index for services

Source: The Conference Board (http://www.conference-board.org)

Analysts should be aware that the classifications *leading, coincident,* and *lagging* indicators reflect tendencies in the timing of their turning points, not exact relationships with the business cycle. Not all changes in direction of leading indicator indexes have been followed by corresponding changes in the business cycle, and even when they have, the lead time has varied. This common criticism is summed up in the often repeated comment, "Declines in stock prices have predicted nine of the last four recessions."

Professor's Note: Analysts who use economic indicators in forecasting models must guard against look-ahead bias. The data are not available immediately. For example, data for May are typically first released in mid- to late June and may be revised in July and August.

KEY CONCEPTS

LOS 18.a

The business cycle has four phases:

1. Expansion: Real GDP is increasing.
2. Peak: Real GDP stops increasing and begins decreasing.
3. Contraction: Real GDP is decreasing.
4. Trough: Real GDP stops decreasing and begins increasing.

Expansions feature increasing output, employment, consumption, investment, and inflation. Contractions are characterized by decreases in these indicators.

Business cycles are recurring but do not occur at regular intervals, can differ in strength or severity, and do not persist for specific lengths of time.

LOS 18.b

Inventory to sales ratios typically increase late in expansions when sales slow and decrease near the end of contractions when sales begin to accelerate. Firms decrease or increase production to restore their inventory-sales ratios to their desired levels.

Because hiring and laying off employees have high costs, firms prefer to adjust their utilization of current employees. As a result, firms are slow to lay off employees early in contractions and slow to add employees early in expansions.

Firms use their physical capital more intensively during expansions, investing in new capacity only if they believe the expansion is likely to continue. They use physical capital less intensively during contractions, but they are more likely to reduce capacity by deferring maintenance and not replacing equipment than by selling their physical capital.

The level of activity in the housing sector is affected by mortgage rates, demographic changes, the ratio of income to housing prices, and investment or speculative demand for homes resulting from recent price trends.

Domestic imports tend to rise with increases in GDP growth and domestic currency appreciation, while increases in foreign incomes and domestic currency depreciation tend to increase domestic export volumes.

LOS 18.c

Neoclassical economists believe business cycles are temporary and driven by changes in technology, and that rapid adjustments of wages and other input prices cause the economy to move to full-employment equilibrium.

Keynesian economists believe excessive optimism or pessimism among business managers causes business cycles and that contractions can persist because wages are slow to move downward. New Keynesians believe input prices other than wages are also slow to move downward.

Monetarists believe inappropriate changes in the rate of money supply growth cause business cycles, and that money supply growth should be maintained at a moderate and predictable rate to support the growth of real GDP.

Austrian-school economists believe business cycles are initiated by government intervention that drives interest rates to artificially low levels.

Real business cycle theory holds that business cycles can be explained by utility-maximizing actors responding to real economic forces such as external shocks and changes in technology, and that policymakers should not intervene in business cycles.

LOS 18.d

Frictional unemployment results from the time it takes for employers looking to fill jobs and employees seeking those jobs to find each other. Structural unemployment results from long-term economic changes that require workers to learn new skills to fill available jobs. Cyclical unemployment is positive (negative) when the economy is producing less (more) than its potential real GDP.

A person is considered unemployed if he is not working, is available for work, and is actively seeking work. The labor force includes all people who are either employed or unemployed. The unemployment rate is the percentage of labor force participants who are unemployed.

LOS 18.e

Inflation is a persistent increase in the price level over time. An inflation rate is a percentage increase in the price level from one period to the next.

Disinflation is a decrease in the inflation rate over time. Deflation refers to a persistent decrease in the price level (i.e., a negative inflation rate).

LOS 18.f

A price index measures the cost of a specific basket of goods and services relative to its cost in a prior (base) period. The inflation rate is most often calculated as the annual percentage change in a price index.

The most widely followed price index is the consumer price index (CPI), which is based on the purchasing patterns of a typical household. The GDP deflator and the producer or wholesale price index are also used as measures of inflation.

Headline inflation is a percentage change in a price index for all goods. Core inflation is calculated by excluding food and energy prices from a price index because of their high short-term volatility.

LOS 18.g

A Laspeyres price index is based on the cost of a specific basket of goods and services that represents actual consumption in a base period. New goods, quality improvements, and consumers' substitution of lower-priced goods for higher-priced goods over time cause a Laspeyres index to be biased upward.

A Paasche price index uses current consumption weights for the basket of goods and services for both periods and thereby reduces substitution bias. A Fisher price index is the geometric mean of a Laspeyres and a Paasche index.

LOS 18.h

Cost-push inflation results from a decrease in aggregate supply caused by an increase in the real price of an important factor of production, such as labor or energy.

Demand-pull inflation results from persistent increases in aggregate demand that increase the price level and temporarily increase economic output above its potential or full-employment level.

The non-accelerating inflation rate of unemployment (NAIRU) represents the unemployment rate below which upward pressure on wages is likely to develop.

Wage demands reflect inflation expectations.

LOS 18.i

Leading indicators have turning points that tend to precede those of the business cycle.

Coincident indicators have turning points that tend to coincide with those of the business cycle.

Lagging indicators have turning points that tend to occur after those of the business cycle.

A limitation of using economic indicators to predict business cycles is that their relationships with the business cycle are inexact and can vary over time.

CONCEPT CHECKERS

1. In the early part of an economic expansion, inventory-sales ratios are *most likely* to:
    A. increase because sales are unexpectedly low.
    B. increase because businesses plan for expansion.
    C. decrease because of unexpected increases in sales.

2. The contraction phase of the business cycle is *least likely* accompanied by decreasing:
    A. unemployment.
    B. inflation pressure.
    C. economic output.

3. According to which business cycle theory should expansionary monetary policy be used to fight a recession?
    A. Keynesian school.
    B. Monetarist school.
    C. New classical school.

4. The unemployment rate is defined as the number of unemployed as a percentage of the:
    A. labor force.
    B. number of employed.
    C. working-age population.

5. A country's year-end consumer price index over a 5-year period is as follows:

    Year 1   106.5
    Year 2   114.2
    Year 3   119.9
    Year 4   124.8
    Year 5   128.1

    The behavior of inflation as measured by this index is *best* described as:
    A. deflation.
    B. disinflation.
    C. hyperinflation.

6. Core inflation is *best* described as an inflation rate:
    A. for producers' raw materials.
    B. the central bank views as acceptable.
    C. that excludes certain volatile goods prices.

7. Which of the following is *least likely* to reduce substitution bias in a consumer price index?
    A. Use a chained index.
    B. Use a Paasche index.
    C. Adjust for the bias directly using hedonic pricing.

8.	In which of the following inflation scenarios does short-run aggregate supply decrease due to increasing wage demands?
	A.	Cost-push inflation.
	B.	Demand-pull inflation.
	C.	Both cost-push and demand-pull inflation.

9.	An economic indicator that has turning points which tend to occur after the turning points in the business cycle is classified as a:
	A.	lagging indicator.
	B.	leading indicator.
	C.	trailing indicator.

ANSWERS – CONCEPT CHECKERS

1. **C** Early in an expansion, inventory-sales ratios typically decrease below their normal levels as accelerating sales draw down inventories of produced goods.

2. **A** An economic contraction is likely to feature increasing unemployment (i.e., decreasing employment), along with declining economic output and decreasing inflation pressure.

3. **A** Keynesian school economists recommend monetary or fiscal policy action to stimulate aggregate demand and restore full employment. Monetarists believe the rate of money supply growth should be kept stable and predictable. The new classical school recommends against monetary or fiscal policy intervention because recessions reflect individuals' and firms' utility-maximizing response to real factors in the economy.

4. **A** The unemployment rate is the number of unemployed as a percentage of the labor force.

5. **B** The yearly inflation rate is as follows:

   Year 2 (114.2 − 106.5) / 106.5 = 7.2%
   Year 3 (119.9 − 114.2) / 114.2 = 5.0%
   Year 4 (124.8 − 119.9) / 119.9 = 4.1%
   Year 5 (128.1 − 124.8) / 124.8 = 2.6%

   The inflation rate is decreasing, but the price level is still increasing. This is best described as disinflation.

6. **C** Core inflation is measured using a price index that excludes food and energy prices.

7. **C** Adopting a chained price index method addresses substitution bias, as does using a Paasche index. Hedonic pricing adjusts for improvements in the quality of products over time, not substitution bias.

8. **C** Both inflation scenarios can involve a decrease in short-run aggregate supply due to increasing wage demands. In a wage-push scenario, which is a form of cost-push inflation, the decrease in aggregate supply causes real GDP to fall below full employment. In a demand-pull inflation scenario, an increase in aggregate demand causes real GDP to increase beyond full employment, which creates wage pressure that results in a decrease in short-run aggregate supply.

9. **A** Lagging indicators have turning points that occur after business cycle turning points.

MONETARY AND FISCAL POLICY

EXAM FOCUS

This topic review covers the supply and demand for money, as well as fiscal and monetary policy. This is a lot of material, but you really need to get it all down to be prepared for the exam. Concentrate initially on all the definitions and the basics of expansionary and contractionary fiscal and monetary policy. When you read it the second time, try to understand every cause-and-effect relationship so you can trace the effects of a policy change through the economy. In this way, you will be able to answer questions about the effect of, for example, open market purchases of securities by the central bank on interest rates, consumption, saving, private investment, and, of course, real GDP in the short and long run. You should understand the role of the central bank in a developed economy, including its limitations in achieving its stated objectives.

LOS 19.a: Compare monetary and fiscal policy.

CFA® Program Curriculum, Volume 2, page 347

Fiscal policy refers to a government's use of spending and taxation to influence economic activity. The budget is said to be *balanced* when tax revenues equal government expenditures. A **budget surplus** occurs when government tax revenues exceed expenditures, and a **budget deficit** occurs when government expenditures exceed tax revenues.

Monetary policy refers to the central bank's actions that affect the quantity of money and credit in an economy in order to influence economic activity. Monetary policy is said to be **expansionary** (or *accommodative* or *easy*) when the central bank increases the quantity of money and credit in an economy. Conversely, when the central bank is reducing the quantity of money and credit in an economy, the monetary policy is said to be **contractionary** (or *restrictive* or *tight*).

Both monetary and fiscal policies are used by policymakers with the goals of maintaining stable prices and producing positive economic growth. Fiscal policy can also be used as a tool for redistribution of income and wealth.

LOS 19.b: Describe functions and definitions of money.

CFA® Program Curriculum, Volume 2, page 349

Money is most commonly defined as a generally accepted medium of exchange. Rather than exchanging goods and services directly (bartering), using money facilitates indirect exchange.

Money has three primary functions:

- Money serves as a **medium of exchange** or **means of payment** because it is accepted as payment for goods and services.
- Money also serves as a **unit of account** because prices of all goods and services are expressed in units of money: dollars, yen, rupees, pesos, and so forth. This allows us to determine how much of any good we are foregoing when consuming another.
- Money provides a **store of value** because money received for work or goods now can be saved to purchase goods later.

Narrow money is the amount of notes (currency) and coins in circulation in an economy plus balances in checkable bank deposits. **Broad money** includes narrow money plus any amount available in liquid assets, which can be used to make purchases.

Measures of money differ among monetary authorities, but there is consistency in that broad measures of money include money that is less liquid (immediately spendable) than that included in narrow money measures. We have included definitions of narrow and broad monetary aggregates used by the U.S. Federal Reserve and by the European Central Bank as examples.

According to the Federal Reserve Bank of New York:

> The money supply measures reflect the different degrees of liquidity—or spendability—that different types of money have. The narrowest measure, M1, is restricted to the most liquid forms of money; it consists of currency in the hands of the public; travelers checks; demand deposits, and other deposits against which checks can be written. M2 includes M1, plus savings accounts, time deposits of under $100,000, and balances in retail money market mutual funds.

The European Central Bank describes their monetary aggregates as follows:

	M1	M2	M3
Currency in circulation	X	X	X
Overnight deposits	X	X	X
Deposits with an agreed maturity of up to 2 years		X	X
Deposits redeemable at notice of up to 3 months		X	X
Repurchase agreements			X
Money market fund shares/units			X
Debt securities issued with a maturity of up to 2 years			X

LOS 19.c: Explain the money creation process.

CFA® Program Curriculum, Volume 2, page 350

In the early stages of money development, **promissory notes** were developed. When customers deposited gold (or other precious metal) with early bankers, they were issued a promissory note, which was a promise by the banker to return that gold on demand from the depositor. Promissory notes themselves then became a medium of exchange. Bankers, recognizing that all the deposits would never be withdrawn at the same time, started lending a portion of deposits to earn interest. This led to what is called **fractional reserve banking**.

In a fractional reserve banking system, a bank holds a proportion of deposits in reserve. In most countries, banks are required to hold a minimum percentage of deposits as reserves.

When cash is deposited in a bank, the portion that is not required to be held in reserve can be loaned out. When a bank makes a cash loan and the borrower spends the money, the sellers who receive this cash may deposit it in banks as well. These funds can now be loaned out by these banks, except for the portion that must be held as reserves by each bank. This process of lending, spending, and depositing can continue until deposits are some multiple of the original cash amount.

Consider a bank that has $1,000 in **excess reserves** (cash not needed for reserves) that it lends. Assume the required reserve ratio is 25%. If the borrower of the $1,000 deposits the cash in a second bank, the second bank will be able to lend its excess reserves of $750 (0.75 × $1,000). Those funds may be deposited in a third bank, which can then lend its excess reserve of $563 (0.75 × $750). If this lending and depositing continues, the money supply can expand to $4,000 [(1 / 0.25) × $1,000]. One dollar of excess reserves can generate a $4 increase in the money supply.

The total amount of money that can be created is calculated as:

$$\text{money created} = \frac{\text{new deposit}}{\text{reserve requirement}} = \frac{1,000}{0.25} = \$4,000$$

With 25% of deposits held as reserves, the original deposit can result in total deposits four times as large, and we say that the **money multiplier** is four.

$$\text{money multiplier} = \frac{1}{\text{reserve requirement}} = \frac{1}{0.25} = 4$$

If the required reserve percentage is decreased, the money multiplier increases, and the quantity of money that can be created increases. If the reserve requirement was reduced from 25% to 10%, the money multiplier would increase from 4 to 10.

Relationship of Money and the Price Level

The **quantity theory of money** states that quantity of money is some proportion of the total spending in an economy and implies the **quantity equation of exchange**:

$$\text{money supply} \times \text{velocity} = \text{price} \times \text{real output} \quad (MV = PY)$$

Price multiplied by real output is total spending so that **velocity** is the average number of times per year each unit of money is used to buy goods or services. The equation of exchange must hold with velocity defined in this way.

Monetarists believe that velocity and the real output of the economy change only slowly. Assuming that velocity and real output remain constant, any increase in the money supply will lead to a proportionate increase in the price level. For example, a 5% increase in the money supply will increase average prices by 5%. For this reason, monetarists argue that monetary policy can be used to control and regulate inflation. The belief that real variables (real GDP and velocity) are not affected by monetary variables (money supply and prices) is referred to as **money neutrality**.

LOS 19.d: Describe theories of the demand for and supply of money.

CFA® Program Curriculum, Volume 2, page 355

The amount of wealth that households and firms in an economy choose to hold in the form of money is known as **demand for money**. There are three reasons for holding money:

1. *Transaction demand*: Money held to meet the need for undertaking transactions. As the level of real GDP increases, the size and number of transactions will increase, and the demand for money to carry out transactions increases.

2. *Precautionary demand*: Money held for unforeseen future needs. The demand for money for precautionary reasons is higher for large firms. In the aggregate, the total amount of precautionary demand for money increases with the size of the economy.

3. *Speculative demand*: Money that is available to take advantage of investment opportunities that arise in the future. It is inversely related to returns available in the market. As bonds and other financial instruments provide higher returns, investors would rather invest their money now than hold speculative money balances. Conversely, the demand for money for speculative reasons is positively related to perceived risk in other financial instruments. If the risk is perceived to be higher, people choose to hold money rather than invest it.

The relation between short-term interest rates and the quantity of money that firms and households demand to hold is illustrated in Figure 1. At lower interest rates, firms and households choose to hold more money. At higher interest rates, the opportunity cost of holding money increases, and firms and households will desire to hold less money and more interest-bearing financial assets.

The **supply of money** is determined by the central bank (the Fed in the United States) and is independent of the interest rate. This accounts for the vertical (perfectly inelastic) supply curve in Figure 1.

Short-term interest rates are determined by the equilibrium between money supply and money demand. As illustrated in Figure 1, if the interest rate is above the equilibrium rate (i_{high}), there is excess supply of real money. Firms and households are holding more real money balances than they desire to, given the opportunity cost of holding money balances. They will purchase securities to reduce their money balances, which will decrease the interest rate as securities prices are bid up. If interest rates are below equilibrium (i_{low}), there is excess demand for real money balances, as illustrated in Figure 1. Firms and households will sell securities to increase their money holdings to the desired level, decreasing securities prices and increasing the interest rate.

Figure 1: The Supply and Demand for Money

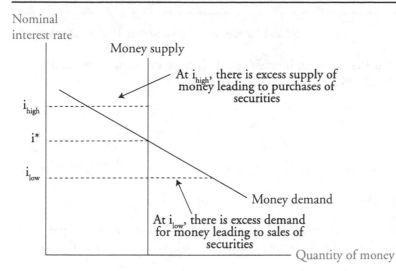

A central bank can affect short-term interest rates by increasing or decreasing the money supply. An increase in the money supply (shift of the money supply curve to the right) will put downward pressure on interest rates, as illustrated in Figure 2. With an increase in the money supply, there is excess supply of money at the previous rate of 5%. To reduce their money holdings, firms and households buy securities, increasing securities prices and decreasing the interest rate until the new equilibrium interest rate of 4% is achieved. If the central bank decreases the money supply, excess demand for money balances results in sales of securities and an increase in the interest rate.

Figure 2: Increase in the Money Supply

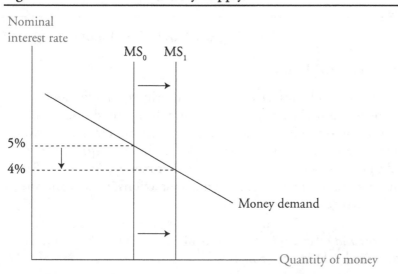

LOS 19.e: Describe the Fisher effect.

CFA® Program Curriculum, Volume 2, page 358

The **Fisher effect** states that the nominal interest rate is simply the sum of the real interest rate and expected inflation.

$$R_{Nom} = R_{Real} + E[I]$$

where:
R_{Nom} = nominal interest rate
R_{Real} = real interest rate
$E[I]$ = expected inflation

The idea behind the Fisher effect is that real rates are relatively stable, and changes in interest rates are driven by changes in expected inflation. This is consistent with money neutrality.

Investors are exposed to the risk that inflation and other future outcomes may be different than expected. Investors require additional return (a risk premium) for bearing this risk, which we can consider a third component of a nominal interest rate.

$$R_{Nom} = R_{Real} + E[I] + RP$$

where:
RP = risk premium for uncertainty

LOS 19.f: Describe roles and objectives of central banks.

CFA® Program Curriculum, Volume 2, page 361

There are several key **roles of central banks**:

1. *Sole supplier of currency*: Central banks have the sole authority to supply money. Traditionally, such money was backed by gold; the central bank stood ready to convert the money into a pre-specified quantity of gold. Later on, the gold backing was removed, and money supplied by the central bank was deemed **legal tender** by law. Money not backed by any tangible value is termed **fiat money**. As long as fiat money holds its value over time and is acceptable for transactions, it can continue to serve as a medium of exchange.

2. *Banker to the government and other banks*: Central banks provide banking services to the government and other banks in the economy.

3. *Regulator and supervisor of payments system*: In many countries, central banks may regulate the banking system by imposing standards of risk-taking allowed and reserve requirements of banks under its jurisdiction. Central banks also oversee the payments system to ensure smooth operations of the clearing system domestically and in conjunction with other central banks for international transactions.

4. *Lender of last resort*: Central banks' ability to print money allows them to supply money to banks with shortages, and this government backing tends to prevent runs on banks (i.e., large scale withdrawals) by assuring depositors their funds are secure.

5. *Holder of gold and foreign exchange reserves:* Central banks are often the repositories of the nation's gold and reserves of foreign currencies.

6. *Conductor of monetary policy:* Central banks control or influence the quantity of money supplied in an economy and growth of money supply over time.

The primary **objective of a central bank** is to *control inflation* so as to promote price stability. High inflation is not conducive to a stable economic environment. High inflation leads to **menu costs** (i.e., cost to businesses of constantly having to change their prices) and **shoe leather costs** (i.e., costs to individuals of making frequent trips to the bank so as to minimize their holdings of cash that are depreciating in value due to inflation).

In addition to price stability, some central banks have other stated goals, such as:

- Stability in exchange rates with foreign currencies.
- Full employment.
- Sustainable positive economic growth.
- Moderate long-term interest rates.

The target inflation rate in most developed countries is a range around 2% to 3%. A target of zero inflation is not used because that increases the risk of deflation, which can be very disruptive for an economy.

While most developed countries have an explicit target inflation rate, the U.S. Fed and the Bank of Japan do not. In the United States, this is because the Fed has the additional goals of maximum employment and moderate long-term interest rates. In Japan, it is because deflation, rather than inflation, has been a persistent problem in recent years.

Some developed countries, and several developing countries, choose a target level for the exchange rate of their currency with that of another country, primarily the U.S. dollar. This is referred to as **pegging** their exchange rate with the dollar. If their currency appreciates (i.e., becomes relatively more valuable), they can sell their domestic currency reserves for dollars to reduce the exchange rate. While such actions may be effective in the short run, for stability of the exchange rate over time, the monetary authorities in the pegging country must manage interest rates and economic activity to achieve their goal. This can lead to increased volatility of their money supply and interest rates. The pegging country essentially commits to a policy intended to make its inflation rate equal to the inflation rate of the country to which they peg their currency.

LOS 19.g: Contrast the costs of expected and unexpected inflation.

CFA® Program Curriculum, Volume 2, page 365

We turn our attention now to the costs to an economy of inflation, why central banks' target inflation rates are low, and why they care about volatility of inflation rates. At any point in time, economic agents have an expected rate of future inflation in the aggregate. The costs of inflation that is equal to the expected rate are different from the costs of inflation that differs from expectations, with the costs imposed on an economy of unanticipated inflation greater than those of perfectly anticipated inflation.

Consider an economy for which expected inflation is 6% and actual inflation will be 6% with certainty, so that inflation is *perfectly anticipated* (i.e., there is no unexpected inflation). The prices of all goods and wages could be indexed to this inflation rate so each month both wages and prices are increased approximately one-half percent. Increased demand for a product would result in monthly price increases of more than one-half percent and decreased demand would be reflected in prices that increased less than one-half percent per month.

One effect of high inflation—even when perfectly anticipated—is that the cost of holding money rather than interest-bearing securities is higher because its purchasing power decreases steadily. This will decrease the quantity of money that people willingly hold and impose some costs of more frequent movement of money from interest-bearing securities to cash or non-interest-bearing deposit accounts to facilitate transactions. To some extent, technology and the Internet have decreased these costs as movement of money between accounts has become much easier.

Much more important are the costs imposed on an economy by *unanticipated inflation*, inflation that is higher or lower than the expected rate of inflation. When inflation is higher than expected, borrowers gain at the expense of lenders as loan payments in the future are made with currency that has less value in real terms. Conversely, inflation that is less than expected will benefit lenders at the expense of borrowers. In an economy with volatile (rather than certain) inflation rates, lenders will require higher interest rates to compensate for the additional risk they face from unexpected changes in inflation. Higher borrowing rates slow business investment and reduce the level of economic activity.

A second cost of unexpected inflation is that information about supply and demand from changes in prices becomes less reliable. Suppose that when expected inflation is 5%, a manufacturer sees that prices for his product have increased 10%. If this is interpreted as an increase in demand for the product, the manufacturer will increase capacity and production in response to the perceived increase in demand. If, in fact, general price inflation is 10% rather than the expected 5% over the recent period, the price increase in the manufacturer's product did not result from an increase in demand. The expansion of production will result in excess inventory and capacity, and the firm will decrease production, laying off workers and reducing or eliminating expenditures on increased capacity for some time. Because of these effects, unexpected inflation can increase the magnitude or frequency of business cycles. The destabilizing effects of inflation, either higher than expected or lower than expected, because of reduced information content of price changes impose real costs on an economy.

LOS 19.h: Describe tools used to implement monetary policy.

CFA® Program Curriculum, Volume 2, page 367

Monetary policy is implemented using the **monetary policy tools** of the central bank. The three main policy tools of central banks are as follows:

1. *Policy rate*: In the United States, banks can borrow funds from the Fed if they have temporary shortfalls in reserves. The rate at which banks can borrow reserves from the Fed is termed the *discount rate*. For the European Central Bank (ECB), it is called the *refinancing rate*.

   One way to lend money to banks is through a *repurchase agreement*. The central bank purchases securities from banks that, in turn, agree to repurchase the securities at a higher price in the future. The percentage difference between the purchase price and the repurchase price is effectively the rate at which the central bank is lending to member banks. The Bank of England uses this method, and its policy rate is called the *two-week repo (repurchase) rate*. A lower rate reduces banks' cost of funds, encourages lending, and tends to decrease interest rates overall. A higher policy rate has the opposite effect, decreasing lending and increasing interest rates.

   In the United States, the *federal funds rate* is the rate that banks charge each other on overnight loans of reserves. The Fed sets a target for this market-determined rate and uses open market operations to move it to the target rate.

2. *Reserve requirements*: By increasing the reserve requirement (the percentage of deposits banks are required to retain as reserves), the central bank effectively decreases the funds that are available for lending and the money supply, which will tend to increase interest rates. A decrease in the reserve requirement will increase the funds available for lending and the money supply, which will tend to decrease interest rates. This tool only works well to increase the money supply if banks are willing to lend and customers are willing to borrow.

3. *Open market operations*: Buying and selling of securities by the central bank is referred to as open market operations. When the central bank buys securities, cash replaces securities in investor accounts, banks have excess reserves, more funds are available for lending, the money supply increases, and interest rates decrease. Sales of securities by the central bank have the opposite effect, reducing cash in investor accounts, excess reserves, funds available for lending, and the money supply, which will tend to cause interest rates to increase. In the United States, open market operations are the Fed's most commonly used tool and are important in achieving the federal funds target rate.

LOS 19.i: Describe the monetary transmission mechanism.

CFA® Program Curriculum, Volume 2, page 369

The **monetary transmission mechanism** refers to the ways in which a change in monetary policy, specifically the central bank's policy rate, affects the price level and inflation. There are four channels through which a change in the policy rates the monetary authorities control directly are transmitted to prices. They are transmitted through their effect on other short-term rates, asset values, currency exchange rates, and expectations. We can examine the transmission mechanism in more detail by considering the effects of a change to a contractionary monetary policy implemented through an increase in the policy rate.

- Banks' *short-term lending rates will increase* in line with the increase in the policy rate. The higher rates will decrease aggregate demand as consumers reduce credit purchases and businesses cut back on investment in new projects.
- Bond prices, equity prices, and *asset prices in general will decrease* as the discount rates applied to future expected cash flows are increased. This may have a wealth effect because a decrease in the value of households' assets may increase the savings rate and decrease consumption.
- Both consumers and businesses may decrease their expenditures because their *expectations for future economic growth decrease*.
- The increase in interest rates may attract foreign investment in debt securities, leading to an *appreciation of the domestic currency relative to foreign currencies*. An appreciation of the domestic currency increases the foreign currency prices of exports and can reduce demand for the country's export goods.

Taken together, these effects act to decrease aggregate demand and put downward pressure on the price level. A decrease in the policy rate would affect the price level through the same channels, but in the opposite direction.

LOS 19.j: Describe qualities of effective central banks.

CFA® Program Curriculum, Volume 2, page 371

For a central bank to succeed in its inflation-targeting policies, it should have **three essential qualities:**

1. *Independence*: For a central bank to be effective in achieving its goals, it should be free from political interference. Reducing the money supply to reduce inflation can also be expected to decrease economic growth and employment. The political party in power has an incentive to boost economic activity and reduce unemployment prior to elections. For this reason, politicians may interfere with the central bank's activities, compromising its ability to manage inflation. Independence should be thought of in relative terms (degrees of independence) rather than absolute terms. Even in the case of relatively independent central banks, the heads of the banks may be appointed by politicians.

   Independence can be evaluated based on both **operational independence** and **target independence**. Operational independence means that the central bank is allowed to independently determine the policy rate. Target independence means the central bank also defines how inflation is computed, sets the target inflation level, and determines the horizon over which the target is to be achieved. The ECB has both target and operational independence, while most other central banks have only operational independence.

2. *Credibility*: To be effective, central banks should follow through on their stated intentions. If a government with large debts, instead of a central bank, set an inflation target, the target would not be credible because the government has an incentive to allow inflation to exceed the target level. On the other hand, a credible central bank's targets can become self-fulfilling prophecies. If the market believes that a central bank is serious about achieving a target inflation rate of 3%, wages and other nominal contracts will be based on 3% inflation, and actual inflation will then be close to that level.

3. *Transparency*: Transparency on the part of central banks aids their credibility. Transparency means central banks periodically disclose the state of the economic environment by issuing **inflation reports**. Transparent central banks periodically report their views on the economic indicators and other factors they consider in their interest rate setting policy. When a central bank makes clear the economic indicators that it uses in establishing monetary policy and how they will be used, it not only gains credibility but makes policy changes easier to anticipate and implement.

LOS 19.k: Explain the relationships between monetary policy and economic growth, inflation, interest, and exchange rates.

CFA® Program Curriculum, Volume 2, page 369

If money neutrality holds, changes in monetary policy and the policy rate will have no effect on real output. In the short run, however, changes in monetary policy can affect real economic growth as well as interest rates, inflation, and foreign exchange rates. The effects of a change to a more expansionary monetary policy may include any or all of the following:

- The central bank buys securities, which increases bank reserves.
- The interbank lending rate decreases as banks are more willing to lend each other reserves.
- Other short-term rates decrease as the increase in the supply of loanable funds decreases the equilibrium rate for loans.
- Longer-term interest rates also decrease.
- The decrease in real interest rates causes the currency to depreciate in the foreign exchange market.
- The decrease in long-term interest rates increases business investment in plant and equipment.
- Lower interest rates cause consumers to increase their purchases of houses, autos, and durable goods.
- Depreciation of the currency increases foreign demand for domestic goods.
- These increases in consumption, investment, and net exports all increase aggregate demand.
- The increase in aggregate demand increases inflation, employment, and real GDP.

The transmission mechanism for a decrease in interbank lending rates affects four things simultaneously:

1. Market rates decrease due to banks adjusting their lending rates for the short and long term.

2. Asset prices increase because lower discount rates are used for computing present values.

3. Firms and individuals raise their expectations for economic growth and profitability. They may also expect the central bank to follow up with further interest rate decreases.

4. The domestic currency depreciates due to an outflow of foreign money as real interest rates decline.

Together, these four factors increase domestic demand as people consume more (they have less incentive to save given lower interest rates) and increase net external demand (exports minus imports) because depreciation of the domestic currency makes exports less expensive to foreigners and imports more expensive in the domestic economy. The increase in overall demand and import prices tends to increase aggregate demand and domestic inflation.

LOS 19.l: Contrast the use of inflation, interest rate, and exchange rate targeting by central banks.

CFA® Program Curriculum, Volume 2, page 371

Central banks have used various economic variables and indicators over the years to make monetary policy decisions. In the past, some have used **interest rate targeting**, increasing the money supply when specific interest rates rose above the target band and decreasing the money supply (or the rate of money supply growth) when rates fell below the target band. Currently, **inflation targeting** is the most widely used tool for making monetary policy decisions and is, in fact, the method required by law in some countries. Central banks that currently use inflation targeting include the U.K., Brazil, Canada, Australia, Mexico, and the European Central Bank.

The most common inflation rate target is 2%, with a permitted deviation of ±1% so the target band is 1% to 3%. The reason the inflation target is not 0% is that variations around that rate would allow for negative inflation (i.e., deflation), which is considered disruptive to the smooth functioning of an economy. Central banks are not necessarily targeting current inflation, which is the result of prior policy and events, but inflation in the range of two years in the future.

Some countries, especially developing countries, use **exchange rate targeting**. That is, they target a foreign exchange rate between their currency and another (often the U.S. dollar), rather than targeting inflation. As an example, consider a country that has targeted an exchange rate for its currency versus the U.S. dollar. If the foreign exchange value of the domestic currency falls relative to the U.S. dollar, the monetary authority must use foreign reserves to purchase their domestic currency (which will reduce money supply growth and increase interest rates) in order to reach the target exchange rate. Conversely, an increase in the foreign exchange value of the domestic currency above the target rate will require sale of the domestic currency in currency markets to reduce its value (increasing the domestic money supply and decreasing interest rates) to move towards the target exchange rate. One result of exchange rate targeting may be greater volatility of the money supply because domestic monetary policy must adapt to the necessity of maintaining a stable foreign exchange rate.

Over the short term, the targeting country can purchase or sell its currency in the foreign exchange markets to influence the exchange rate. There are limits, however, on how much influence currency purchases or sales can have on exchange rates over time. For example, a country may run out of foreign reserves with which to purchase its currency when the exchange value of its currency is still below the target exchange rate.

The net effect of exchange rate targeting is that the targeting country will have the same inflation rate as the targeted currency and the targeting country will need to follow monetary policy and accept interest rates that are consistent with this goal, regardless of domestic economic circumstances.

LOS 19.m: Determine whether a monetary policy is expansionary or contractionary.

CFA® Program Curriculum, Volume 2, page 380

An economy's long-term sustainable real growth rate is called the **real trend rate** or, simply, the trend rate. The trend rate is not directly observable and must be estimated. The trend rate also changes over time as structural conditions of the economy change. For example, after a prolonged period of heavy debt use, consumers may increase saving and reduce consumption in order to reduce their levels of debt. This structural shift in the economy would reduce the trend growth rate.

The **neutral interest rate** of an economy is the growth rate of the money supply that neither increases nor decreases the economic growth rate:

neutral interest rate = real trend rate of economic growth + inflation target

When the policy rate is above (below) the neutral rate, the monetary policy is said to be **contractionary** (**expansionary**). In general, contractionary policy is associated with a decrease in the *growth rate* of money supply, while expansionary policy increases its growth rate.

Monetary policy is often adjusted to reflect the source of inflation. For example, if inflation is above target due to higher aggregate demand (consumer and business spending), then contractionary monetary policy may be an appropriate response to reduce inflation. Suppose, however, that inflation is higher due to supply shocks, such as higher food or energy prices, and the economy is already operating below full employment. In such a situation, a contractionary monetary policy may make a bad situation worse.

Professor's Note: In the United States, the Federal Reserve focuses on core inflation (i.e., excluding volatile food and energy prices) for this reason.

LOS 19.n: Describe limitations of monetary policy.

CFA® Program Curriculum, Volume 2, page 381

This transmission mechanism for monetary policy previously described does not always produce the intended results. In particular, long-term rates may not rise and fall with short-term rates because of the effect of monetary policy changes on expected inflation.

If individuals and businesses believe that a decrease in the money supply intended to reduce inflation will be successful, they will expect lower future inflation rates. Because long-term bond yields include a premium for expected inflation, long-term rates could fall (tending to increase economic growth), even while the central bank has increased short-term rates in order to slow economic activity. Conversely, increasing the money supply to stimulate economic activity could lead to an increase in expected inflation rates and long-term bond yields, even as short-term rates fall.

From a different perspective, monetary tightening may be viewed as too extreme, increasing the probability of a recession, making long-term bonds more attractive and reducing long-term interest rates. If money supply growth is seen as inflationary, higher expected future asset prices will make long-term bonds relatively less attractive and will increase long-term interest rates. Bond market participants that act in this way have been called **bond market vigilantes.** When the central bank's policy is credible and investors believe that the inflation target rate will be maintained over time, this effect on long-term rates will be small.

Another situation in which the transmission mechanism may not perform as expected is if demand for money becomes very elastic and individuals willingly hold more money even without a decrease in short-term rates. Such a situation is called a **liquidity trap.** Increasing growth of the money supply will not decrease short-term rates under these conditions because individuals hold the money in cash balances instead of investing in interest-bearing securities. If an economy is experiencing deflation even though money supply policy has been expansionary, liquidity trap conditions may be present.

Compared to inflation, deflation is more difficult for central banks to reverse. In a deflationary environment, monetary policy needs to be expansionary. However, the central bank is limited to reducing the nominal policy rate to zero. Once it reaches zero, the central bank has limited ability to further stimulate the economy.

Another reason standard tools for increasing the money supply might not increase economic activity is that even with increasing excess reserves, banks may not be willing to lend. When what has become known as the *credit bubble* collapsed in 2008, banks around the world lost equity capital and desired to rebuild it. For this reason, they decreased their lending, even as money supplies were increased and short-term rates fell. With short-term rates near zero, economic growth still poor, and a real threat of deflation, central banks began a policy termed **quantitative easing**.

In the United Kingdom, quantitative easing entailed large purchases of British government bonds in the maturity range of three to five years. The intent was to reduce interest rates to encourage borrowing and to generate excess reserves in the banking system to encourage lending. Uncertainty about the economy's future caused banks to behave quite conservatively and willingly hold more excess reserves, rather than make loans.

In the United States, billions of dollars were made available for the Fed to buy assets other than short-term Treasury securities. Large amounts of mortgage securities were purchased from banks to encourage bank lending and to reduce mortgage rates in an attempt to revive the housing market, which had collapsed. When this program did not have the desired effect, a second round of quantitative easing (QE2) was initiated. The Fed purchased long-term Treasury bonds in large quantities (hundreds of billions of dollars) with the goal of bringing down longer-term interest rates and generating excess reserves to increase lending and economic growth. The Fed has also purchased securities with credit risk as part of its quantitative easing, improving banks' balance sheets but perhaps just shifting risk from the private sector to the public sector.

Monetary Policy in Developing Economies

Developing countries face problems in successfully implementing monetary policy. Without a liquid market in their government debt interest rate, information may be distorted and open market operations difficult to implement. In a very rapidly developing economy it may be quite difficult to determine the neutral rate of interest for policy purposes. Rapid financial innovation may change the demand to hold monetary aggregates. Central banks may lack credibility because of past failure to maintain inflation rates in a target band and may not be given independence by the political authority.

LOS 19.o: Describe roles and objectives of fiscal policy.

CFA® Program Curriculum, Volume 2, page 386

Fiscal policy refers to a government's use of spending and taxation to meet macroeconomic goals. A government budget is said to be *balanced* when tax revenues equal government expenditures. A *budget surplus* occurs when government tax revenues exceed expenditures, and a *budget deficit* occurs when government expenditures exceed tax revenues.

In general, decreased taxes and increased government spending both *increase* a budget deficit, overall demand, economic growth, and employment. Increased taxes and decreased government spending *decrease* a budget deficit, overall demand, economic growth, and employment. Budget deficits are increased in response to recessions, and budget deficits are decreased to slow growth when inflation is too high.

Keynesian economists believe that fiscal policy, through its effect on aggregate demand, can have a strong effect on economic growth when the economy is operating at less than full employment. Monetarists believe that the effect of fiscal stimulus is only temporary and that monetary policy should be used to increase or decrease inflationary pressures over time. Monetarists do not believe that monetary policy should be used in an attempt to influence aggregate demand to counter cyclical movements in the economy.

Discretionary fiscal policy refers to the spending and taxing decisions of a national government that are intended to stabilize the economy. In contrast, **automatic stabilizers** are built-in fiscal devices triggered by the state of the economy. For example, during a recession, tax receipts will fall, and government expenditures on unemployment insurance payments will increase. Both of these tend to increase budget deficits and are expansionary. Similarly, during boom times, higher tax revenues coupled with lower outflows for social programs tend to decrease budget deficits and are contractionary.

Objectives of fiscal policy may include:

- Influencing the level of economic activity and aggregate demand.
- Redistributing wealth and income among segments of the population.
- Allocating resources among economic agents and sectors in the economy.

LOS 19.p: Describe tools of fiscal policy, including their advantages and disadvantages.

CFA® Program Curriculum, Volume 2, page 394

Fiscal policy tools include spending tools and revenue tools.

Spending Tools

Transfer payments, also known as entitlement programs, redistribute wealth, taxing some and making payments to others. Examples include Social Security and unemployment insurance benefits. Transfer payments are not included in GDP computations.

Current spending refers to government purchases of goods and services on an ongoing and routine basis.

Capital spending refers to government spending on infrastructure, such as roads, schools, bridges, and hospitals. Capital spending is expected to boost future productivity of the economy.

Justification for spending tools:

- Provide services such as national defense that benefit all the residents in a country.
- Invest in infrastructure to enhance economic growth.
- Support the country's growth and unemployment targets by directly affecting aggregate demand.

- Provide a minimum standard of living.
- Subsidize investment in research and development for certain high-risk ventures consistent with future economic growth or other goals (e.g., green technology).

Revenue Tools

Direct taxes are levied on income or wealth. These include income taxes, taxes on income for national insurance, wealth taxes, estate taxes, corporate taxes, capital gains taxes, and Social Security taxes. Some progressive taxes (such as income and wealth taxes) generate revenue for wealth and income redistributing.

Indirect taxes are levied on goods and services. These include sales taxes, value-added taxes (VATs), and excise taxes. Indirect taxes can be used to reduce consumption of some goods and services (e.g., alcohol, tobacco, gambling).

Desirable attributes of tax policy:

- Simplicity to use and enforce.
- Efficiency; having the least interference with market forces and not acting as a deterrent to working.
- Fairness is quite subjective, but two commonly held beliefs are:
    - Horizontal equality: people in similar situations should pay similar taxes.
    - Vertical equality: richer people should pay more in taxes.
- Sufficiency, in that taxes should generate sufficient revenues to meet the spending needs of the government.

Advantages of fiscal policy tools:

- Social policies, such as discouraging tobacco use, can be implemented very quickly via indirect taxes.
- Quick implementation of indirect taxes also means that government revenues can be increased without significant additional costs.

Disadvantages of fiscal policy tools:

- Direct taxes and transfer payments take time to implement, delaying the impact of fiscal policy.
- Capital spending also takes a long time to implement. The economy may have recovered by the time its impact is felt.

Announcing a change in fiscal policy may have significant effects on expectations. For example, an announcement of future increase in taxes may immediately reduce current consumption, rapidly producing the desired goal of reducing aggregate demand. Note that not all fiscal policy tools affect economic activity equally. Spending tools are most effective in increasing aggregate demand. Tax reductions are somewhat less effective, as people may not spend the entire amount of the tax savings. Tax reductions for those with low incomes will be more effective in increasing aggregate demand, as those with lower incomes tend to spend a larger proportion of income on consumption; that is, they save a smaller proportion of income and have a higher marginal propensity to consume.

Fiscal Multiplier

Changes in government spending have magnified effects on aggregate demand because those whose incomes increase from increased government spending will in turn increase their spending, which increases the incomes and spending of others. The magnitude of the *multiplier effect* depends on the tax rate and on the marginal propensity to consume.

To understand the calculation of the multiplier effect, consider an increase in government spending of $100 when the MPC is 80%, and the tax rate is 25%. The increase in spending increases incomes by $100, but $25 (100 × 0.25) of that will be paid in taxes. **Disposable income** is equal to income after taxes, so disposable income increases by $100 × (1 − 0.25) = $75. With an MPC of 80%, additional spending by those who receive the original $100 increase is $75 × 0.8 = $60.

This additional spending will increase others' incomes by $60 and disposable incomes by $60 × 0.75 = $45, from which they will spend $45 × 0.8 = $36.

Because each iteration of this process reduces the amount of additional spending, the effect reaches a limit. The **fiscal multiplier** determines the potential increase in aggregate demand resulting from an increase in government spending:

$$\text{fiscal multiplier} = \frac{1}{1 - \text{MPC}(1 - t)}$$

Here, with a tax rate of 25% and an MPC of 80%, the fiscal multiplier is 1 / [1 − 0.8(1 − 0.25)] = 2.5, and the increase of $100 in government spending has the potential to increase aggregate demand by $250.

The fiscal multiplier is inversely related to the tax rate (higher tax rate decreases the multiplier) and directly related to the marginal propensity to consume (higher MPC increases the multiplier).

Balanced Budget Multiplier

In order to balance the budget, the government could increase taxes by $100 to just offset a $100 increase in spending. Changes in taxes also have a magnified effect on aggregate demand. An increase in taxes will decrease disposable income and consumption expenditures, thereby decreasing aggregate demand. The initial decrease in spending from a tax increase of $100 is 100 × MPC = 100 × 0.8 = $80; beyond that, the multiplier effect is the same as we described for a direct increase in government spending, and the overall decrease in aggregate demand for a $100 tax increase is 100(MPC) × fiscal multiplier, or, for our example, 100(0.8)(2.5) = $200.

Combining the total increase in aggregate demand from a $100 increase in government spending with the total decrease in aggregate demand from a $100 tax increase shows that the net effect on aggregate demand of both is an increase of $250 − $200 = $50, so we can say that the balanced budget multiplier is positive.

If instead of a $100 increase in taxes, we increased taxes by 100 / MPC = 100 / 0.8 = $125 and increased government spending by $100, the net effect on aggregate demand would be zero.

Ricardian Equivalence

Increases in the current deficit mean greater taxes in the future. To maintain their preferred pattern of consumption over time, taxpayers may increase current savings (reduce current consumption) in order to offset the expected cost of higher future taxes. If taxpayers reduce current consumption and increase current saving by just enough to repay the principal and interest on the debt the government issued to fund the increased deficit, there is no effect on aggregate demand. This is known as **Ricardian equivalence** after economist David Ricardo. If taxpayers underestimate their future liability for servicing and repaying the debt, so that aggregate demand is increased by equal spending and tax increases, Ricardian equivalence does not hold. Whether it does is an open question.

LOS 19.q: Describe the arguments about whether the size of a national debt relative to GDP matters.

CFA® Program Curriculum, Volume 2, page 393

When a government runs fiscal deficits, it incurs debt that needs to be repaid as well as ongoing interest expense. Total deficits, annual deficits, and interest expense can all be evaluated relative to annual GDP. When these ratios increase beyond certain levels, it may be a cause for concern, and the solvency of the country may be questioned.

A country's **debt ratio** is the ratio of aggregate debt to GDP. Because taxes are linked to GDP, when an economy grows in real terms, tax revenues will also grow in real terms. If the real interest rate on the government's debt is higher than the real growth rate of the economy, then the debt ratio will increase over time (keeping tax rates constant). Similarly, if the real interest rate on government's debt is lower than real growth in GDP, the debt ratio will decrease (i.e., improve) over time.

Arguments *for* being concerned with the size of fiscal deficit:

- Higher deficits lead to higher future taxes. Higher future taxes will lead to disincentives to work and entrepreneurship. This leads to lower long-term economic growth.
- If markets lose confidence in the government, investors may not be willing to refinance the debt. This can lead to the government defaulting (if debt is in a foreign currency) or having to simply print money (if the debt is in local currency). Printing money would ultimately lead to higher inflation.
- Increased government borrowing will tend to increase interest rates, and firms may reduce their borrowing and investment spending as a result, decreasing the impact on aggregate demand of deficit spending. This is referred to as the **crowding-out effect** because government borrowing is taking the place of private sector borrowing.

Arguments *against* being concerned with the size of fiscal deficit:

- If the debt is primarily being held by domestic citizens, the scale of the problem is overstated.
- If the debt is used to finance productive capital investment, future economic gains will be sufficient to repay the debt.
- Fiscal deficits may prompt needed tax reform.
- Deficits would not matter if private sector savings in anticipation of future tax liabilities just offsets the government deficit (Ricardian equivalence holds).
- If the economy is operating at less than full capacity, deficits do not divert capital away from productive uses. On the contrary, deficits can aid in increasing GDP and employment.

LOS 19.r: Explain the implementation of fiscal policy and difficulties of implementation.

CFA® Program Curriculum, Volume 2, page 400

Fiscal policy is implemented through changes in taxes and spending. This is called **discretionary fiscal policy** (as opposed to automatic stabilizers discussed previously). Discretionary fiscal policy would be designed to be expansionary when the economy is operating below full employment. Fiscal policy aims to stabilize aggregate demand. During recessions, actions can be taken to increase government spending or decrease taxes. Either change tends to strengthen the economy by increasing aggregate demand, putting more money in the hands of corporations and consumers to invest and spend. During inflationary economic booms, actions can be taken to decrease government spending or increase taxes. Either change tends to slow the economy by decreasing aggregate demand, taking money out of the hands of corporations and consumers, causing both investment and consumption spending to fall.

Discretionary fiscal policy is not an exact science. First, economic forecasts might be wrong, leading to incorrect policy decisions. Second, complications arise in practice that delay both the implementation of discretionary fiscal policy and the impact of policy changes on the economy. The lag between recessionary or inflationary conditions in the economy and the impact on the economy of fiscal policy changes can be divided into three types:

- **Recognition lag:** Discretionary fiscal policy decisions are made by a political process. The state of the economy is complex, and it may take policymakers time to recognize the nature and extent of the economic problems.
- **Action lag:** The time governments take to discuss, vote on, and enact fiscal policy changes.
- **Impact lag:** The time between the enactment of fiscal policy changes and when the impact of the changes on the economy actually takes place. It takes time for corporations and individuals to act on the fiscal policy changes, and fiscal multiplier effects occur only over time as well.

These lags can actually make fiscal policy counterproductive. For example, if the economy is in a recession phase, fiscal stimulus may be deemed appropriate. However, by the time fiscal stimulus is implemented and has its full impact, the economy may already be on a path to a recovery driven by the private sector.

Additional macroeconomic issues may hinder usefulness of fiscal policy:

- *Misreading economic statistics:* The full employment level for an economy is not precisely measurable. If the government relies on expansionary fiscal policy mistakenly at a time when the economy is already at full capacity, it will simply drive inflation higher.
- *Crowding-out effect:* Expansionary fiscal policy may crowd out private investment, reducing the impact on aggregate demand.
- *Supply shortages:* If economic activity is slow due to resource constraints (low availability of labor or other resources) and not due to low demand, expansionary fiscal policy will fail to achieve its objective and will probably lead to higher inflation.
- *Limits to deficits:* There is a limit to expansionary fiscal policy. If the markets perceive that the deficit is already too high as a proportion of GDP, funding the deficit will be problematic. This could lead to higher interest rates and actually make the situation worse.
- *Multiple targets:* If the economy has high unemployment coupled with high inflation, fiscal policy cannot address both problems simultaneously.

LOS 19.s: Determine whether a fiscal policy is expansionary or contractionary.

CFA® Program Curriculum, Volume 2, page 386

Fiscal policy entails setting taxes and spending. A budget surplus (deficit) occurs when tax revenues exceed (fall short of) spending. Economists often focus on *changes* in the surplus or deficit to determine if the fiscal policy is expansionary or contractionary. An increase (decrease) in surplus is indicative of a contractionary (expansionary) fiscal policy. Similarly, an increase (decrease) in deficit is indicative of an expansionary (contractionary) fiscal policy.

Professor's Note: For the exam, an increase (decrease) in a revenue item (e.g., sales tax) should be considered contractionary (expansionary), and an increase (decrease) in a spending item (e.g., construction of highways) should be considered expansionary (contractionary).

A government's intended fiscal policy is not necessarily obvious from just examining the current deficit. Consider an economy that is in recession so that transfer payments are increased and tax revenue is decreased, leading to a deficit. This does not necessarily indicate that fiscal policy is expansionary as, at least to some extent, the deficit is a natural outcome of the recession without any explicit action of the government. Economists often use a measure called the **structural** (or **cyclically adjusted**) **budget deficit** to gauge fiscal policy. This is the deficit that would occur based on current policies if the economy were at full employment.

LOS 19.t: Explain the interaction of monetary and fiscal policy.

CFA® Program Curriculum, Volume 2, page 404

Monetary policy and fiscal policy may each be either expansionary or contractionary, so there are four possible scenarios:

1. **Expansionary fiscal and monetary policy:** In this case, the impact will be highly expansionary taken together. Interest rates will usually be lower (due to monetary policy), and the private and public sectors will both expand.

2. **Contractionary fiscal and monetary policy:** In this case, aggregate demand and GDP would be lower, and interest rates would be higher due to tight monetary policy. Both the private and public sectors would contract.

3. **Expansionary fiscal policy + contractionary monetary policy:** In this case, aggregate demand will likely be higher (due to fiscal policy), while interest rates will be higher (due to increased government borrowing and tight monetary policy). Government spending as a proportion of GDP will increase.

4. **Contractionary fiscal policy + expansionary monetary policy:** In this case, interest rates will fall from decreased government borrowing and from the expansion of the money supply, increasing both private consumption and output. Government spending as a proportion of GDP will decrease due to contractionary fiscal policy. The private sector would grow as a result of lower interest rates.

Not surprisingly, the fiscal multipliers for different types of fiscal stimulus differ, and the effects of expansionary fiscal policy are greater when it is combined with expansionary monetary policy. The fiscal multiplier for direct government spending increases has been much higher than the fiscal multiplier for increases in transfers to individuals or tax reductions for workers. Within this latter category, government transfer payments to the poor have the greatest relative impact, followed by tax cuts for workers, and broader-based transfers to individuals (not targeted). For all types of fiscal stimulus, the impact is greater when the fiscal actions are combined with expansionary monetary policy. This may reflect the impact of greater inflation, falling real interest rates, and the resulting increase in business investment.

KEY CONCEPTS

LOS 19.a
Fiscal policy is a government's use of taxation and spending to influence the economy. Monetary policy deals with determining the quantity of money supplied by the central bank. Both policies aim to achieve economic growth with price level stability, although governments use fiscal policy for social and political reasons as well.

LOS 19.b
Money is defined as a widely accepted medium of exchange. Functions of money include a medium of exchange, a store of value, and a unit of account.

LOS 19.c
In a fractional reserve system, new money created is a multiple of new excess reserves available for lending by banks. The potential multiplier is equal to the reciprocal of the reserve requirement and, therefore, is inversely related to the reserve requirement.

LOS 19.d
Three factors influence money demand:
- Transaction demand, for buying goods and services.
- Precautionary demand, to meet unforseen future needs.
- Speculative demand, to take advantage of investment opportunities.

Money supply is determined by central banks with the goal of managing inflation and other economic objectives.

LOS 19.e
The Fisher effect states that a nominal interest rate is equal to the real interest rate plus the expected inflation rate.

LOS 19.f
Central bank roles include supplying currency, acting as banker to the government and to other banks, regulating and supervising the payments system, acting as a lender of last resort, holding the nation's gold and foreign currency reserves, and conducting monetary policy.

Central banks have the objective of controlling inflation, and some have additional goals of maintaining currency stability, full employment, positive sustainable economic growth, or moderate interest rates.

LOS 19.g
High inflation, even when it is perfectly anticipated, imposes costs on the economy as people reduce cash balances because of the higher opportunity cost of holding cash. More significant costs are imposed by unexpected inflation, which reduces the information value of price changes, can make economic cycles worse, and shifts wealth from lenders to borrowers. Uncertainty about the future rate of inflation increases risk, resulting in decreased business investment.

LOS 19.h

Policy tools available to central banks include the policy rate, reserve requirements, and open market operations. The policy rate is called the discount rate in the United States, the refinancing rate by the ECB, and the 2-week repo rate in the United Kingdom.

Decreasing the policy rate, decreasing reserve requirements, and making open market purchases of securities are all expansionary. Increasing the policy rate, increasing reserve requirements, and making open market sales of securities are all contractionary.

LOS 19.i

The transmission mechanism for changes in the central bank's policy rate through to prices and inflation includes one or more of the following:
- Short-term bank lending rates.
- Asset prices.
- Expectations for economic activity and future policy rate changes.
- Exchange rates with foreign currencies.

LOS 19.j

Effective central banks exhibit independence, credibility, and transparency.
- Independence: The central bank is free from political interference.
- Credibility: The central bank follows through on its stated policy intentions.
- Transparency: The central bank makes it clear what economic indicators it uses and reports on the state of those indicators.

LOS 19.k

A contractionary monetary policy (increase in policy rate) will tend to decrease economic growth, increase market interest rates, decrease inflation, and lead to appreciation of the domestic currency in foreign exchange markets. An expansionary monetary policy (decrease in policy rate) will have opposite effects, tending to increase economic growth, decrease market interest rates, increase inflation, and reduce the value of the currency in foreign exchange markets.

LOS 19.l

Most central banks set target inflation rates, typically 2% to 3%, rather than targeting interest rates as was once common. When inflation is expected to rise above (fall below) the target band, the money supply is decreased (increased) to reduce (increase) economic activity.

Developing economies sometimes target a stable exchange rate for their currency relative to that of a developed economy, selling their currency when its value rises above the target rate and buying their currency with foreign reserves when the rate falls below the target. The developing country must follow a monetary policy that supports the target exchange rate and essentially commits to having the same inflation rate as the developed country.

LOS 19.m

The real trend rate is the long-term sustainable real growth rate of an economy. The neutral interest rate is the sum of the real trend rate and the target inflation rate. Monetary policy is said to be contractionary when the policy rate is above the neutral rate and expansionary when the policy rate is below the neutral rate.

LOS 19.n

Reasons that monetary policy may not work as intended:

- Monetary policy changes may affect inflation expectations to such an extent that long-term interest rates move opposite to short-term interest rates.
- Individuals may be willing to hold greater cash balances without a change in short-term rates (liquidity trap).
- Banks may be unwilling to lend greater amounts, even when they have increased excess reserves.
- Short-term rates cannot be reduced below zero.
- Developing economies face unique challenges in utilizing monetary policy due to undeveloped financial markets, rapid financial innovation, and lack of credibility of the monetary authority.

LOS 19.o

Fiscal policy refers to the taxing and spending policies of the government. Objectives of fiscal policy can include (1) influencing the level of economic activity, (2) redistributing wealth or income, and (3) allocating resources among industries.

LOS 19.p

Fiscal policy tools include spending tools and revenue tools. Spending tools include transfer payments, current spending (goods and services used by government), and capital spending (investment projects funded by government). Revenue tools include direct and indirect taxation.

An advantage of fiscal policy is that indirect taxes can be used to quickly implement social policies and can also be used to quickly raise revenues at a low cost.

Disadvantages of fiscal policy include time lags for implementing changes in direct taxes and time lags for capital spending changes to have an impact.

LOS 19.q

Arguments for being concerned with the size of fiscal deficit:

- Higher future taxes lead to disincentives to work, negatively affecting long-term economic growth.
- Fiscal deficits may not be financed by the market when debt levels are high.
- Crowding-out effect as government borrowing increases interest rates and decreases private sector investment.

Arguments against being concerned with the size of fiscal deficit:

- Debt may be financed by domestic citizens.
- Deficits for capital spending can boost the productive capacity of the economy.
- Fiscal deficits may prompt needed tax reform.
- Ricardian equivalence may prevail: private savings rise in anticipation of the need to repay principal on government debt.
- When the economy is operating below full employment, deficits do not crowd out private investment.

LOS 19.r

Fiscal policy is implemented by governmental changes in taxing and spending policies. Delays in realizing the effects of fiscal policy changes limit their usefulness. Delays can be caused by:

- Recognition lag: Policymakers may not immediately recognize when fiscal policy changes are needed.
- Action lag: Governments take time to enact needed fiscal policy changes.
- Impact lag: Fiscal policy changes take time to affect economic activity.

LOS 19.s

A government has a budget surplus when tax revenues exceed government spending and a deficit when spending exceeds tax revenue.

An increase (decrease) in a government budget surplus is indicative of a contractionary (expansionary) fiscal policy. Similarly, an increase (decrease) in a government budget deficit is indicative of an expansionary (contractionary) fiscal policy.

LOS 19.t

Interaction of monetary and fiscal policies:

Monetary Policy	Fiscal Policy	Interest Rates	Output	Private Sector Spending	Public Sector Spending
Tight	Tight	higher	lower	lower	lower
Easy	Easy	lower	higher	higher	higher
Tight	Easy	higher	higher	lower	higher
Easy	Tight	lower	varies	higher	lower

CONCEPT CHECKERS

1.   Both monetary and fiscal policy are used to:
      A. balance the budget.
      B. achieve economic targets.
      C. redistribute income and wealth.

2.   Which of the following statements is *least accurate*? The existence and use of money:
      A. permits individuals to perform economic transactions.
      B. requires the central bank to control the supply of currency.
      C. increases the efficiency of transactions compared to a barter system.

3.   Assume the Federal Reserve purchases $1 billion of securities in the open market. What is the maximum increase in the money supply that can result from this action, if the required reserve ratio is 15%?
      A. $850 million.
      B. $1.00 billion.
      C. $6.67 billion.

4.   If money neutrality holds, the effect of an increase in the money supply is.
      A. higher prices.
      B. higher output.
      C. lower unemployment.

5.   If the money supply is increasing and velocity is decreasing:
      A. prices will decrease.
      B. real GDP will increase.
      C. the impact on prices and real GDP is uncertain.

6.   According to the quantity theory of money, if nominal GDP is $7 trillion, the price index is 150, and the money supply is $1 trillion, then the velocity of the money supply is *closest* to:
      A. 4.7.
      B. 7.0.
      C. 10.5.

7.   The money supply curve is perfectly inelastic because the:
      A. money supply is independent of interest rates.
      B. money demand schedule is downward-sloping.
      C. money supply is dependent upon interest rates.

8.   The Fisher effect states that the nominal interest rate is equal to the real rate plus:
      A. actual inflation.
      B. average inflation.
      C. expected inflation.

9. A central bank's policy goals *least likely* include:
   A. price stability.
   B. minimizing long-term interest rates.
   C. maximizing the sustainable growth rate of the economy.

10. Which of the following is *least likely* a function or objective of a central bank?
    A. Issuing currency.
    B. Lending money to government agencies.
    C. Keeping inflation within an acceptable range.

11. A country that targets a stable exchange rate with another country's currency *least likely*:
    A. accepts the inflation rate of the other country.
    B. will sell its currency if its foreign exchange value rises.
    C. must also match the money supply growth rate of the other country.

12. A central bank conducts monetary policy primarily by altering the:
    A. policy rate.
    B. inflation rate.
    C. long-term interest rate.

13. Purchases of securities in the open market by the monetary authorities are *least likely* to increase:
    A. excess reserves.
    B. cash in investor accounts.
    C. the interbank lending rate.

14. An increase in the policy rate will *most likely* lead to an increase in:
    A. business investment in fixed assets.
    B. consumer spending on durable goods.
    C. the foreign exchange value of the domestic currency.

15. If a country's inflation rate is below the central bank's target rate, the central bank is *most likely* to:
    A. sell government securities.
    B. increase the reserve requirement.
    C. decrease the overnight lending rate.

16. Suppose an economy has a real trend rate of 2%. The central bank has set an inflation target of 4.5%. To achieve the target, the central bank has set the policy rate at 6%. Monetary policy is *most likely*:
    A. balanced.
    B. expansionary.
    C. contractionary.

17. Monetary policy is *most likely* to fail to achieve its objectives when the economy is:
    A. growing rapidly.
    B. experiencing deflation.
    C. experiencing disinflation.

18. A government enacts a program to subsidize farmers with an expansive spending program of $10 billion. At the same time, the government enacts a $10 billion tax increase over the same period. Which of the following statements *best* describes the impact on aggregate demand?
    A. Lower growth because the tax increase will have a greater effect.
    B. No effect because the tax and spending effects just offset each other.
    C. Higher growth because the spending increase will have a greater effect.

19. A government reduces spending by $50 million. The tax rate is 30%, and consumers exhibit a marginal propensity to consume of 80%. The change in aggregate demand caused by the change in government spending is *closest* to:
    A. –$66 million.
    B. –$114 million.
    C. –$250 million.

20. Sales in the retail sector have been sluggish, and consumer confidence has recently declined, indicating fewer planned purchases. In response, the president sends an expansionary government spending plan to the legislature. The plan is submitted on March 30, and the legislature refines and approves the terms of the spending plan on June 30. What type of fiscal plan is being considered, and what type of delay did the plan experience between March 30 and June 30?

	Fiscal plan	Type of lag
A.	Discretionary	Recognition
B.	Automatic	Action
C.	Discretionary	Action

21. A government is concerned about the timing of the impact of fiscal policy changes and is considering requiring the compilation and reporting of economic statistics weekly, rather than quarterly. The new reporting frequency is intended to decrease the:
    A. action lag.
    B. impact lag.
    C. recognition lag.

22. In the presence of tight monetary policy and loose fiscal policy, the *most likely* effect on interest rates and the private sector share in GDP are:

	Interest rates	Share of private sector
A.	lower	lower
B.	higher	higher
C.	higher	lower

ANSWERS – CONCEPT CHECKERS

1. **B**   Both monetary and fiscal policies primarily strive to achieve economic targets such as inflation and GDP growth. Balancing the budget is not a goal for monetary policy and is a potential outcome of fiscal policy. Fiscal policy (but not monetary policy) may secondarily be used as a tool to redistribute income and wealth.

2. **B**   Money functions as a unit of account, a medium of exchange, and a store of value. Money existed long before the idea of central banking was conceived.

3. **C**   The money multiplier is 1 / 0.15 = 6.67, so the open market purchase can increase the money supply by a maximum of $6.67 billion.

4. **A**   Money neutrality is the theory that changes in the money supply do not affect real output or the velocity of money. Therefore, an increase in the money supply can only increase the price level.

5. **C**   Given the equation of exchange, MV = PY, an increase in the money supply is consistent with an increase in nominal GDP (PY). However, a decrease in velocity is consistent with a decrease in nominal GDP. Unless we know the size of the changes in the two variables, there is no way to tell what the net impact is on real GDP (Y) and prices (P).

6. **B**   The equation of exchange is MV = PY.

Nominal GDP = PY, so that MV = nominal GDP.

Therefore, ($1.0 trillion)(V) = $7.0 trillion.

V = $7.0 trillion / $1.0 trillion

V = 7.0

7. **A**   The money supply schedule is vertical because the money supply is independent of interest rates. Central banks control the money supply.

8. **C**   The Fisher effect states that nominal interest rates are equal to the real interest rate plus the expected inflation rate.

9. **B**   Central bank goals often include maximum employment, which is interpreted as the maximum sustainable growth rate of the economy; stable prices; and *moderate* (not minimum) long-term interest rates.

10. **B**   Lending money to government agencies is not typically a function of a central bank. Central bank functions include controlling the country's money supply to keep inflation within acceptable levels and promoting a sustainable rate of economic growth, as well as issuing currency and regulating banks.

11. **C**   The money supply growth rate may need to be adjusted to keep the exchange rate within acceptable bounds, but is not necessarily the same as that of the other country. The other two statements are true.

12. **A**   The primary method by which a central bank conducts monetary policy is through changes in the target short-term rate or policy rate.

13. **C** Open market purchases by monetary authorities *decrease* the interbank lending rate by increasing excess reserves that banks can lend to one another and therefore increasing their willingness to lend.

14. **C** An increase in the policy rate is likely to increase longer-term interest rates, causing decreases in consumption spending on durable goods and business investment in plant and equipment. The increase in rates, however, makes investment in the domestic economy more attractive to foreign investors, increasing demand for the domestic currency and causing the currency to appreciate.

15. **C** Decreasing the overnight lending rate would add reserves to the banking system, which would encourage bank lending, expand the money supply, reduce interest rates, and allow GDP growth and the rate of inflation to increase. Selling government securities or increasing the reserve requirement would have the opposite effect, reducing the money supply and decreasing the inflation rate.

16. **B** neutral rate = trend rate + inflation target = 2% + 4.5% = 6.5%

    Because the policy rate is less than the neutral rate, monetary policy is expansionary.

17. **B** Monetary policy has limited ability to act effectively against deflation because the policy rate cannot be reduced below zero and demand for money may be highly elastic (liquidity trap).

18. **C** The amount of the spending program exactly offsets the amount of the tax increase, leaving the budget unaffected. The multiplier for government spending is greater than the multiplier for a tax increase. Therefore, the balanced budget multiplier is positive. All of the government spending enters the economy as increased expenditure, whereas spending is reduced by only a portion of the tax increase.

19. **B** fiscal multiplier = 1 / [1 – MPC (1 – T)] = 1 / [1 – 0.80(1 – 0.3)] = 2.27

    change in government spending = –$50 million

    change in aggregate demand = –(50 × 2.27) = –$113.64 million

20. **C** The expansionary plan initiated by the president and approved by the legislature is an example of discretionary fiscal policy. The lag from the time of the submission (March 30) through time of the vote (June 30) is known as action lag. It took the legislature three months to write and pass the necessary laws.

21. **C** More frequent and current economic data would make it easier for authorities to monitor the economy and to recognize problems. The reduction in the time between economic reports should reduce the recognition lag.

22. **C** Tight monetary policy and loose fiscal policy both lead to higher interest rates. Tight monetary policy decreases private sector growth, while loose fiscal policy expands the public sector, reducing the overall share of private sector in the GDP.

INTERNATIONAL TRADE AND CAPITAL FLOWS

EXAM FOCUS

International trade and currency exchange rates are key topics for both Level I and Level II. First, learn how comparative advantage results in a welfare gain from international trade and the two models of the sources of comparative advantage. Learn the types of trade restrictions and their effects on domestic price and quantity. For the balance of payments, focus on how a surplus or deficit in the broadly defined capital account must offset a deficit or surplus in the merchandise trade account. Finally, focus on how the difference between domestic income and expenditures and the difference between domestic savings and investment are related to a country's balance of trade.

WARM-UP: INTERNATIONAL TRADE

Before we address specific topics and learning outcomes, it will help to define some terms as follows.

Imports: Goods and services that firms, individuals, and governments purchase from producers in other countries.

Exports: Goods and services that firms, individuals, and governments from other countries purchase from domestic producers.

Autarky or **closed economy:** A country that does not trade with other countries.

Free trade: A government places no restrictions or charges on import and export activity.

Trade protection: A government places restrictions, limits, or charges on exports or imports.

World price: The price of a good or service in world markets for those to whom trade is not restricted.

Domestic price: The price of a good or service in the domestic country, which may be equal to the world price if free trade is permitted or different from the world price when the domestic country restricts trade.

Net exports: The value of a country's exports minus the value of its imports over some period.

Trade surplus: Net exports are positive; the value of the goods and services a country exports are greater than the value of the goods and services it imports.

Trade deficit: Net exports are negative; the value of the goods and services a country exports is less than the value of the goods and services it imports.

Terms of trade: The ratio of an index of the prices of a country's exports to an index of the prices of its imports expressed relative to a base value of 100. If a country's terms of trade are currently 102, the prices of the goods it exports have risen relative to the prices of the goods it imports since the base period.

Foreign direct investment: Ownership of productive resources (land, factories, natural resources) in a foreign country.

Multinational corporation: A firm that has made foreign direct investment in one or more foreign countries, operating production facilities and subsidiary companies in foreign countries.

LOS 20.a: Compare gross domestic product and gross national product.

CFA® Program Curriculum, Volume 2, page 422

Gross domestic product over a period, typically a year, is the total value of goods and services produced within a country's borders. **Gross national product** is similar but measures the total value of goods and services produced by the labor and capital of a country's citizens. The difference is due to non-citizen incomes of foreigners working within a country, the income of citizens who work in other countries, the income of foreign capital invested within a country, and the income of capital supplied by its citizens to foreign countries. The income to capital owned by foreigners invested within a country is included in the domestic country's GDP but not in its GNP. The income of a country's citizens working abroad is included in its GNP but not in its GDP.

GDP is more closely related to economic activity within a country and so to its employment and growth.

LOS 20.b: Describe benefits and costs of international trade.

CFA® Program Curriculum, Volume 2, page 429

The benefits of trade are not hard to understand. As an example, consider China, and really Asia as a whole, which has had rapidly growing exports to the United States and other countries. The benefit to the importing countries has been lower-cost goods, from textiles to electronics. The benefits to the Chinese economy have been in increasing employment, increasing wages for workers, and the profits from its export products.

The costs of trade are primarily borne by those in domestic industries that compete with imported goods. Textile workers who have lost their jobs in the United States, as more and more textiles are imported, are certainly worse off in the short run. As other industries, such as health care, have grown, these workers have had to retrain to qualify for the new jobs in those fields. At the same time, U.S. firms that produce textile products using capital and technology intensive production methods have expanded. We address the reasons for this and the underlying economic theory in this topic review.

Overall, economics tells us that the benefits of trade are greater than the costs for economies as a whole, so that the winners could conceivably compensate the losers and still be better off. We now turn to the economic theory that supports this view.

LOS 20.c: Distinguish between comparative advantage and absolute advantage.

CFA® Program Curriculum, Volume 2, page 433

A country is said to have an **absolute advantage** in the production of a good if it can produce the good at lower cost in terms of resources than that of another country. A country is said to have a **comparative advantage** in the production of a good if its opportunity cost in terms of other goods that could be produced instead is lower than that of another country. Economic analysis tells us that regardless of which country has an absolute advantage, there are potential gains from trade as long as the opportunity costs of one good in terms of another are different.

This analysis was first published by David Ricardo in 1817. He used the example of the production of cloth and wine in England and Portugal. The costs of labor to produce one unit of cloth and one unit of wine for both countries were given as shown in Figure 1.

Figure 1: Labor Costs Per Unit

	Cloth	*Wine*
England	100	110
Portugal	90	80

Ricardo argued that, in the absence of trading costs, England could trade cloth for wine and, by doing so, get wine for 100 instead of 110. Portugal would get cloth for 80 (the cost in Portugal of the traded wine), and both countries would be better off. Note that Portugal has an absolute advantage in the production of both goods but a comparative advantage in the production of wine. In England, the opportunity cost of one unit of wine is 110 / 100 = 1.10 units of cloth. In Portugal, the opportunity cost of one unit of wine is 80 / 90 = 0.89 units of cloth.

Since Portugal has a comparative advantage in the production of wine, England must have a comparative advantage in the production of cloth. We can confirm this by noting that the opportunity cost of cloth is 100 / 110 = 0.91 units of wine in England and 90 / 80 = 1.125 units of wine in Portugal.

The conclusion is that, in the absence of trading costs, trade can make both countries better off by increasing total consumption of both goods in both countries. However, if trading costs are high enough, they will prevent gains from trade. An important point of the analysis is that whether one country has an absolute advantage in the production of one or both goods, as long as the opportunity costs of the goods in each country are different, there are possible gains from trade.

An example will illustrate the gains from trade in terms of expanded consumption opportunities for two countries. Figures 2 and 3 show the *production possibility frontiers* (PPF) for two countries, Alton and Borton, for two generic goods, food and machinery.

 Professor's Note: Ricardo's example is stated in terms of input costs (labor) per unit of output. The example that follows is stated in terms of output that can be produced from a given amount of input. In either form, the goal is to determine the opportunity cost of production: how much of one good each country must give up to produce one more unit of the other good.

Figure 2: Production Possibility Frontier for Alton

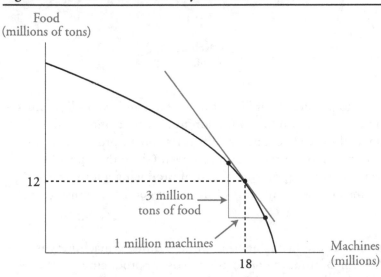

Figure 3: Production Possibility Frontier for Borton

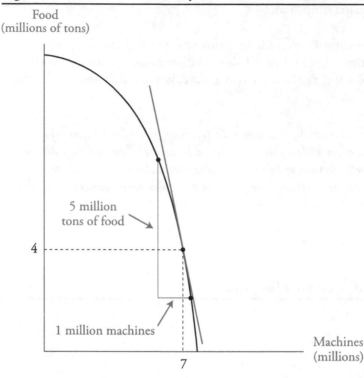

Without trade, Alton chooses to produce 12 million tons of food and 18 million units of machinery, while Borton chooses to produce 4 million tons of food and 7 million units of machinery. The slope of the each country's PPF at its chosen production point represents the opportunity cost of food in terms of machinery. Given their possible production levels of the two goods, the opportunity cost of producing a unit of one good can be expressed in terms of how many units of the other good they must give up to produce it.

For Alton, the opportunity cost of producing another million units of machinery is 3 million tons of food, while for Borton, the opportunity cost of producing another million units of machinery is 5 million tons of food. The opportunity costs of food are simply the reciprocals of these amounts. For Alton, the opportunity cost of producing another million tons of food is 1/3 million units of machinery, and for Borton, the opportunity cost of producing another million tons of food is 1/5 million units of machinery. If one country has a lower opportunity cost of producing one good, the other country must have a comparative advantage in the production of the other good. Alton has a comparative advantage in the production of (the lowest opportunity cost of producing) machinery, and Borton has a comparative advantage in the production of food. Next we will show that, as long as their opportunity costs of production differ, trade will allow both countries to consume more than they can without trade.

Since Alton has a comparative advantage in the production of machinery, it will be advantageous for Alton to produce more machinery and to trade with Borton for food. For example, Alton could produce 2 million more units of machinery and 6 million tons less food. Borton could produce 6 million more tons of food and, given that their opportunity cost of a million tons of food is one-fifth of a million units of machinery, produce 1.2 million fewer units of machinery.

The table in Figure 4 illustrates the total output of both countries with and without specialization and trade.

Figure 4: Gain From Trade

	Without Trade		With Trade	
	Machinery	*Food*	*Machinery*	*Food*
Alton	18 million	12 million tons	20.0 million	6 million tons
Borton	7 million	4 million tons	5.8 million	10 million tons
Total	25 million	16 million tons	25.8 million	16 million tons

When each country specializes in the good for which they have a comparative advantage and trades with the other, there are clear gains in our example. Total food production can remain at 16 million tons while the total output of machinery is increased by 0.8 million units. Alton will export machinery, since they are the low (opportunity) cost producer of machinery, and import food from Borton. Borton has a comparative advantage in the production of food and will export food to Alton and import Alton-produced machinery.

How the gains from specialization and trade will be shared between the two countries is not determined here, but clearly there is a possible exchange that will allow both countries to enjoy a combination of food and machinery that they could not reach on their own without trade. In terms of our PPF graphs, each country can consume at a point *outside* its PPF through specialization and trade. That's the important point here: as long as opportunity costs differ, two countries can both benefit from trade.

LOS 20.d: Explain the Ricardian and Heckscher–Ohlin models of trade and the source(s) of comparative advantage in each model.

CFA® Program Curriculum, Volume 2, page 440

The **Ricardian model of trade** has only one factor of production—labor. The source of differences in production costs in Ricardo's model is *differences in labor productivity* due to differences in technology.

Heckscher and Ohlin presented a model in which there are two factors of production—capital and labor. The source of comparative advantage (differences in opportunity costs) in this model is *differences in the relative amounts of each factor* the countries possess. We can view the England and Portugal example in these terms by assuming that England has more capital (machinery) compared to labor than Portugal. Additionally, we need to assume that cloth production is more capital intensive than wine production. The result of their analysis is that the country that has more capital will specialize in the capital intensive good and trade for the less capital intensive good with the country that has relatively more labor and less capital.

In the **Heckscher-Ohlin model**, there is a redistribution of wealth within each country between labor and the owners of capital. The price of the relatively less scarce (more available) factor of production in each country will increase so that owners of capital will earn more in England, and workers will earn more in Portugal compared to what they were without trade. This is easy to understand in the context of prices of the two goods. The good that a country imports will fall in price (that is why they import it), and the good that a country exports will rise in price. In our example, this means that the price of wine falls, and the price of cloth rises in England. Because with trade, more of the capital-intensive good, cloth, is produced in England, demand for capital and the price of capital will increase in England. As a result, capital receives more income at the expense of labor in England. In Portugal, increasing the production of wine (which is labor intensive) increases the demand for and price of labor, and workers gain at the expense of the owners of capital.

Professor's Note: Remember that the model named after one economist has one factor of production, and the model named after two economists has two factors of production.

LOS 20.e: Compare types of trade and capital restrictions and their economic implications.

CFA® Program Curriculum, Volume 2, page 442

There are many reasons (at least stated reasons) why governments impose trade restrictions. Some have support among economists as conceivably valid in terms of increasing a country's welfare, while others have little or no support from economic theory. Some of the reasons for trade restrictions that have support from economists are:

- *Infant industry.* Protection from foreign competition is given to new industries to give them an opportunity to grow to an internationally competitive scale and get up the learning curve in terms of efficient production methods.
- *National security.* Even if imports are cheaper, it may be in the country's best interest to protect producers of goods crucial to the country's national defense so that those goods are available domestically in the event of conflict.

Other arguments for trade restrictions that have little support in theory are:

- *Protecting domestic jobs.* While some jobs are certainly lost, and some groups and regions are negatively affected by free trade, other jobs (in export industries or growing domestic goods and services industries) will be created, and prices for domestic consumers will be less without import restrictions.
- *Protecting domestic industries.* Industry firms often use political influence to get protection from foreign competition, usually to the detriment of consumers, who pay higher prices.

Other arguments include retaliation for foreign trade restrictions; government collection of tariffs (like taxes on imported goods); countering the effects of government subsidies paid to foreign producers; and preventing foreign exports at less than their cost of production (*dumping*).

Types of trade restrictions include:

- **Tariffs:** Taxes on imported good collected by the government.
- **Quotas:** Limits on the amount of imports allowed over some period.
- **Export subsidies:** Government payments to firms that export goods.
- **Minimum domestic content:** Requirement that some percentage of product content must be from the domestic country.
- **Voluntary export restraint:** A country voluntarily restricts the amount of a good that can be exported, often in the hope of avoiding tariffs or quotas imposed by their trading partners.

Economic Implications of Trade Restrictions

We will now examine the effects of the primary types of trade restrictions, tariffs, and subsidies.

A **tariff** placed on an imported good increases the domestic price, decreases the quantity imported, and increases the quantity supplied domestically. Domestic producers gain, foreign exporters lose, and the domestic government gains by the amount of the tariff revenues.

A **quota** restricts the quantity of a good imported to the quota amount. Domestic producers gain, and domestic consumers lose from an increase in the domestic price. The right to export a specific quantity to the domestic country is granted by the domestic government, which may or may not charge for the import licenses to foreign countries. If the import licenses are sold, the domestic government gains the revenue.

We illustrate the overall welfare effects of quotas and tariffs for a small country in Figure 5. We define a quota that is equivalent to a given tariff as a quota that will result in the same decrease in the quantity of a good imported as the tariff. Defined this way, a tariff and an equivalent quota both increase the domestic price from P_{world}, the price that prevails with no trade restriction, to $P_{protection}$.

At P_{world}, prior to any restriction, the domestic quantity supplied is QS_1, and the domestic quantity demanded is QD_1, with the difference equal to the quantity imported, $QD_1 - QS_1$. Placing a tariff on imports increases the domestic price to $P_{protection}$, increases the domestic quantity supplied to QS_2, and decreases the domestic quantity demanded to QD_2. The difference is the new quantity imported. An equivalent quota will have the same effect, decreasing the quantity imported to $QD_2 - QS_2$.

The entire shaded area in Figure 5 represents the loss of consumer surplus in the domestic economy. The portion with vertical lines, the area to the left of the domestic supply curve between $P_{protection}$ and P_{world}, represents the gain in the producer surplus of domestic producers. The portion with horizontal lines, the area bounded by $QD_2 - QS_2$ and $P_{protection} - P_{world}$, represents the gain to the domestic government from tariff revenue. The two remaining triangular areas are the deadweight loss from the restriction on free trade.

In the case of a quota, if the domestic government collects the full value of the import licenses, the result is the same as for a tariff. If the domestic government does not charge for the import licenses, this amount is a gain to those foreign exporters who receive the import licenses under the quota and are termed **quota rents**.

Figure 5: Effects of Tariffs and Quotas

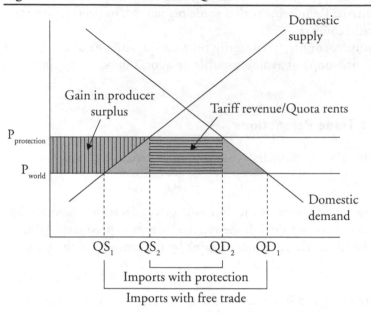

In terms of overall economic gains from trade, the deadweight loss is the amount of lost welfare from the imposition of the quota or tariff. From the viewpoint of the domestic country, the loss in consumer surplus is only partially offset by the gains in domestic producer surplus and the collection of tariff revenue.

If none of the quota rents are captured by the domestic government, the overall welfare loss to the domestic economy is greater by the amount of the quota rents. It is the entire difference between the gain in producer surplus and the loss of consumer surplus.

A **voluntary export restraint** (VER) is just as it sounds. It refers to a voluntary agreement by a government to limit the quantity of a good that can be exported. VERs are another way of protecting the domestic producers in the importing country. They result in a welfare loss to the importing country equal to that of an equivalent quota with no government charge for the import licenses; that is, no capture of the quota rents.

Export subsidies are payments by a government to its country's exporters. Export subsidies benefit producers (exporters) of the good but increase prices and reduce consumer surplus in the exporting country. In a small country, the price will increase by the amount of the subsidy to equal the world price plus the subsidy. In the case of a large exporter of the good, the world price decreases and some benefits from the subsidy accrue to foreign consumers, while foreign producers are negatively affected.

Most of the effects of all four of these protectionist policies are the same. With respect to the domestic (importing) country, import quotas, tariffs, and VERs all:

- Reduce imports.
- Increase price.
- Decrease consumer surplus.
- Increase domestic quantity supplied.
- Increase producer surplus.

With one exception, all will decrease national welfare. Quotas and tariffs in a large country could increase national welfare under a specific set of assumptions, primarily because for a country that imports a large amount of the good, setting a quota or tariff could reduce the world price for the good.

Capital Restrictions

Some countries impose **capital restrictions** on the flow of financial capital across borders. Restrictions include outright prohibition of investment in the domestic country by foreigners, prohibition of or taxes on the income earned on foreign investments by domestic citizens, prohibition of foreign investment in certain domestic industries, and restrictions on repatriation of earnings of foreign entities operating in a country.

Overall, capital restrictions are thought to decrease economic welfare. However, over the short term, they have helped developing countries avoid the impact of great inflows of foreign capital during periods of optimistic expansion and the impact of large outflows of foreign capital during periods of correction and market unease or outright panic. Even these short-term benefits may not offset longer-term costs if the country is excluded from international markets for financial capital flows.

LOS 20.f: Explain motivations for and advantages of trading blocs, common markets, and economic unions.

CFA® Program Curriculum, Volume 2, page 448

There are various types of agreements among countries with respect to trade policy. The essence of all of them is to reduce trade barriers among the countries. Reductions in trade restrictions among countries have some, by now familiar, positive and negative effects on economic welfare. The positive effects result from increased trade according to comparative advantage, as well as increased competition among firms in member countries. The negative effects result because some firms, some industries, and some groups of workers will see their wealth and incomes decrease. Workers in affected industries may need to learn new skills to get new jobs.

On balance, economic welfare is improved by reducing or eliminating trade restrictions. Note, however, that to the extent that a trade agreement increases trade restrictions on imports from non-member countries, economic welfare gains are reduced and, in an extreme case, could be outweighed by the costs such restrictions impose. This could result if restrictions on trade with non-member countries increases a country's (unrestricted) imports from a member that has higher prices than the country's previous imports from a non-member.

We list these types of agreements, generally referred to as **trading blocs** or **regional trading agreements** (RTA), in order of their degrees of integration.

Free Trade Areas

1. All barriers to import and export of goods and services among member countries are removed.

Customs Union

1. All barriers to import and export of goods and services among member countries are removed.
2. All countries adopt a common set of trade restrictions with non-members.

Common Market

1. All barriers to import and export of goods and services among the countries are removed.
2. All countries adopt a common set of trade restrictions with non-members.
3. All barriers to the movement of labor and capital goods among member countries are removed.

Economic Union

1. All barriers to import and export of goods and services among the countries are removed.
2. All countries adopt a common set of trade restrictions with non-members.
3. All barriers to the movement of labor and capital goods among member countries are removed.
4. Member countries establish common institutions and economic policy for the union.

Monetary Union

1. All barriers to import and export of goods and services among the countries are removed.
2. All countries adopt a common set of trade restrictions with non-members.
3. All barriers to the movement of labor and capital goods among member countries are removed.
4. Member countries establish common institutions and economic policy for the union.
5. Member countries adopt a single currency.

The North American Free Trade Agreement (NAFTA) is an example of a free trade area, the European Union (EU) is an example of an economic union, and the euro zone is an example of a monetary union.

LOS 20.g: Describe common objectives of capital restrictions imposed by governments.

CFA® Program Curriculum, Volume 2, page 452

Governments sometimes place restrictions on the flow of investment capital into their country, out of their country, or both. Commonly cited objectives of capital flow restrictions include the following:

- *Reduce the volatility of domestic asset prices.* In times of macroeconomic crisis, capital flows out of the country can drive down asset prices drastically, especially prices of liquid assets such as stocks and bonds. With no restrictions on inflows or outflows of foreign investment capital, the asset markets of countries with economies that are small relative to the amount of foreign investment can be quite volatile over a country's economic cycle.
- *Maintain fixed exchange rates.* For countries with fixed exchange rate targets, limiting flows of foreign investment capital makes it easier to meet the exchange rate target and, therefore, to be able to use monetary and fiscal policy to pursue only the economic goals for the domestic economy.
- *Keep domestic interest rates low.* By restricting the outflow of investment capital, countries can keep their domestic interest rates low and manage the domestic economy with monetary policy, as investors cannot pursue higher rates in foreign countries. China is an example of a country with a fixed exchange rate regime where restrictions on capital flows allow policymakers to maintain the target exchange rate as well as to pursue a monetary policy independent of concerns about its effect on currency exchange rates.
- *Protect strategic industries.* Governments sometimes prohibit investment by foreign entities in industries considered to be important for national security, such as the telecommunications and defense industries.

LOS 20.h: Describe the balance of payments accounts including their components.

CFA® Program Curriculum, Volume 2, page 455

When a country's firms and individuals pay for their purchases of foreign goods, services, and financial assets, they must buy the currencies of the foreign countries in order to accomplish those transactions. Similarly, payment for sales of goods, services, and financial assets to foreigners requires them to purchase the currency of the domestic country. With adjustment for changes in foreign debt to the domestic country and domestic debt to foreign countries, these amounts must balance each other.

According to the U.S. Federal Reserve, "The BOP [**balance of payments**] includes the **current account**, which mainly measures the flows of goods and services; the **capital account**, which consists of capital transfers and the acquisition and disposal of non-produced, non-financial assets; and the **financial account**, which records investment flows."[1]

---

1. Federal Reserve Bank of New York, *Fedpoints*, May 2009. Emphasis added.

Drawing on the N.Y. Fed's explanation, the items recorded in each account are as follows.

Current Account

The current account comprises three sub-accounts:

- **Merchandise and services.** Merchandise consists of all raw materials and manufactured goods bought, sold, or given away. Services include tourism, transportation, and business and engineering services, as well as fees from patents and copyrights on new technology, software, books, and movies.
- **Income receipts** include foreign income from dividends on stock holdings and interest on debt securities.
- **Unilateral transfers** are one-way transfers of assets, such as money received from those working abroad and direct foreign aid. In the case of foreign aid and gifts, the capital account of the donor nation is debited.

Capital Account

The capital account comprises two sub-accounts:

- **Capital transfers** include debt forgiveness and goods and financial assets that migrants bring when they come to a country or take with them when they leave. Capital transfers also include the transfer of title to fixed assets and of funds linked to the purchase or sale of fixed assets, gift and inheritance taxes, death duties, and uninsured damage to fixed assets.
- **Sales and purchases of non-financial assets** that are not produced assets include rights to natural resources and intangible assets, such as patents, copyrights, trademarks, franchises, and leases.

Financial Account

The financial account comprises two sub-accounts:

- **Government-owned assets abroad** include gold, foreign currencies, foreign securities, reserve position in the International Monetary Fund, credits and other long-term assets, direct foreign investment, and claims against foreign banks.
- **Foreign-owned assets in the country** are divided into foreign official assets and other foreign assets in the domestic country. These assets include domestic government and corporate securities, direct investment in the domestic country, domestic country currency, and domestic liabilities to foreigners reported by domestic banks.

A country that has imports valued more than its exports is said to have a *current account (trade) deficit*, while countries with more exports than imports are said to have a *current account surplus*. For a country with a trade deficit, it must be balanced by a net surplus in the capital and financial accounts. As a result, investment analysts often think of all financing flows as a single capital account that combines items in the capital and financial accounts. Thinking in this way, any deficit in the current account must be made up by a surplus in the combined capital account. That is, the excess of imports over exports must be offset by sales of assets and debt incurred to foreign entities. A current account surplus is similarly offset by purchases of foreign physical or financial assets.

LOS 20.i: Explain how decisions by consumers, firms, and governments affect the balance of payments.

CFA® Program Curriculum, Volume 2, page 460

The primary influences referred to here are on the current account deficit or surplus. If a country's net savings (both government savings and private savings) are less than the amount of investment in domestic capital, this investment must be financed by foreign borrowing. Foreign borrowing results in a capital account surplus, which means there is a trade deficit.

We can write the relation between the trade deficit, saving, and domestic investment as:

X – M = private savings + government savings – investment

Lower levels of private saving, larger government deficits, and high rates of domestic investment all tend to result in or increase a current account deficit. The intuition here is that low private or government savings in relation to private investment in domestic capital requires foreign investment in domestic capital.

We can make a distinction, however, between a trade deficit resulting from high government or private consumption and one resulting from high private investment in capital. In the first case, borrowing from foreign countries to finance high consumption (low savings) increases the domestic country's liabilities without any increase to its future productive power. In the second case, borrowing from foreign countries to finance a high level of private investment in domestic capital, the added liability is accompanied by an increase in future productive power because of the investment in capital.

LOS 20.j: Describe functions and objectives of the international organizations that facilitate trade, including the World Bank, the International Monetary Fund, and the World Trade Organization.

CFA® Program Curriculum, Volume 2, page 467

Perhaps the best way to understand the roles of the organizations designed to facilitate trade is to examine their own statements.

According to the **International Monetary Fund** (IMF; more available at *www.IMF.org*):

Article I of the Articles of Agreement sets out the IMF's main goals:

- promoting international monetary cooperation;
- facilitating the expansion and balanced growth of international trade;
- promoting exchange stability;
- assisting in the establishment of a multilateral system of payments; and
- making resources available (with adequate safeguards) to members experiencing balance of payments difficulties.

According to the **World Bank** (more available at *www.WorldBank.org*):

> The World Bank is a vital source of financial and technical assistance to developing countries around the world. Our mission is to fight poverty with passion and professionalism for lasting results and to help people help themselves and their environment by providing resources, sharing knowledge, building capacity and forging partnerships in the public and private sectors.
>
> We are not a bank in the common sense; we are made up of two unique development institutions owned by 187 member countries: the International Bank for Reconstruction and Development (IBRD) and the International Development Association (IDA).
>
> Each institution plays a different but collaborative role in advancing the vision of inclusive and sustainable globalization. The IBRD aims to reduce poverty in middle-income and creditworthy poorer countries, while IDA focuses on the world's poorest countries.
>
> …Together, we provide low-interest loans, interest-free credits and grants to developing countries for a wide array of purposes that include investments in education, health, public administration, infrastructure, financial and private sector development, agriculture and environmental and natural resource management.

According to the **World Trade Organization** (WTO; more available at *www.WTO.org*):

> The World Trade Organization (WTO) is the only international organization dealing with the global rules of trade between nations. Its main function is to ensure that trade flows as smoothly, predictably and freely as possible.
>
> …Trade friction is channeled into the WTO's dispute settlement process where the focus is on interpreting agreements and commitments, and how to ensure that countries' trade policies conform with them. That way, the risk of disputes spilling over into political or military conflict is reduced.
>
> …At the heart of the system—known as the multilateral trading system—are the WTO's agreements, negotiated and signed by a large majority of the world's trading nations, and ratified in their parliaments. These agreements are the legal ground-rules for international commerce. Essentially, they are contracts, guaranteeing member countries important trade rights. They also bind governments to keep their trade policies within agreed limits to everybody's benefit.

KEY CONCEPTS

LOS 20.a

Gross domestic product is the total value of goods and services produced within a country's borders. Gross national product measures the total value of goods and services produced by the labor and capital supplied by a country's citizens, regardless of where the production takes place.

LOS 20.b

Free trade among countries increases overall economic welfare. Countries can benefit from trade because one country can specialize in the production of an export good and benefit from economies of scale. Economic welfare can also be increased by greater product variety, more competition, and a more efficient allocation of resources.

Costs of free trade are primarily losses to those in domestic industries that lose business to foreign competition, especially less efficient producers who leave an industry. While other domestic industries will benefit from freer trade policies, unemployment may increase over the period in which workers are retrained for jobs in the expanding industries. Some argue that greater income inequality may result, but overall the gains from liberalization of trade policies are thought to exceed the costs, so that the winners could conceivably compensate the losers and still be better off.

LOS 20.c

A country is said to have an absolute advantage in the production of a good if it can produce the good at lower cost in terms of resources relative to another country.

A country is said to have a comparative advantage in the production of a good if its opportunity cost in terms of other goods that could be produced instead is lower than that of another country.

LOS 20.d

The Ricardian model of trade has only one factor of production—labor. The source of differences in production costs and comparative advantage in Ricardo's model is differences in labor productivity due to differences in technology.

Heckscher and Ohlin presented a model in which there are two factors of production—capital and labor. The source of comparative advantage (differences in opportunity costs) in this model is differences in the relative amounts of each factor that countries possess.

LOS 20.e

Types of trade restrictions include:

- Tariffs: Taxes on imported good collected by the government.
- Quotas: Limits on the amount of imports allowed over some period.
- Minimum domestic content: Requirement that some percentage of product content must be from the domestic country.
- Voluntary export restraints: A country voluntarily restricts the amount of a good that can be exported, often in the hope of avoiding tariffs or quotas imposed by their trading partners.

Within each importing country, all of these restrictions will tend to:

- Increase prices of imports and decrease quantities of imports.
- Increase demand for and quantity supplied of domestically produced goods.
- Increase producer's surplus and decrease consumer surplus.

Export subsidies decrease export prices and benefit importing countries at the expense of the government of the exporting country.

Restrictions on the flow of financial capital across borders include outright prohibition of investment in the domestic country by foreigners, prohibition of or taxes on the income earned on foreign investments by domestic citizens, prohibition of foreign investment in certain domestic industries, and restrictions on repatriation of earnings of foreign entities operating in a country.

LOS 20.f

Trade agreements, which increase economic welfare by facilitating trade among member countries, take the following forms:

- Free trade area: All barriers to the import and export of goods and services among member countries are removed.
- Customs union: Member countries *also* adopt a common set of trade restrictions with non-members.
- Common market: Member countries *also* remove all barriers to the movement of labor and capital goods among members.
- Economic union: Member countries *also* establish common institutions and economic policy for the union.
- Monetary union: Member countries *also* adopt a single currency.

LOS 20.g

Commonly cited objectives of capital flow restrictions include:

- Reducing the volatility of domestic asset prices.
- Maintaining fixed exchange rates.
- Keeping domestic interest rates low and enabling greater independence regarding monetary policy.
- Protecting strategic industries from foreign ownership.

LOS 20.h

The balance of payments refers to the fact that increases in a country's assets and decreases in its liabilities must equal (balance with) decreases in its assets and increases in its liabilities. These financial flows are classified into three types:

- The current account includes imports and exports of merchandise and services, foreign income from dividends on stock holdings and interest on debt securities, and unilateral transfers such as money received from those working abroad and direct foreign aid.
- The capital account includes debt forgiveness, assets that migrants bring to or take away from a country, transfer of funds for the purchase or sale of fixed assets, and purchases of non-financial assets, including rights to natural resources, patents, copyrights, trademarks, franchises, and leases.
- The financial account includes government-owned assets abroad such as gold, foreign currencies and securities, and direct foreign investment and claims against foreign banks. The financial account also includes foreign-owned assets in the country, domestic government and corporate securities, direct investment in the domestic country, and domestic country currency.

Overall, any surplus (deficit) in the current account must be offset by a deficit (surplus) in the capital and financial accounts.

LOS 20.i

In equilibrium, we have the relationship:

exports – imports = private savings + government savings – domestic investment

When total savings is less than domestic investment, exports must be less than imports so that there is a deficit in the current account. Lower levels of private saving, larger government deficits, and high rates of domestic investment all tend to result in or increase a current account deficit. The intuition here is that low private or government savings in relation to private investment in domestic capital requires foreign investment in domestic capital.

LOS 20.j

The International Monetary Fund facilitates trade by promoting international monetary cooperation and exchange rate stability, assists in setting up international payments systems, and makes resources available to member countries with balance of payments problems.

The World Bank provides low-interest loans, interest-free credits, and grants to developing countries for many specific purposes. It also provides resources and knowledge and helps form private/public partnerships with the overall goal of fighting poverty.

The World Trade Organization has the goal of ensuring that trade flows freely and works smoothly. Its main focus is on instituting, interpreting, and enforcing a number of multilateral trade agreements that detail global trade policies for a large majority of the world's trading nations.

CONCEPT CHECKERS

1. The income from a financial investment in Country P by a citizen of Country Q is *most likely* included in:
    A. Country P's GDP but not its GNP.
    B. Country Q's GNP and GDP.
    C. Country P's GDP and GNP

2. Which of the following effects is *most likely* to occur in a country that increases its openness to international trade?
    A. Increased prices of consumer goods.
    B. Greater specialization in domestic output.
    C. Decreased employment in exporting industries.

3. Which of the following statements about international trade is *least accurate*? If two countries have different opportunity costs of production for two goods, by engaging in trade:
    A. each country gains by importing the good for which it has a comparative advantage.
    B. each country can achieve a level of consumption outside its domestic production possibility frontier.
    C. the low opportunity cost producer of each good will export to the high opportunity cost producer of that good.

4. With regard to the Ricardian and Heckscher-Ohlin models of international trade, the amount of capital relative to labor within a country is a factor in:
    A. both of these models.
    B. neither of these models.
    C. only one of these models.

5. An agreement with another country to limit the volume of goods and services sold to them is *best* described as a:
    A. quota.
    B. voluntary export restraint.
    C. minimum domestic content rule.

6. The *least likely* result of import quotas and voluntary export restraints is:
    A. increased revenue for the government.
    B. a decrease in the quantity of imports of the product.
    C. a shift in production toward higher-cost suppliers.

7. Which of the following groups would be *most likely* to suffer losses from the imposition of a tariff on steel imports?
    A. Domestic steel producers.
    B. Workers in the domestic auto industry.
    C. Workers in the domestic steel industry.

8. The *most likely* motivation for establishing a trading bloc is to:
    A. increase economic welfare in the member countries.
    B. increase tariff revenue for the member governments.
    C. protect domestic industries in the member economies.

9. In which type of regional trade agreement are economic policies conducted independently by the member countries, while labor and capital are free to move among member countries?
    A. Free trade area.
    B. Common market.
    C. Economic union.

10. Which of the following is *least likely* a component of the current account?
    A. Unilateral transfers.
    B. Payments for fixed assets.
    C. Payments for goods and services.

11. A current account deficit is *most likely* to decrease as a result of an increase in:
    A. domestic savings.
    B. private investment.
    C. the fiscal budget deficit.

12. Which international organization is primarily concerned with providing economic assistance to developing countries?
    A. World Bank.
    B. World Trade Organization.
    C. International Monetary Fund.

ANSWERS – CONCEPT CHECKERS

1. **A** The income from a financial investment in Country P of a citizen of Country Q is included in Country P's GDP but not its GNP. It is included in Country Q's GNP but not its GDP.

2. **B** Openness to international trade increases specialization as production shifts to those products in which domestic producers have a comparative advantage. Greater competition from imports will tend to decrease prices for consumer goods. Increasing international trade is likely to increase profitability and employment in exporting industries but may decrease profitability and employment in industries that compete with imported goods.

3. **A** Each country gains by *exporting* the good for which it has a comparative advantage.

4. **C** In the Ricardian model, labor is the only factor of production considered. In the Heckscher-Ohlin model, comparative advantage results from the relative amounts of labor and capital available in different countries.

5. **B** Voluntary export restraints are agreements to limit the volume of goods and services exported to another country. Minimum domestic content rules are limitations imposed by a government on its domestic firms. Import quotas are limitations on imports, not on exports.

6. **A** Import quotas and voluntary export restraints, unlike tariffs, do not necessarily generate tax revenue. The other choices describe effects that result from tariffs, quotas, and VERs.

7. **B** Imposing a tariff on steel imports benefits domestic steel producers and workers by increasing the domestic price of steel and benefits the national government by increasing tax (tariff) revenue. However, the increase in the domestic price of steel would increase costs in industries that use significant amounts of steel, such as the automobile industry. The resulting increase in the price of automobiles reduces the quantity of automobiles demanded and ultimately reduces employment in that industry.

8. **A** The motivation for trading blocs is to increase economic welfare in the member countries by eliminating barriers to trade. Joining a trading bloc may have negative consequences for some domestic industries and may decrease tariff revenue for the government.

9. **B** These characteristics describe a common market. In a free trade area, member countries remove restrictions on goods and services trade with one another but may still restrict movement of labor and capital among member countries. In an economic union, member countries also coordinate their economic policies and institutions.

10. **B** Purchases and sales of fixed assets are recorded in the capital account. Goods and services trade and unilateral transfers are components of the current account.

11. **A** Other things equal, an increase in domestic savings would tend to decrease the current account deficit, while an increase in private investment or an increase in the fiscal budget deficit would tend to increase the current account deficit.

12. **A** The World Bank provides technical and financial assistance to economically developing countries. The World Trade Organization is primarily concerned with settling disputes among countries concerning international trade. The International Monetary Fund promotes international trade and exchange rate stability and assists member countries that experience balance of payments trouble.

CURRENCY EXCHANGE RATES

EXAM FOCUS

Candidates must understand spot exchange rates, forward exchange rates, and all the calculations having to do with currency appreciation and depreciation. Additionally, candidates should understand the steps a country can take to decrease a trade deficit and the requirements for these to be effective under both the elasticities and absorption approaches. Finally, candidates should make sure to know the terms for and definitions of the various exchange rate regimes countries may adopt.

LOS 21.a: Define an exchange rate, and distinguish between nominal and real exchange rates and spot and forward exchange rates.

CFA® Program Curriculum, Volume 2, page 487

An **exchange rate** is simply the price or cost of units of one currency in terms of another. For the purposes of this book we will write 1.416 USD/EUR to mean that each euro costs $1.416. If you read the "/" as *per*, you will have no trouble with the notation. We say the exchange rate is $1.416 per euro. Sometimes we will write *d/f* to mean the cost of a foreign currency unit in terms of domestic currency units.

 Professor's Note: There are many notations for foreign exchange quotes, but expressing them as the price of the denominator currency in terms of the numerator currency is what we will use and what you can expect on the Level I exam.

In a foreign currency quotation we have the price of one currency in units of another currency. These are often referred to as the **base currency** and the **price currency**. In the quotation 1.25 USD/EUR, the USD is the price currency and the EUR is the base currency. The price of one euro (base currency) is 1.25 USD (the price currency) so 1.25 is the price of one unit of the base currency in terms of the other. It may help to remember that the euro in this example is in the bottom or "base" of the exchange rate given in terms of USD/EUR.

At a point in time, the **nominal exchange rate** $1.416/euro suggests that in order to purchase one euro's worth of goods and services in Euroland, the cost in U.S. dollars will be $1.416. As time passes, the **real exchange rate** tells us the dollar cost of purchasing that same unit of goods and services based on the new (current) dollar/euro exchange rate and the relative changes in the price levels of both countries.

The formula for this calculation is:

$$\text{real exchange rate (d/f)} = \text{nominal exchange rate (d/f)} \left(\frac{CPI_{foreign}}{CPI_{domestic}} \right)$$

A numerical example will help in understanding this concept.

Example: Real exchange rate

At a base period, the CPIs of the U.S. and U.K. are both 100, and the exchange rate is $1.70/£. Three years later, the exchange rate is $1.60/£, and the CPI has risen to 110 in the United States and 112 in the U.K. What is the real exchange rate?

Answer:

The real exchange rate is $1.60/£ × 112/110 = $1.629/£ which means that U.S. goods and services that cost $1.70 at the base period now cost only $1.629 (in real terms) if purchased in the U.K. and the real exchange rate, $/£, has fallen.

The intuition in this example is that the USD has appreciated versus the GBP by just over 6.0% in nominal terms, and the price level in the U.K. has increased by approximately 1.8% (112/110 – 1) relative to the U.S. price level. Because the dollar has appreciated in nominal terms by more than the price level in the U.K. has risen relative to the price level in the United States, the purchasing power of one USD in terms of U.K. goods and services has increased. The real rate of exchange has decreased from $1.70/£ to $1.629/£, which is a decrease of approximately 6.0% – 1.8% = 4.2%. Note that the real rate of exchange is the same as the nominal rate of exchange at the base period because both CPIs are equal to 100 at that point in time.

It will help your understanding to examine how a change in each of the variables affects the real rate. Holding other things equal:

- Inflation in the U.K., by itself, increases the real $/£ exchange rate so that a unit of real goods and services in the U.K. costs relatively more in USD than it did at the base period.
- Inflation in the U.S., by itself, decreases the real $/£ exchange rate so that a unit of real goods and services in the U.K. costs relatively less in USD than it did at the base period.
- An increase (decrease) in the nominal $/£ exchange rate when inflation in both countries is equal increases (decreases) the real $/£ exchange rate, and the cost of a unit of real goods and services in the U.K. increases (decreases) relative to what it was in the base period.

Changes in real exchange rates can be used when analyzing economic changes over time. When the real exchange rate (d/f) increases, exports of goods and services have gotten relatively less expensive to foreigners, and imports of goods and services from the foreign country have gotten relatively more expensive over time.

A **spot exchange rate** is the currency exchange rate for immediate delivery, which for most currencies means the exchange of currencies takes place two days after the trade.

A **forward exchange rate** is a currency exchange rate for an exchange to be done in the future. Forward rates are quoted for various future dates (e.g., 30 days, 60 days, 90 days, or one year). A forward is actually an agreement to exchange a specific amount of one currency for a specific amount of another on a future date specified in the forward agreement.

A French firm that will receive 10 million GBP from a British firm six months from now has uncertainty about the amount of euros that payment will be equivalent to six months from now. By entering into a forward agreement covering 10 million GBP at the 6-month forward rate of 1.192 EUR/GBP, the French firm has agreed to exchange 10 million GBP for 11.92 million euros in six months.

LOS 21.b: Describe functions of and participants in the foreign exchange market.

CFA® Program Curriculum, Volume 2, page 492

Foreign currency markets serve companies and individuals that purchase or sell foreign goods and services denominated in foreign currencies. An even larger market, however, exists for capital flows. Foreign currencies are needed to purchase foreign physical assets as well as foreign financial securities.

Many companies have foreign exchange risk arising from their cross-border transactions. A Japanese company that expects to receive 10 million euros when a transaction is completed in 90 days has yen/euro exchange rate risk as a result. By entering into a **forward currency contract** to sell 10 million euros in 90 days for a specific quantity of yen, the firm can reduce or eliminate its foreign exchange risk associated with the transaction. When a firm takes a position in the foreign exchange market to reduce an existing risk, we say the firm is **hedging** its risk.

Alternatively, when a transaction in the foreign exchange markets increases currency risk, we term it a **speculative** transaction or position. Investors, companies, and financial institutions, such as banks and investment funds, all regularly enter into speculative foreign currency transactions.

The primary dealers in currencies and originators of forward foreign exchange (FX) contracts are large multinational banks. This part of the FX market is often called the **sell side**. On the other hand, the **buy side** consists of the many buyers of foreign currencies and forward FX contracts. These buyers include the following:

- **Corporations** regularly engage in cross-border transactions, purchase and sell foreign currencies as a result, and enter into FX forward contracts to hedge the risk of expected future receipts and payments denominated in foreign currencies.
- **Investment accounts** of many types transact in foreign currencies, hold foreign securities, and may both speculate and hedge with currency derivatives. **Real money accounts** refer to mutual funds, pension funds, insurance companies, and other institutional accounts that do not use derivatives. **Leveraged accounts** refer to the various types of investment firms that do use derivatives, including hedge funds, firms that trade for their own accounts, and other trading firms of various types.

- **Governments** and **government entities**, including **sovereign wealth funds** and pension funds, acquire foreign exchange for transactional needs, investment, or speculation. Central banks sometimes engage in FX transactions to affect exchange rates in the short term in accordance with government policy.
- The **retail market** refers to FX transactions by households and relatively small institutions and may be for tourism, cross-border investment, or speculative trading.

LOS 21.c: Calculate and interpret the percentage change in a currency relative to another currency.

CFA® Program Curriculum, Volume 2, page 504

Consider a USD/EUR exchange rate that has changed from 1.42 to 1.39 USD/EUR. The percentage change in the USD price of a euro is simply 1.39 / 1.42 − 1 = −0.0211 = −2.11%. Because the USD price of a euro has fallen, the euro has *depreciated* relative to the dollar, and a euro now buys 2.11% fewer U.S. dollars. It is correct to say that the EUR has depreciated by 2.11% relative to the USD.

On the other hand, it is *not* correct to say that the USD has appreciated by 2.11%. To calculate the percentage appreciation of the USD, we need to convert the quotes to EUR/USD. So our beginning quote of 1.42 USD/EUR becomes 1/1.42 USD/EUR = 0.7042 EUR/USD, and our ending quote of 1.39 USD/EUR becomes 1/1.39 USD/EUR = 0.7194 EUR/USD. Using these exchange rates, we can calculate the change in the euro price of a USD as 0.7194 / 0.7042 − 1 = 0.0216 = 2.16%. In this case, it is correct to say that the USD has appreciated 2.16% with respect to the EUR. For the same quotes, the percentage appreciation of the USD is not the same as the percentage depreciation in the EUR.

The key point to remember is that we can correctly calculate the percentage change of the *base currency* in a foreign exchange quotation.

LOS 21.d: Calculate and interpret currency cross-rates.

CFA® Program Curriculum, Volume 2, page 507

The **cross rate** is the exchange rate between two currencies implied by their exchange rates with a common third currency. Cross rates are necessary when there is no active FX market in the currency pair. The rate must be computed from the exchange rates between each of these two currencies and a third currency, usually the USD or EUR.

Let's return to our previous quotation for the Australian dollar and the U.S. dollar (USD/AUD = 0.60). Let's assume that we also have the following quotation for Mexican pesos: MXN/USD = 10.70. The cross rate between Australian dollars and pesos (MXN/AUD) is:

$$MXN/AUD = USD/AUD \times MXN/USD = 0.60 \times 10.70 = 6.42$$

So our MXN/AUD cross rate is 6.42 pesos per Australian dollar. The key to calculating cross rates is to note that the basis of the quotations must be such that we get the desired result algebraically. If we had started with an AUD/USD quotation of 1.67, we would have taken the inverse to get the quotation into USD/AUD terms. Another approach is to divide through, as is illustrated in the following example.

Example: Cross rate calculation

The spot exchange rate between the Swiss franc (CHF) and the USD is CHF/USD = 1.7799, and the spot exchange rate between the New Zealand dollar (NZD) and the U.S. dollar is NZD/USD = 2.2529. Calculate the CHF/NZD spot rate.

Answer:

The CHF/NZD cross rate is:

(CHF/USD) / (NZD/USD) = 1.7799 / 2.2529 = 0.7900

LOS 21.e: Convert forward quotations expressed on a points basis or in percentage terms into an outright forward quotation.

CFA® Program Curriculum, Volume 2, page 511

A forward exchange rate quote typically differs from the spot quotation and is expressed in terms of the difference between the spot exchange rate and the forward exchange rate. One way to indicate this is with points. The unit of points is the last decimal place in the spot rate quote. For a spot currency quote to four decimal places, such as 2.3481, each point is 0.0001 or 1/10,000th. A quote of +18.3 points for a 90-day forward exchange rate means that the forward rate is 0.00183 more than the spot exchange rate.

Example: Forward exchange rates in points

The AUD/EUR spot exchange rate is 0.7313 with the 1-year forward rate quoted at +3.5 points. What is the 1-year forward AUD/EUR exchange rate?

Answer:

The forward exchange rate is 0.7313 + 0.00035 = 0.73165.

> **Example: Forward exchange rates in percent**
>
> The AUD/EUR spot rate is quoted at 0.7313, and the 120-day forward exchange rate is given as –0.062%. What is the 120-day forward AUD/EUR exchange rate?
>
> **Answer:**
>
> The forward exchange rate is 0.7313 (1 – 0.00062) = 0.7308.

LOS 21.f: Explain the arbitrage relationship between spot rates, forward rates, and interest rates.

CFA® Program Curriculum, Volume 2, page 513

When currencies are freely traded and forward currency contracts exist, the percentage difference between forward and spot exchange rates is approximately equal to the difference between the two countries' interest rates. This is because there is an arbitrage trade with a riskless profit to be made when this relation does not hold.

We call this a no-arbitrage condition because if it doesn't hold there is an opportunity to make a profit without risk. The possible arbitrage is as follows: borrow Currency A at interest rate A, convert it to Currency B at the spot rate and invest it to earn interest rate B, and sell the proceeds from this investment forward at the forward rate to turn it back into Currency A. If the forward rate does not correctly reflect the difference between interest rates, such an arbitrage could generate a profit to the extent that the return from investing Currency B and converting it back to Currency A with a forward contract is greater than the cost of borrowing Currency A for the period. We consider a numerical analysis of such an arbitrage later in this topic review.

For spot and forward rates expressed as domestic/foreign, the no-arbitrage relation (commonly referred to as *interest rate parity*) is:

$$\frac{\text{forward}}{\text{spot}} = \frac{(1 + \text{interest rate}_{\text{domestic}})}{(1 + \text{interest rate}_{\text{foreign}})}$$

This formula can be rearranged as necessary in order to solve for specific values of the relevant terms.

 Professor's Note: If the spot and forward rates are expressed as domestic / foreign, then the domestic interest rate goes in the numerator on the right-hand side of this equation. If the spot and forward quotes are given as foreign / domestic, then the foreign interest rate goes in the numerator on the right-hand side.

LOS 21.g: Calculate and interpret a forward discount or premium.

CFA® Program Curriculum, Volume 2, page 511

The **forward discount** or **forward premium** for a currency is calculated relative to the spot exchange rate. The forward discount or premium *for the base currency* is the percentage difference between the forward price and the spot price.

Consider the following spot and forward exchange rates as the price in U.S. dollars of one euro.

USD/EUR spot = $1.312   USD/EUR 90-day forward = $1.320

The (90-day) forward premium or discount on the euro = forward/spot – 1 = 1.320/1.312 – 1 = 0.609%. Because this is positive, it is interpreted as a forward premium on the euro of 0.609%. Since we have the forward rate for 3 months, we could annualize the discount simply by multiplying by (12/3=) 4.

Because the forward quote is greater than the spot quote, it will take more dollars to buy one euro 90 days from now, so the euro is expected to appreciate versus the dollar, and the dollar is expected to depreciate relative to the euro.

If the forward quote were less than the spot quote, the calculated amount would be negative and we would interpret that as a forward discount for the euro relative to the U.S. dollar.

LOS 21.h: Calculate and interpret the forward rate consistent with the spot rate and the interest rate in each currency.

CFA® Program Curriculum, Volume 2, page 513

Example: Calculating the arbitrage-free forward exchange rate

Consider two currencies, the ABE and the DUB. The spot ABE/DUB exchange rate is 4.5671, the 1-year riskless ABE rate is 5%, and the 1-year riskless DUB rate is 3%. What is the 1-year forward exchange rate that will prevent arbitrage profits?

Answer:

Rearranging our formula, we have:

$$\text{forward} = \text{spot}\left(\frac{1+I_{ABE}}{1+I_{DUB}}\right) \text{ and we can calculate the forward rate as}$$

$$\text{forward} = 4.5671\left(\frac{1.05}{1.03}\right) = 4.6558\left(\text{ABE}\big/\text{DUB}\right)$$

Note that the forward rate is greater than the spot rate by $4.6558 / 4.5671 - 1 = 1.94\%$. This is approximately equal to the interest rate differential of $5\% - 3\% = 2\%$. The currency with the higher interest rate should depreciate over time by approximately the amount of the interest rate differential.

If we are calculating a 90-day or 180-day forward exchange rate, we need to use interest rates for 90-day or 180-day periods rather than annual rates.

Example: Calculating the arbitrage-free forward exchange rate with 90-day interest rates

The spot ABE/DUB exchange rate is 4.5671, the 90-day riskless ABE rate is 5%, and the 90-day riskless DUB rate is 3%. What is the 90-day forward exchange rate that will prevent arbitrage profits?

Answer:

$$\text{forward} = 4.5671\left[\frac{1+\dfrac{0.05}{4}}{1+\dfrac{0.03}{4}}\right] = 4.5671\left(\frac{1.0125}{1.0075}\right) = 4.5898\left(\text{ABE}\big/\text{DUB}\right)$$

Now, let's build on the first example by examining the arbitrage opportunity when the forward rate does not satisfy the equation that describes interest rate parity between two currencies. Consider a forward rate of 4.6000 so that the depreciation in the ABE is less than that implied by interest rate parity. This makes the ABE attractive to a DUB investor who can earn a riskless profit as follows:

- Borrow 1,000 DUB for one year at 3% to purchase ABE and get 4,567.1 ABE.
- Invest the 4,567.1 ABE at the ABE rate of 5% to have 1.05(4,567.1) = 4,795.45 ABE at the end of one year.
- Enter into a currency forward contract to exchange 4,795.45 ABE in one year at the forward rate of 4.6000 ABE/DUB in order to receive 4,795.45 / 4.6000 = 1,042.49 DUB.

The investor has ended the year with a 4.249% return on his 1,000 DUB investment, which is higher than the 3% 1-year DUB interest rate. After repaying the 1,000 DUB loan plus interest (1,030 DUB), the investor has a profit of 1,042.49 – 1,030 = 12.49 DUB with no risk and no initial out-of-pocket investment (i.e., a pure arbitrage profit).

Arbitrageurs will pursue this opportunity, buying ABE (driving down the spot ABE/DUB exchange rate) and selling ABE forward (driving up the forward ABE/DUB exchange rate), until the interest rate parity relation is restored and arbitrage profits are no longer available.

LOS 21.i: Describe exchange rate regimes.

CFA® Program Curriculum, Volume 2, page 518

The IMF categorizes **exchange rate regimes** into the following types, two for countries that do not issue their own currencies and seven for countries that issue their own currencies.

Countries That Do Not Have Their Own Currency

- A country can use the currency of another country (**formal dollarization**). The country cannot have its own monetary policy, as it does not create money/currency.
- A country can be a member of a **monetary union** in which several countries use a common currency. Within the European Union, for example, most countries use the euro. While individual countries give up the ability to set domestic monetary policy, they all participate in determining the monetary policy of the European Central Bank.

Countries That Have Their Own Currency

- A **currency board arrangement** is an explicit commitment to exchange domestic currency for a specified foreign currency at a fixed exchange rate. A notable example of such an arrangement is Hong Kong. In Hong Kong, currency is (and may be) only issued when fully backed by holdings of an equivalent amount of U.S. dollars. The Hong Kong Monetary Authority can earn interest on its U.S. dollar balances. With dollarization, there is no such income, as the income is earned by the U.S. Federal Reserve when it buys interest-bearing assets with the U.S. currency it issues. While the monetary authority gives up the ability to conduct independent monetary policy and essentially imports the inflation rate of the outside currency, there may be some latitude to affect interest rates over the short term.

- In a **conventional fixed peg arrangement,** a country pegs its currency within margins of ±1% versus another currency or a basket that includes the currencies of its major trading or financial partners. The monetary authority can maintain exchange rates within the band by purchasing or selling foreign currencies in the foreign exchange markets (*direct intervention*). In addition, the country can use *indirect intervention,* including changes in interest rate policy, regulation of foreign exchange transactions, and convincing people to constrain foreign exchange activity. The monetary authority retains more flexibility to conduct monetary policy than with dollarization, a monetary union, or a currency board. However, changes in policy are constrained by the requirements of the peg.

- In a system of pegged exchange rates within horizontal bands or a **target zone,** the permitted fluctuations in currency value relative to another currency or basket of currencies are wider (e.g., ±2%). Compared to a conventional peg, the monetary authority has more policy discretion because the bands are wider.

- With a **crawling peg,** the exchange rate is adjusted periodically, typically to adjust for higher inflation versus the currency used in the peg. This is termed a *passive crawling peg,* as opposed to an *active crawling peg* in which a series of exchange rate adjustments over time is announced and implemented. An active crawling peg can influence inflation expectations, adding some predictability to domestic inflation. Monetary policy is restricted in much the same way it is with a fixed peg arrangement.

- With **management of exchange rates within crawling bands,** the width of the bands that identify permissible exchange rates is increased over time. This method can be used to transition from a fixed peg to a floating rate when the monetary authority's lack of credibility makes an immediate change to floating rates impractical. Again, the degree of monetary policy flexibility increases with the width of the bands.

- With a system of **managed floating exchange rates,** the monetary authority attempts to influence the exchange rate in response to specific indicators such as the balance of payments, inflation rates, or employment without any specific target exchange rate or predetermined exchange rate path. Intervention may be direct or indirect. Such management of exchange rates may induce trading partners to respond in ways that reduce stability.

- When a currency is **independently floating,** the exchange rate is market-determined, and foreign exchange market intervention is used only to slow the rate of change and reduce short-term fluctuations, not to keep exchange rates at a certain target level.

LOS 21.j: Explain the effects of exchange rates on countries' international trade and capital flows.

CFA® Program Curriculum, Volume 2, page 529

We address the question of how a change in exchange rates affects a country's balance of trade using two approaches. The **elasticities approach** focuses on the impact of exchange rate changes on the total value of imports and on the total value of exports. Because a trade deficit (surplus) must be offset by a surplus (deficit) in the capital account, we can also view the effects of a change in exchange rates on capital flows rather than on goods flows. The **absorption approach** to analyzing the effect of a change in exchange rates focuses on capital flows.

The relation between the balance of trade and capital flows is expressed by the identity we presented in the topic review of Aggregate Output, Prices, and Economic Growth. This identity is:

exports – imports ≡ (private savings – investment in physical capital) + (tax revenue – government spending)

or

$$X - M \equiv (S - I) + (T - G)$$

The intuition is that a trade deficit (X – M < 0) means that the right-hand side must also be negative so that the total savings (private savings + government savings) is less than domestic investment in physical capital. The additional amount to fund domestic investment must come from foreigners, so there is a surplus in the capital account to offset the deficit in the trade account. Another thing we can see from this identity is that any government deficit not funded by an excess of domestic saving over domestic investment is consistent with a trade deficit (imports > exports) which is offset by an inflow of foreign capital (a surplus in the capital account).

Elasticities Approach

This approach to understanding the impact of exchange rate changes on the balance of trade focuses on how exchange rate changes affect total expenditures on imports and exports. Consider an initial situation in which a country has a merchandise trade deficit (i.e., its imports exceed its exports). Depreciation of the domestic currency will make imports more expensive in domestic currency terms and exports less expensive in foreign currency terms. Thus, depreciation of the domestic currency will increase exports and decrease imports and would seem to unambiguously reduce the trade deficit. However, it is not the *quantity* of imports and exports, but the total *expenditures* on imports and exports that must change in order to affect the trade deficit. Thus, the elasticity of demand for export goods and import goods is a crucial part of the analysis.

The condition under which a depreciation of the domestic currency will decrease a trade deficit are given in what is called the generalized **Marshall-Lerner condition**:

$$W_X\, \varepsilon_X + W_M\, (\varepsilon_M - 1) > 0$$

where:
W_x = proportion of total trade that is exports
W_m = proportion of total trade that is imports
ε_X = price elasticity of demand for exports
ε_m = price elasticity of demand for imports

In the case where import expenditures and export revenues are equal, $W_X = W_M$, this condition reduces to $\varepsilon_X + \varepsilon_M > 1$, which is most often cited as the classic Marshall-Lerner condition.

The elasticities approach tells us that currency depreciation will result in a greater improvement in the trade deficit when either import or export demand is elastic. For this reason, the compositions of export goods and import goods are an important determinant of the success of currency depreciation in reducing a trade deficit. In general, elasticity of demand is greater for goods with close substitutes, goods that represent a high proportion of consumer spending, and luxury goods in general. Goods that are necessities, have few or no good substitutes, or represent a small proportion of overall expenditures tend to have less elastic demand. Thus, currency depreciation will have a greater effect on the balance of trade when import or export goods are primarily luxury goods, goods with close substitutes, and goods that represent a large proportion of overall spending.

The J-Curve

Because import and export contracts for the delivery of goods most often require delivery and payment in the future, import and export quantities may be relatively insensitive to currency depreciation in the short run. This means that a currency depreciation may worsen a trade deficit initially. Importers adjust over time by reducing quantities. The Marshall-Lerner conditions take effect and the currency depreciation begins to improve the trade balance.

This short-term increase in the deficit followed by a decrease when the Marshall-Lerner condition is met is referred to as the **J-curve** and is illustrated in Figure 1.

Figure 1: J-Curve Effect

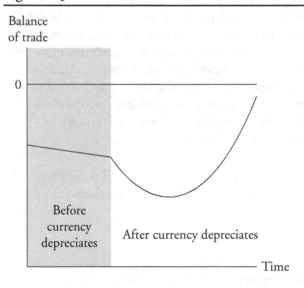

The Absorption Approach

One shortcoming of the elasticities approach is that it only considers the microeconomic relationship between exchange rates and trade balances. It ignores capital flows, which must also change as a result of a currency depreciation that improves the balance of trade. The absorption approach is a macroeconomic technique that focuses on the capital account and can be represented as:

BT = Y − E

where:
Y = domestic production of goods and services or national income
E = domestic absorption of goods and services, which is total expenditure
BT = balance of trade

Viewed in this way, we can see that income relative to expenditure must increase (domestic absorption must fall) for the balance of trade to improve in response to a currency depreciation. For the balance of trade to improve, domestic saving must increase relative to domestic investment in physical capital (which is a component of *E*). Thus, for a depreciation of the domestic currency to improve the balance of trade towards surplus, it must increase national income relative to expenditure. We can also view this as a requirement that national saving increase relative to domestic investment in physical capital.

Whether a currency depreciation has these effects depends on the current level of capacity utilization in the economy. When an economy is operating at less than full employment, the currency depreciation makes domestic goods and assets relatively more attractive than foreign goods and assets. The resulting shift in demand away from foreign goods and assets and towards domestic goods and assets will increase both expenditures and income. Because part of the income increase will be saved, national income will increase more than total expenditure, improving the balance of trade.

In a situation where the economy is operating at full employment (capacity), an increase in domestic spending will translate to higher domestic prices, which can reverse the relative price changes of the currency depreciation, resulting in a return to the previous deficit in the balance of trade. A currency depreciation at full capacity does result in a decline in the value of domestic assets. This decline in savers' real wealth will induce an increase in saving to rebuild wealth, initially improving the balance of trade from the currency depreciation. As the real wealth of savers increases, however, the positive impact on saving will decrease, eventually returning the economy to its previous state and balance of trade.

KEY CONCEPTS

LOS 21.a

Currency exchange rates are given as the price of one unit of currency in terms of another. A nominal exchange rate of 1.44 USD/EUR is interpreted as $1.44 per euro. We refer to the USD as the price currency and the EUR as the base currency.

A decrease (increase) in a direct exchange rate represents an appreciation (depreciation) of the domestic currency relative to the foreign currency.

A spot exchange rate is the rate for immediate delivery. A forward exchange rate is a rate for exchange of currencies at some future date.

A real exchange rate measures changes in relative purchasing power over time.

$$\text{real exchange rate}(\text{domestic/foreign}) = \text{spot exchange rate}(\text{domestic/foreign}) \times \frac{CPI_{foreign}}{CPI_{domestic}}$$

LOS 21.b

The market for foreign exchange is the largest financial market in terms of the value of daily transactions and has a variety of participants, including large multinational banks (the sell side) and corporations, investment fund managers, hedge fund managers, investors, governments, and central banks (the buy side).

Participants in the foreign exchange markets are referred to as hedgers if they enter into transactions that decrease an existing foreign exchange risk and as speculators if they enter into transactions that increase their foreign exchange risk.

LOS 21.c

For a change in an exchange rate, we can calculate the percentage appreciation (price goes up) or depreciation (price goes down) of the base currency. For example, a decrease in the USD/EUR exchange rate from 1.44 to 1.42 represents a depreciation of the EUR relative to the USD of 1.39% (1.42 / 1.44 − 1 = −0.0139) because the price of a euro has fallen 1.39%.

To calculate the appreciation or depreciation of the price currency, we first invert the quote so it is now the base currency and then proceed as above. For example, a decrease in the USD/EUR exchange rate from 1.44 to 1.42 represents an appreciation of the USD relative to the EUR of 1.41%: $(1 / 1.42) / (1 / 1.44) - 1 = \frac{1.44}{1.42} - 1 = 0.0141$.

The appreciation is the inverse of the depreciation, $\frac{1}{(1 - 0.0139)} - 1 = 0.0141$.

LOS 21.d

Given two exchange rate quotes for three different currencies, we can calculate a currency cross rate. If the MXN/USD quote is 12.1 and the USD/EUR quote is 1.42, we can calculate the cross rate of MXN/EUR as 12.1 × 1.42 = 17.18.

LOS 21.e

Points in a foreign currency quotation are in units of the last digit of the quotation. For example, a forward quote of +25.3 when the USD/EUR spot exchange rate is 1.4158 means that the forward exchange rate is 1.4158 + 0.00253 = 1.41833 USD/EUR.

For a forward exchange rate quote given as a percentage, the percentage (change in the spot rate) is calculated as forward / spot – 1. A forward exchange rate quote of +1.787%, when the spot USD/EUR exchange rate is 1.4158, means that the forward exchange rate is 1.4158 (1 + 0.01787) = 1.4411 USD/EUR.

LOS 21.f

If a forward exchange rate does not correctly reflect the difference between the interest rates for two currencies, an arbitrage opportunity for a riskless profit exists. In this case, borrowing one currency, converting it to the other currency at the spot rate, investing the proceeds for the period, and converting the end-of-period amount back to the borrowed currency at the forward rate will produce more than enough to pay off the initial loan, with the remainder being a riskless profit on the arbitrage transaction.

LOS 21.g

To calculate a forward premium or forward discount for Currency B using exchange rates quoted as units of Currency A per unit of Currency B, use the following formula:

$$(\text{forward}/\text{spot}) - 1$$

LOS 21.h

The condition that must be met so that there is no arbitrage opportunity available is:

$$\frac{\text{forward}}{\text{spot}} = \frac{\left(1 + i_{\text{price currency}}\right)}{\left(1 + i_{\text{base currency}}\right)} \text{ so that forward} = \text{spot} \times \frac{\left(1 + i_{\text{price currency}}\right)}{\left(1 + i_{\text{base currency}}\right)}$$

If the spot exchange rate for the euro is 1.25 USD/EUR, the euro interest rate is 4% per year, and the dollar interest rate is 3% per year, the no-arbitrage one-year forward rate can be calculated as:

$$1.25 \times (1.03 / 1.04) = 1.238 \text{ USD/EUR.}$$

LOS 21.i

Exchange rate regimes for countries that do not have their own currency:

- With *formal dollarization*, a country uses the currency of another country.
- In a *monetary union*, several countries use a common currency.

Exchange rate regimes for countries that have their own currency:

- A *currency board arrangement* is an explicit commitment to exchange domestic currency for a specified foreign currency at a fixed exchange rate.
- In a *conventional fixed peg arrangement*, a country pegs its currency within margins of ±1% versus another currency.
- In a system of *pegged exchange rates within horizontal bands* or a *target zone*, the permitted fluctuations in currency value relative to another currency or basket of currencies are wider (e.g., ±2 %).
- With a *crawling peg*, the exchange rate is adjusted periodically, typically to adjust for higher inflation versus the currency used in the peg.
- With *management of exchange rates within crawling bands*, the width of the bands that identify permissible exchange rates is increased over time.
- With a system of *managed floating exchange rates*, the monetary authority attempts to influence the exchange rate in response to specific indicators, such as the balance of payments, inflation rates, or employment without any specific target exchange rate.
- When a currency is *independently floating*, the exchange rate is market-determined.

LOS 21.j

Elasticities (ε) of export and import demand must meet the Marshall-Lerner condition for a depreciation of the domestic currency to reduce an existing trade deficit:

$$W_X \varepsilon_X + W_M(\varepsilon_M - 1) > 0$$

Under the absorption approach, national income must increase relative to national expenditure in order to decrease a trade deficit. This can also be viewed as a requirement that national saving must increase relative to domestic investment in order to decrease a trade deficit.

CONCEPT CHECKERS

1. One year ago, the nominal exchange rate for USD/EUR was 1.300. Since then, the real exchange rate has increased by 3%. This *most likely* implies that:
   A. the nominal exchange rate is less than USD/EUR 1.235.
   B. the purchasing power of the euro has increased approximately 3% in terms of U.S. goods.
   C. inflation in the euro zone was approximately 3% higher than inflation in the United States.

2. Sell-side participants in the foreign exchange market are *most likely* to include:
   A. banks.
   B. hedge funds.
   C. insurance companies.

3. Suppose that the quote for British pounds (GBP) in New York is USD/GBP 1.3110. What is the quote for U.S. dollars (USD) in London (GBP/USD)?
   A. 0.3110.
   B. 0.7628.
   C. 1.3110.

4. The Canadian dollar (CAD) exchange rate with the Japanese yen (JPY) changes from JPY/CAD 75 to JPY/CAD 78. The CAD has:
   A. depreciated by 3.8%, and the JPY has appreciated by 4.0%.
   B. appreciated by 3.8%, and the JPY has depreciated by 4.0%.
   C. appreciated by 4.0%, and the JPY has depreciated by 3.8%.

5. Today's spot rate for the Indonesian rupiah (IDR) is IDR/USD 2,400.00, and the New Zealand dollar trades at NZD/USD 1.6000. The NZD/IDR cross rate is:
   A. 0.00067.
   B. 1,492.53.
   C. 3,840.00.

6. The NZD is trading at USD/NZD 0.3500, and the SEK is trading at NZD/SEK 0.3100. The USD/SEK cross rate is:
   A. 0.1085.
   B. 8.8573.
   C. 9.2166.

7. The spot CHF/GBP exchange rate is 1.3050. In the 180-day forward market, the CHF/GBP exchange rate is –42.5 points. The 180-day forward CHF/GBP exchange rate is *closest* to:
   A. 1.2625.
   B. 1.3008.
   C. 1.3093.

8. The current spot rate for the British pound in terms of U.S. dollars is $1.533 and the 180-day forward rate is $1.508. Relative to the pound, the dollar is trading *closest* to a 180-day forward:
   A. discount of 1.63%.
   B. premium of 1.66%.
   C. discount of 1.66%.

9. The annual interest rates in the United States (USD) and Sweden (SEK) are 4% and 7% per year, respectively. If the current spot rate is SEK/USD 9.5238, then the 1-year forward rate in SEK/USD is:
   A. 9.2568.
   B. 9.7985.
   C. 10.2884.

10. The annual risk-free interest rate is 10% in the United States (USD) and 4% in Switzerland (CHF), and the 1-year forward rate is USD/CHF 0.80. Today's USD/CHF spot rate is *closest* to:
    A. 0.7564.
    B. 0.8462.
    C. 0.8888.

11. The spot rate on the New Zealand dollar (NZD) is NZD/USD 1.4286, and the 180-day forward rate is NZD/USD 1.3889. This difference means:
    A. interest rates are lower in the United States than in New Zealand.
    B. interest rates are higher in the United States than in New Zealand.
    C. it takes more NZD to buy one USD in the forward market than in the spot market.

12. The monetary authority of The Stoddard Islands will exchange its currency for U.S. dollars at a one-for-one ratio. As a result, the exchange rate of the Stoddard Islands currency with the U.S. dollar is 1.00, and many businesses in the Islands will accept U.S. dollars in transactions. This exchange rate regime is *best* described as:
    A. a fixed peg.
    B. dollarization.
    C. a currency board.

13. A country that wishes to narrow its trade deficit devalues its currency. If domestic demand for imports is perfectly price-inelastic, whether devaluing the currency will result in a narrower trade deficit is *least likely* to depend on:
    A. the size of the currency devaluation.
    B. the country's ratio of imports to exports.
    C. price elasticity of demand for the country's exports.

14. A devaluation of a country's currency to improve its trade deficit would *most likely* benefit a producer of:
    A. luxury goods for export.
    B. export goods that have no close substitutes.
    C. an export good that represents a relatively small proportion of consumer expenditures.

15.   Other things equal, which of the following is *most likely* to decrease a country's
       trade deficit?
       A. Increase its capital account surplus.
       B. Decrease expenditures relative to income.
       C. Decrease domestic saving relative to domestic investment.

ANSWERS – CONCEPT CHECKERS

1. **B** An increase in the real exchange rate USD/EUR (the number of USD per one EUR) means a euro is worth more in purchasing power (real) terms in the United States. Changes in a real exchange rate depend on the change in the nominal exchange rate relative to the difference in inflation. By itself, a real exchange rate does not indicate the directions or degrees of change in either the nominal exchange rate or the inflation difference.

2. **A** Large multinational banks make up the sell side of the foreign exchange market. The buy side includes corporations, real money and leveraged investment accounts, governments and government entities, and retail purchasers of foreign currencies.

3. **B** 1 / 1.311 = 0.7628 GBP/USD.

4. **C** The CAD has appreciated because it is worth a larger number of JPY. The percent appreciation is (78 – 75) / 75 = 4.0%. To calculate the percentage depreciation of the JPY against the CAD, convert the exchange rates to direct quotations for Japan: 1 / 75 = 0.0133 CAD/JPY and 1 / 78 = 0.0128 CAD/JPY. Percentage depreciation = (0.0128 – 0.0133) / 0.0133 = –3.8%.

5. **A** Start with one NZD and exchange for 1 / 1.6 = 0.625 USD. Exchange the USD for 0.625 × 2,400 = 1,500 IDR. We get a cross rate of 1,500 IDR/NZD or 1 / 1,500 = 0.00067 NZD/IDR.

6. **A** USD/NZD 0.3500 × NZD/SEK 0.3100 = USD/SEK 0.1085.

   Notice that the NZD term cancels in the multiplication.

7. **B** The 180-day forward exchange rate is 1.3050 – 0.00425 = CHF/GBP 1.30075.

8. **B** To calculate a percentage forward premium or discount for the U.S. dollar, we need the dollar to be the base currency. The spot and forward quotes given are U.S. dollars per British pound (USD/GBP), so we must invert them to GBP/USD. The spot GBP/USD price is 1 / 1.533 = 0.6523 and the forward GBP/USD price is 1 / 1.508 = 0.6631. Because the forward price is greater than the spot price, we say the dollar is at a forward premium of 0.6631 / 0.6523 – 1 = 1.66%. Alternatively, we can calculate this premium with the given quotes as spot/forward – 1 to get 1.533 / 1.508 – 1 = 1.66%.

9. **B** The forward rate in SEK/USD is $9.5238\left(\dfrac{1.07}{1.04}\right) = 9.7985$. Since the SEK interest rate is the higher of the two, the SEK must depreciate approximately 3%.

10. **A** We can solve interest rate parity for the spot rate as follows:

    With the exchange rates quoted as USD/CHF, the spot is $0.80\left(\dfrac{1.04}{1.10}\right) = 0.7564$. Since the interest rate is higher in the United States, it should take fewer USD to buy CHF in the spot market. In other words, the forward USD must be depreciating relative to the spot.

11. **B** Interest rates are higher in the United States than in New Zealand. It takes fewer NZD to buy one USD in the forward market than in the spot market.

12. **C**   This exchange rate regime is a currency board arrangement. The country has not formally dollarized because it continues to issue a domestic currency. A conventional fixed peg allows for a small degree of fluctuation around the target exchange rate.

13. **A**   With perfectly inelastic demand for imports, currency devaluation of any size will increase total expenditures on imports (same quantity at higher prices in the home currency). The trade deficit will narrow only if the increase in export revenues is larger than the increase in import spending. To satisfy the Marshall-Lerner condition when import demand elasticity is zero, export demand elasticity must be larger than the ratio of imports to exports in the country's international trade.

14. **A**   A devaluation of the currency will reduce the price of export goods in foreign currency terms. The greatest benefit would be to producers of goods with more elastic demand. Luxury goods tend to have higher elasticity of demand, while goods that have no close substitutes or represent a small proportion of consumer expenditures tend to have low elasticities of demand.

15. **B**   An improvement in a trade deficit requires that domestic savings increase relative to domestic investment, which would decrease a capital account surplus. Decreasing expenditures relative to income means domestic savings increase. Decreasing domestic saving relative to domestic investment is consistent with a larger capital account surplus (an increase in net foreign borrowing) and a greater trade deficit.

12 questions: 18 minutes

1. An analyst is evaluating the degree of competition in an industry and compiles the following information:
   - Few significant barriers to entry or exit exist.
   - Firms in the industry produce slightly differentiated products.
   - Each firm faces a demand curve that is largely unaffected by the actions of other individual firms in the industry.

   The analyst should characterize the competitive structure of this industry as:
   A. oligopoly.
   B. monopoly.
   C. monopolistic competition.

2. Which of the following statements about the behavior of firms in a perfectly competitive market is *least accurate*?
   A. A firm experiencing economic losses in the short run will continue to operate if its revenues are greater than its variable costs.
   B. A firm that is producing less than the quantity for which marginal cost equals the market price would lose money by increasing production.
   C. If firms are earning economic profits in the short run, new firms will enter the market and reduce economic profits to zero in the long run.

3. Compared to a customs union or a common market, the primary advantage of an economic union is that:
   A. its members adopt a common currency.
   B. its members have a common economic policy.
   C. it removes barriers to imports and exports among its members.

4. Which of the following statements about consumer surplus and producer surplus is *most accurate*?
   A. Economic gains to society are maximized at the price and quantity where consumer surplus and producer surplus are equal.
   B. No producer surplus is realized on the sale of an additional unit of a good if the opportunity cost of producing it is greater than the price received.
   C. A consumer is not willing to buy an additional unit of a good if his consumer surplus from the next unit is less than his consumer surplus from the previous unit.

5. Other things equal, an increase of 2.0% in the price of Product X results in a 1.4% increase in the quantity demanded of Product Y and a 0.7% decrease in the quantity demanded of Product Z. Which statement about products X, Y and Z is *least accurate*?
   A. Products X and Y are substitutes.
   B. Products X and Z are complements.
   C. Products Y and Z are complements.

6.   The EUR/USD spot exchange rate is 0.70145, and 1-year interest rates are 3% in EUR and 2% in USD. The forward USD/EUR exchange rate is *closest* to:
     A. 1.1426.
     B. 1.4118.
     C. 1.4396.

7.   Depreciation of a country's currency is *most likely* to narrow its trade deficit when:
     A. its imports are greater in value than its exports.
     B. price elasticity of import demand is greater than one.
     C. investment increases relative to private and government savings.

8.   According to real business cycle theory, business cycles result from:
     A. rational responses to external shocks.
     B. inappropriate changes in monetary policy.
     C. increases and decreases in business confidence.

9.   A decrease in the target U.S. federal funds rate is *least likely* to result in:
     A. a proportionate decrease in long-term interest rates.
     B. an increase in consumer spending on durable goods.
     C. depreciation of the U.S. dollar on the foreign exchange market.

10. For an economy that is initially at full-employment real GDP, an increase in aggregate demand will *most likely* have what effects on the price level and real GDP in the short run?
     A. Both will increase in the short run.
     B. Neither will increase in the short run.
     C. Only one will increase in the short run.

11. Potential real GDP is *least likely* to increase as a result of an:
     A. improvement in technology.
     B. increase in the money wage rate.
     C. increase in the labor force participation ratio.

12. When the economy is operating at the natural rate of unemployment, it is *most likely* that:
     A. inflation is accelerating.
     B. frictional unemployment is absent.
     C. structural unemployment is present.

SELF-TEST ANSWERS – ECONOMICS

1. **C** Both oligopoly and monopolistic competition are consistent with firms that produce slightly differentiated products. However, with few significant barriers to entry and little interdependence among competitors, the industry does not fit the definition of an oligopoly and would be best characterized as monopolistic competition.

2. **B** A firm that is producing *more* than the quantity where its marginal revenue (the market price in perfect competition) is equal to its marginal cost is losing money on sales of additional units. A firm producing where marginal cost is less than price is foregoing additional profit by not increasing production. The other responses accurately describe characteristics of firms in perfectly competitive markets.

3. **B** The advantage of an economic union is that its members establish common economic policies and institutions. A common currency is a characteristic of a monetary union. All regional trading agreements remove barriers to imports and exports among their members.

4. **B** Producers realize a producer surplus on the next unit of a good when the price they receive for it is greater than the opportunity cost of producing it. Economic gains to society are greatest when the sum of consumer surplus and producer surplus is maximized, regardless of which is larger. A consumer is willing to buy an additional unit of a good as long as it will generate *any* additional consumer surplus.

5. **C** It does not necessarily follow from the information given in the question that products Y and Z are complements.

   The increase in the price of Product X caused the quantity demanded of Product Y to increase (positive cross price elasticity) and caused the quantity demanded of Product Z to decrease (negative cross price elasticity). This suggests that Product Y is a substitute for Product X, and Product Z is a complement to Product X.

   But this does not mean Product Y is a complement to Product Z. For example, gasoline is a complement to automobiles; bicycles are a substitute for automobiles; but gasoline is not a complement to bicycles.

6. **B** $0.70145 \times 1.03 / 1.02 = 0.7083$; $1 / 0.7083 = 1.4118$

7. **B** The elasticities approach to evaluating the effect of exchange rates on the trade balance suggests that the more elastic both import demand and export demand are, the more likely currency depreciation is to narrow a trade deficit. A country with a trade deficit imports more than its exports by definition. An increase in investment relative to savings would tend to increase the trade deficit (net exports equal private and government savings minus investment).

8. **A** Real business cycle theory holds that economic cycles are driven by utility-maximizing individuals and firms responding to changes in real economic factors, such as changes in technology. Keynesian cycle theory attributes the business cycle to changes in business confidence. Monetarist theory attributes the business cycle to inappropriate changes in the rate of money supply growth.

9. **A** Changes in the U.S. federal funds rate and changes in long-term interest rates are unlikely to be proportionate. Long-term rates are the sum of short-term rates and a premium for the expected rate of inflation. If a decrease (increase) in the target federal funds rate by the Fed causes economic agents to increase (decrease) their inflation expectations, the change in long-term rates will be less than the change in the federal funds rate. Increases in spending on consumer durables and a decrease in the foreign exchange value of the U.S. dollar are among the expected results of a decrease in the target U.S. federal funds rate.

10. **A** An increase in aggregate demand will cause short-run equilibrium to move along the short-run aggregate supply curve (SAS). This will tend to increase both real GDP and the price level in the short run.

11. **B** An increase in the money wage rate would not increase long-run aggregate supply (potential real GDP), but instead would decrease the short-run aggregate supply curve. An improvement in technology would tend to increase potential real GDP. An increase in the participation ratio increases the full-employment quantity of labor supplied and potential real GDP.

12. **C** Structural and frictional unemployment are always present. The natural rate of unemployment is the lowest rate consistent with non-accelerating inflation.

FORMULAS

$$\text{own price elasticity} = \frac{\text{\% change in quantity demanded}}{\text{\% change in own price}}$$

$$\text{income elasticity} = \frac{\text{\% change in quantity demanded}}{\text{\% change in income}}$$

$$\text{cross price elasticity} = \frac{\text{\% change in quantity demanded}}{\text{\% change in price of related good}}$$

accounting profit = total revenue − total accounting (explicit) costs

economic profit = accounting profit − implicit opportunity costs = total revenue − total economic costs

= total revenue − explicit costs − implicit costs

normal profit = accounting profit − economic profit

total revenue (TR) = P × Q

average revenue (AR) = TR / Q

marginal revenue (MR) = ΔTR / ΔQ

total cost = total fixed cost + total variable cost

$$\text{marginal cost} = \frac{\text{change in total cost}}{\text{change in output}}, \text{ or } MC = \frac{\Delta TC}{\Delta Q}$$

average total costs (ATC) = total costs / total product

average fixed costs (AFC) = total fixed costs / total product

average variable costs (AVC) = total variable costs / total product

breakeven points:

    perfect competition: AR = ATC
    imperfect competition: TR = TC

short-run shutdown points:

    perfect competition: AR < AVC
    imperfect competition: TR < TVC

cost minimizing combination of inputs:

$$\frac{MP_1}{P_1} = \frac{MP_2}{P_2} = ... = \frac{MP_N}{P_N}$$

where:
MP_N = marginal product of input N
P_N = cost of input N
N = number of inputs

profit maximizing combination of inputs:

$$\frac{MRP_1}{P_1} = \frac{MRP_2}{P_2} = ... = \frac{MRP_N}{P_N} = 1$$

where:
MRP_N = marginal revenue product of input N
P_N = cost of input N
N = number of inputs

nominal GDP for year $t = \sum_{i=1}^{N} P_{i,t} Q_{i,t}$

$$= \sum_{i=1}^{N} \left(\text{price of good } i \text{ in year } t \right) \times \left(\text{quantity of good } i \text{ produced in year } t \right)$$

real GDP for year $t = \sum_{i=1}^{N} P_{i,\text{base year}} Q_{i,t}$

$$= \sum_{i=1}^{N} \left(\text{price of good } i \text{ in base year} \right) \times \left(\text{quantity of good } i \text{ produced in year } t \right)$$

GDP deflator for year t

$$\frac{\sum_{i=1}^{N} P_{i,t} Q_{i,t}}{\sum_{i=1}^{N} P_{i,\text{base year}} Q_{i,t}} \times 100 = \frac{\text{nominal GDP in year } t}{\text{value of year } t \text{ output at base year prices}} \times 100$$

GDP, expenditure approach:

$$GDP = C + I + G + (X - M)$$

where:
C = consumption spending
I = business investment (capital equipment, inventories)
G = government purchases
X = exports
M = imports

GDP, income approach:

$$GDP = \text{national income} + \text{capital consumption allowance} + \text{statistical discrepancy}$$

national income = compensation of employees (wages and benefits)
+ corporate and government enterprise profits before taxes
+ interest income
+ unincorporated business net income (business owners' incomes)
+ rent
+ indirect business taxes – subsidies (taxes and subsidies that are included in final prices)

personal income = national income
+ transfer payments to households
– indirect business taxes
– corporate income taxes
– undistributed corporate profits

personal disposable income = personal income – personal taxes

growth in potential GDP = growth in technology + W_L(growth in labor) + W_C(growth in capital)
where:
W_L = labor's percentage share of national income
W_C = capital's percentage share of national income

growth in per-capita potential GDP = growth in technology + W_C(growth in the capital-to-labor ratio)
where:
W_C = capital's percentage share of national income

$$\text{consumer price index} = \frac{\text{cost of basket at current prices}}{\text{cost of basket at base period prices}} \times 100$$

$$\text{money multiplier} = \frac{1}{\text{reserve requirement}}$$

equation of exchange: money supply $\times$ velocity = price $\times$ real output $(MV = PY)$

Fisher effect: nominal interest rate = real interest rate + expected inflation rate

neutral interest rate = real trend rate of economic growth + inflation target

fiscal multiplier:

$$\frac{1}{1 - MPC(1 - t)}$$

where:
t $\quad$ = tax rate
MPC = marginal propensity to consume

real exchange rate (d/f) = nominal exchange rate (d/f) $\left(\dfrac{CPI_{foreign}}{CPI_{domestic}} \right)$

forward discount (+) or premium (–):

$$\frac{forward}{spot} - 1$$

interest rate parity:

$$\frac{forward\ (d/f)}{spot\ (d/f)} = \frac{(1 + interest\ rate_{domestic})}{(1 + interest\ rate_{foreign})}$$

Marshall-Lerner condition:

$$W_X\, \varepsilon_X + W_M\, (\varepsilon_M - 1) > 0$$

where:
W_M = proportion of trade that is imports
W_X = proportion of trade that is exports
ε_M $\quad$ = elasticity of demand for imports
ε_X $\quad$ = elasticity of demand for exports

INDEX

©2014 Kaplan, Inc.

©2014 Kaplan, Inc.

Notes

Notes

Notes

Notes

Notes

Notes

Notes

Notes

Notes